TASTE LIKE A WINE CRITIC

A Guide to Understanding Wine Quality

For anyone wanting more out of wine

by LISA PERROTTI-BROWN MW

Text, Photographs and Artwork copyright
© Lisa Perrotti-Brown MW 2014

Published in 2015 by The Wine Advocate, Inc.

Library of Congress Control Number: 2014922720

ISBN 978-0-692-39213-3

Creative Direction, Design & Layout:
Catherine Wong, Burda Singapore, Pte. Ltd.

Illustrations for " The Wine Purposes Pyramid"
(p30) and "Stages of Grape Berry Ripening" (p66):
Matthew Teo, Burda Singapore, Pte. Ltd.

LISA PERROTTI-BROWN MW

Born and raised in rural Maine, USA, Lisa graduated from Colby College with a degree in English Literature and Performing Arts. Her wine career began by accident when, living as a struggling playwright in London after college, she stumbled into a job as the manager of a wine bar. She progressed through wine sales and marketing roles in the UK wine trade before moving to Tokyo in 2002 where she worked as a wine buyer for one of Japan's top fine wine importers and a wine educator at Tokyo's Academie du Vin. In 2008 Lisa began writing a column for Robert Parker's website, eRobertParker.com, and later that year she achieved her Master of Wine qualification and the Madame Bollinger Medal for excellence in wine tasting. Now living in Singapore, she is the Editor in Chief for Robert Parker's Wine Advocate and eRobertParker.com and remains the publication's critic for the wines of Australia and New Zealand.

Dedication

For Rick, Mia & Scarlett.

Contents

About this Book

With so many great books about wine out there comprehensively covering the fundamentals of tasting, viticulture and vinification, broadly and minutely detailing every style, region and grape variety known to mankind as well as a whole library of geeky topics for the more scientifically inclined, for many of my wine career years I never felt compelled to write a book about wine. It was around the time when I started my Master of Wine studies that I identified a gap; there were no advanced level tasting guides that took that incredible library of knowledge of wine that we now possess and put it into practical context when addressing the most fundamental aspect of wine: quality. When I looked high and low for a guide to help me in my advanced tasting studies I realised that in fact precious little has been written about the topic of evaluating wine quality. So during my time as a wine educator I attempted to address this gap by developing a lecture and then series of lectures that helped members of the wine trade learn how to "assess wine quality". The popularity of these lectures followed by my time spent as a wine critic and Editor in Chief for the world's most influential wine publication - Robert Parker's Wine Advocate - sparked my determination to write this book...which is essentially *the book* that I've been searching to buy all these years!

While this guide gets pretty technical in some places, I didn't want to produce a dry textbook that would merely be used as a reference tool. I was hoping to produce a fun read for anyone who had any interest whatsoever in understanding what constitutes a "good" wine. So wherever possible I've tried to bring the topics to life with analogies and stories written in conversational English, although never resorting to dumbing-down any of the higher level concepts. Likewise as the topics expand into side issues and have initiated questions and discussions during my years of lecturing on the assessment of wine quality, I have included a lot of question-asking text boxes throughout the book including the raised-hand queries (✋) which come directly from commonly asked questions by my students.

While writing this book I realised that there is a lot of ambiguity and poorly defined (sometimes outdated) wine jargon surrounding the topic of wine quality. Therefore I've tried to clearly define terms wherever possible and have created new terms where I felt necessary. The **"Glossary of Wine Quality Terms"** at the back of the book is admittedly a bit beefier in its definitions than most glossaries. In an extra effort to clarify and make this book as easy to use as possible, I've cross-referenced all the words in the glossary by highlighting the entries in RED CAPITALS throughout this book.

Enjoy, drink sensibly & always drink well,

GO ON,
I DARE YOU.
SMELL IT.

....

Smell is a potent wizard that transports you
across thousands of miles and
all the years you have lived.

Helen Keller

....

OUR SENSE OF smell is perhaps the most underrated of our five major means of perceiving the world. Most of us hardly ever pay it any heed at all until we come in contact with a foul, recoil-inducing stench or have a cold and the subsequent loss of our ability to smell takes all the fun out of everything we eat.

But think about it. You have a highly sensitive instrument attached to the front of your head composed of hundreds of uniquely sophisticated olfactory receptors – exposed neurons acting as chemoreceptors – that are so mind-bendingly advanced that you'd dismiss the possibility as science fiction were it not as plain as the nose on your face. That we can detect and isolate different molecules and pass corresponding electrical impulse messages on to the olfactory bulb in our brain is complicated enough. But our brains then interpret the impulse patterns and, if recognized as a match within our memory databases, can even prompt us to name the odour from more than 1 trillion different olfactory stimuli (smells) that are said to be discriminable by humans simply by coming into contact with a sufficient concentration. Just by breathing. How awesome is that? Sure, we have to lock-and-load the precise smells of all those molecules in our memories in order to name them. It takes practice, like learning the basic words of a foreign language and then building-up an understanding of the syntactical combinations – smell fluency, if you will - but it's possible. People can and are trained to speak the language of smell. Perfumers for one. And wine dorks.

Wine is slightly unique from other beverages and foods for, amongst other attributes, its COMPLEXITY of AROMAS. There are estimated to be more than 800 different AROMA compounds in a glass of wine as opposed to say a banana, which has closer to 300. What's more, a lot of the AROMAS in wine become volatile, in other words airborne and smell-able, at lower temperatures (generally best at room temperature or slightly below) than many other scents, which may need heating before they enter a gaseous state that can be detected by the nose. You could say that wine and your nose were made for one another.

The world's best-known and most respected wine critic, Robert Parker, famously insured his nose for a million dollars. Far from an episode of nasal paranoia, he and other wine professionals rely so heavily on their natural ability to smell that we would lose our jobs if we lost our noses. Without a fully functioning olfactory system it would be impossible to recognize the triumphs and failings in a glass of wine. So embracing the greatness of your nose is a prerequisite to understanding the meaning of wine quality.

Hold on. We don't drink wine through our noses, do we? Sure, not everyone knows all the hoity-toity ins-and-outs of wine quality but most folks know what they like. So a normal person just out for a good time doesn't need to get their nose sniffing all over the glass to have fun with wine, right?

Let's start by asking this: Why did humans evolve the ability to smell? On a basic level it's obvious that, similar to our other senses, our nose helps us to survive. It helps us to detect danger, such as a gas leak or the smoke from a fire. Awful smells like the stench of rotten meat or the pungency of bleach are so off-putting we'd be out of our minds to want to consume these potential killers. But some foul smelling things are good to eat, like Munster cheese or durian fruit and some enticing AROMAS emanate from poisonous plants and flowers, such as arsenic, cyanide and hemlock. So it isn't all about sorting the wholesome from the deadly.

And while much of this book is devoted to demonstrating how your sense of smell, backed-up by your other senses, can be used a tool to measure the relative greatness of wine, smell offers much more in the search for quality than this.

Did you know that when we eat or drink something it is our sense of smell that largely accounts for the FLAVOURS we "taste"? As we inhale and exhale while drinking or eating we continue to smell via the oral cavity located at the back of the throat. This is known as "RETRONASAL OLFACTION". When RETRONASAL SMELLING is combined with our sense of taste within the mouth the result is very different from smelling or tasting alone, one which we have come to understand as FLAVOUR. Because we can only actually recognize five basic tastes with our tongues, in fact most of the FLAVOURS we "taste" in this manner result from RETRONASAL SMELL. Our brains tend to combine the effects of our 2 senses into 1, which we have come to know and value as the FLAVOURS that we "taste" even though the real heroes here are our noses and our remarkable sense of smell!

The olfactory bulb that controls smell helps to make up our brain's limbic system, an area which also includes the hippocampus and amygdala. This part of the brain is involved in the functioning of our memories, behaviour and moods. So more than hearing, seeing, tasting or touching, our sense of smell is closely connected to our emotions.

It appears that smells are extremely susceptible to inducing conditioned responses because the brain has a tendency to build strong emotional connections between occasions, people, places and times with a smell. So the scent of Chanel No 5 might remind you of your mother and therefore make you feel safe or uneasy, depending on your relationship with your mother. A sniff of a burning coal might take you back to a fun childhood BBQ or a house fire that terrified you. You may not even know why a smell can make you feel a certain way. Perhaps you hate cinnamon because it unconsciously reminds you of an unpleasant place or experience.

These conditioned responses render smell to be a powerful motivator. The invigorating scents of roasted coffee beans and freshly squeezed oranges wake us in the mornings. The lactic sweetness of a baby as we bend to kiss its head bonds us. The yeasty, toasty goodness of baking bread or the saline meatiness of bacon frying makes us salivate with hunger. The musky sweat of a lover arouses us. The clean, comforting scent of lavender relaxes us. The seductively rich smell of melting chocolate drives us nearly insane with a longing to satiate our choc addiction. Our nose draws us to sustenance, emotions and people. It not only feeds and protects us; smell connects us to our lives.

When it comes to savouring epicurean indulgences, our senses of smell and taste work hand in hand. To a certain extent it's true that smell initially pulls us in and taste satisfies us. But smell is also a vital bolster for taste. Bottom line – and you know this - we can smell far more than we can taste. Our tongues can only taste SWEETNESS, salty, bitter, ACIDITY and, that newly discovered sensation, UMAMI, with perhaps a few other moot stragglers like metals and fatty ACIDS. The many FLAVOURS that think we can "taste" are in fact the combined effect of taste and smell in the mouth. Smelling strongly influences FLAVOUR largely through the function of "RETRONASAL OLFACTION" - the detection of AROMAS while drinking or eating via the oral cavity located at the back of the throat. The brain combines the effects of the two senses into one, resulting in what wine tasters have come to recognize as FLAVOUR. Therefore the basic five tastes tend to exist merely as a handful of clear-cut delineations, outlining our FLAVOUR experience like a pencil drawing before the input of AROMAS fill the picture with colours and vividly bring the painting towards something much closer to life.

So although our tongues may be quite limited in terms of taste receptors, we are easily fooled into thinking we can taste much more because we can smell through our mouths. Just by swishing and sloshing liquids or liquefied foods around your mouth you'll get a whole range of FLAVOURS that are in fact mostly scents. If you should travel to Asia sometime, go to a noodle bar and watch a Japanese person eating Ramen or a Vietnamese person eating pho. They slurp…a lot! Why? Because they know that the noodles taste better and of more when they slurp. Taking air in with the soup will better volatise the AROMAS so that when they hit the back of the mouth they can more easily and intensely be picked-up by olfactory receptors through the oral cavity connecting the nose to the top of the windpipe. This is a clear example of RETRONASAL SMELL in common practice. For this reason hard-core wine dorks will go so far as to slurp their wine, but even if you simply leave it in your mouth a few seconds before swallowing there can be a significant boost to the FLAVOURS you "taste".

Widely recognized nowadays as the "fifth taste", UMAMI is a savoury taste found in food items such as meats, parmesan, truffles, tomatoes and seaweed. The taste is also considered to exist in some wines. Personal experience suggests that savoury, meaty and/ or truffle-like UMAMI flavours can be found in some bottle aged red wines such as Rioja, Barolo and Chateauneuf du Pape.

So go on, I dare you. Smell it. Apple juice, iced tea, beer, whisky, Cabernet Sauvignon or Batard-Montrachet – give it a sniff, a slurp and a swirl around your mouth. I'm not saying you have to make a big song and dance out of it. Please don't. All I'm suggesting is an imperceptible whiff of whatever's in your glass before you drink it; suck a little air in with your sip and let the fluid linger languidly in your mouth briefly before you swallow. This little change will make a big difference. Above and beyond all the minor and major wine quality specific details in the pages to follow, the foremost, easiest, cheapest thing you can do to get more from your glass or in fact from anything is simply to smell it.

BUT BEFORE WE BEGIN... ARE WE ALL ON THE SAME SMELL PAGE?

....

No two persons ever read the same book.

Edmund Wilson

....

WE'RE NEARLY READY to get into the nitty-gritty of what wine quality means and how it can be assessed but before we begin I feel I need to fill you in on Part 2 of the background story. Unless you are quite content to simply marvel at your own wine discoveries without ever sharing your observations and evaluations with anyone else, let's first ask ourselves a fundamental question: Are we all on the same page when we talk about what we smell / taste? In short, not always. In fact, hardly at all. Actually, almost never...

VARIABLE 1: We do not all smell and taste with identical equipment: noses & tongues. And so we do not all smell and taste things the same even if we smell and taste the same things. This is because there are slight to pronounced variations amongst the olfactory systems and tongues of individuals.

The Nose: The differences in our senses of smell are genetic since each of our olfactory neurons or receptors are linked to one of around 400 receptor genes that detect "primary scents". So except in the case of identical twins, no two people will have the same genetic make-up or in fact the same sense of smell. If a receptor gene is damaged or gone from your DNA, you might not even be able to smell some AROMAS. The term "specific ANOSMIA" refers to the absence or loss of a particular smell, for instance some people can't smell vanilla, and others can't detect camphor, or violets or types of musk...the list of specific anosmia types goes on and on. The truth is that everyone is specifically anosmic, but most of us aren't aware of our odour failings. In extreme cases "ANOSMIA" is diagnosed as the complete loss of the ability to smell. ANOSMIA has been known to occur with brain damage (e.g after accidents to the head), the onset of Alzheimer's disease or even certain viral infections can cause temporary or permanent loss of smell. Congenital ANOSMIA means that someone was born without a sense of smell. HYPOSMIA is a condition that involves a decrease in an individual's sense of smell while HYPEROSMIA refers to an increase in olfactory sensitivity. Apart from being able to detect a particular scent / molecule, noses vary enormously in the perceived INTENSITY of AROMAS. What may appear quite a strong odour to one person may be relatively weak to another. And there are differing "DETECTION THRESHOLDS" (concentrations at which an odour can be perceived) amongst individuals. In essence, we all have our own unique smell worlds!

The Tongue: The difference in noses is just part of the story. Tongues, our other primary tools for wine evaluation, are also markedly different amongst individuals. The disparity here is once again in the receptors, or taste buds, which like olfactory receptors, are linked to genes. But the major, most easily recognised taste difference amongst individuals is mainly due to the number of taste buds people have – some people can have up to three times more than others! This means there can be a huge variation in the INTENSITY of FLAVOURS that people taste and for "SUPERTASTERS", those with densely budded palates, bitterness in foods can seem particularly prominent whereas those with fewer taste buds may hardly taste a bitter substance or not detect it at all. It's estimated that around 25% of the population are SUPERTASTERS, with a notable tendency towards women. Studies have revealed such basic differences in the tongue can significantly impact our food (and, consequently, wine) preferences and shape our lives as impacted by our diets.

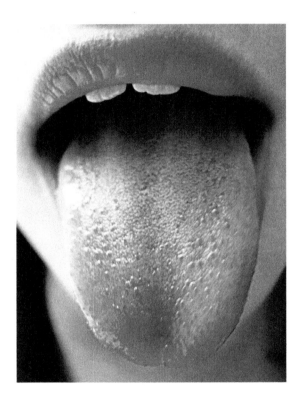

Are you a "SUPERTASTER"? It is easy to find out. Simply place a drop of blue food colouring on your tongue, spread it round with a swish of water, then place a pre-prepared ring-binder made hole over your taste buds and count the number of taste buds within the hole. (A magnifying glass helps.) If you have more than 30 taste buds within the hole, you're likely to be a SUPERTASTER! A more precise test is by placing a bitter PROP (short for the compound 6-n-propylthiouracil) laced tab on your tongue to determine if this bitter substance can be tasted. SUPERTASTERS will hate the bitterness of PROP whereas average tasters may think it's not so bad and "non-tasters" won't taste it at all.

VARIABLE 2: We do not always agree on what to call a smell. Yeah, yeah, yeah, we have Ann C. Noble's famous wine Aroma Wheel and others like it to prompt us with all kinds of wine industry accepted DESCRIPTORS. And we have whole sections of libraries filled with wine books telling us stuff like, "Cabernet Sauvignon smells like cassis", "Merlot smells like plums" and "Sauvignon Blanc smells like gooseberries". Rote learning like this has on the plus side provided the wine world with ready-made lexicons with which to communicate about wine but on the minus side has likely predetermined the drinker's experience and consequently our acceptance of what "good" examples of wines smell like. Ultimately these lexicons can operate as overly simplified and sometimes misleading abstractions that are completely disjointed from what really occurs when we experience and discuss wine. Perhaps the Sauvignon Blanc we're sniffing doesn't smell at all like gooseberries although does measurably (as detected via GC-MS and trained ORGANOLEPTIC methods) contain a high level of METHOXYPYRAZINE (a compound common to green peppers) but what we may have learned is that Sauvignon Blanc smells like gooseberries and, whether we have ever smelled a gooseberry or not, because that's the only varietal DESCRIPTOR we have at hand, that's how we believe and, unfortunately, sometimes do name the smell of Sauvignon.

Our general lack of properly learned / tested ability to precisely detect, isolate and name smells can also be a handicap even when the smells don't have obvious visual or otherwise known markers (e.g. rote learned varietal, regional, winemaking, OAK, etc., DESCRIPTORS). So imagine you are sniffing at some cloves and someone asks you to describe what you smell. You would promptly remark that they smell like "cloves"...and of course they do. The main chemical compound responsible for that very distinctive smell of cloves is known as EUGENOL, which also found in lesser concentrations cinnamon, nutmeg, bay leaves, basil and wine. The eugenol in wine in fact comes from oak barrels during the MATURATION process. An OAK aged wine containing EUGENOL can literally give off the scent of cloves, but wine tasters that are completely unaware of the OAK ageing factor (and even sometimes if they are) may not always name "cloves" in their descriptions and even rarer do they call it EUGENOL. Assuming they have an olfactory receptor to detect the smell, if the taster hasn't learned to isolate and recognize that compound they may not mention it at all. Or they may remark that the wine smells of "cinnamon", "allspice" or is "perfumed", "spicy", "herbal" or automatically associate that compound with OAK and jump to "oaky" or "woody". All these DESCRIPTORS are of course valid in the fuzzy world of wine descriptions but they may mean different things to different people and, most importantly, could well convey an impression of a smell in the wine that is not at all like what it really is: EUGENOL.

VARIABLE 3: The "This wine tasted better on holiday!" Syndrome, as I call it. There is strong evidence to suggest that extrinsic / contextual factors can significantly influence our perception of wine. Recent studies, most notably by Dr. Charles Spence at the Department of Experimental Psychology at the University of Oxford, have revealed that everything from the wine's colour and glassware to scenery, the configuration of a room, room temperature, our mood, ambient smells and music can affect our enjoyment of the wine…and our judgement.

What is the best environment for wine quality tasting assessments?

The most important considerations when creating a tasting space for quality assessments are: smell, temperature, lighting and sound since these can all significantly influence your perception of wine. First of all, make absolutely certain that your chosen area doesn't offer any competing smells such as food, flowers, paint or air freshener. Keep the ambient temperature on the cool side, ideally 18-22 degrees C, to preserve the scents of wines. Oh, but be careful of outdoor breezes, fans or air-conditioning units blowing your way – these could blow the smells right out of your glass! Try to taste in a well-lit room, preferably with access to natural light though bright halogen lamps are also good. Make sure you have ready access to a pure white background up against which your wine glass can be held to check the clarity and colour depth of the wines being assessed, though beyond this I don't get too hung-up on colour. A quiet space is preferred as annoying noises or even favoured music can alter your mood and therefore your judgement. Give yourself plenty of table room for bottles, spittoon (within spitting distance), writing tools / laptop and the wine glasses. Another important consideration is the glassware. When assessing quality I always taste with the same glasses for all wines as the size, shape and thickness of glass can alter not just your perception, but the availability and intensities of smells and in the pursuit of fairness, all wines should be treated equal. Finally, make sure your space is comfortable and without distractions (e.g. phone, internet, children / colleagues, etc.) so that 100% of your focus is on the wines you are assessing.

That's a lot of variables, huh? So how can we all get on the same smell / taste "page"?

Well, some possible solutions are:

Solution to Variable 1: Calibrate our "equipment". Critics should know / ascertain their physiological smell and taste strengths and weaknesses, if merely to compensate for factors should they verge widely off the "norm". Are they, for instance, "SUPERTASTERS" with a freakish ability to taste the slightest hint of bitterness, which can produce quality conclusions that are actually of no use to most of the planet? Or might they have a specific ANOSMIA to 2, 4, 6, TRICHLOROANISOLE (or TCA for short), the compound responsible for "CORKED" wine? Perhaps his or her nose is so unusually sensitive that the critic is detecting many nuances that are lost on the average wine consumer and therefore irrelevant. The bottom line is this: however heightened or lacking a professional's or critic's nose and tongue are, it would be helpful (some would argue essential) to have a definitive, diagnostic awareness of the tools we're using to assess wines.

Solution to Variable 2: Train and test professionals to recognize particular molecule / compound scents that are most common to wine (while simultaneously establishing if they cannot detect certain smells as suggested in 'Solution to Variable 1') and then agree on what to call those scents. This would likely involve isolating particular compounds or finding benchmark examples in wines and training students. There are a few institutions offering courses that only partially address this issue, though in my view not very well. There are also DIY scent-training kits available, like the popular "Nez du Vin" boxed sets that offer for example 12 of the isolated AROMAS of "White Wines" or "Wine FAULTS". (www.nezduvin.co.uk) But perhaps even more precise and valuable is the more recently developed range by a UK company called Aroxa of "FLAVOUR standards" specifically designed for professional tasters. Their taster training kits offer a much wider range of beverage specific (including wine specific) isolated chemical compounds in capsule format (just add water) with accompanying details of the compounds' origins, DETECTION THRESHOLD ranges and suggested DESCRIPTOR names. (www.aroxa.com)

Solution to Variable 3: Standardise our surroundings when assessing wines professionally. (e.g. Always taste with the same glassware, in the same room of a similar temperature, avoid music / noise, etc.) This should preclude professional tasting assessments performed in winery cellars, at tasting events, trade shows, media lunches, etc. as the differing atmospheres are quite likely to alter opinions in some way...although in the wine industry a great many tasting assessments are performed precisely in these aforementioned venues.

A Tasting Room of One's Own – Tasting facilities don't need to look like hospitals. Within certain lighting, ambient smell and temperature guidelines, it's important to create comfortable surroundings for quiet contemplation.

Don't these methods of calibration, testing and standardisation already happen with professional wine tasters, at least to get these guys all on the same page?

In short, not always. In fact, hardly at all. Actually, almost never...

There are almost no incidences of routine scientific testing on tasters within the professional wine community to calibrate let alone evaluate the noses and palates of those "in the trade". Perhaps at the top of the rigor tree, MASTER SOMMELIERS and MASTERS OF WINE need to pass intensive BLIND TASTE tests (i.e. the wine's identity is concealed) that involve wine identification (grape variety, origin, vintage, etc.) in order to achieve the qualification. The AWRI (Australian Wine Research Institute) runs a four-day, "Advanced Wine Assessment Course", which is reasonably thorough albeit brief and needs to be backed-up with real experience. Other organisations may vary enormously in their standards of testing and therefore the validity of accreditation.

But – and I'd like to stress this <u>BUT</u> - with or without a qualification, ultimately the proof in a wine professional's abilities is in the measurement of the following for their opinion. In other words, how many people agree with their tasting notes, reviews and/ or RATINGS of wines and are willing to put their money where that critic's mouth (and nose) is? Wine consumers around the world have embraced particular critics who appeal to their palates and taste with consistency to a well-defined, justly considered and easily understood set of principles. It's not exactly scientific but the wine community has happily muddled along with this system for many years with very few dissenters. And while I may be playing devil's advocate here to present a full-disclosure on the subject and ultimately better balanced view, I wouldn't include myself as a dissenter in this case from the wine status quo. There'll be far better opportunities for dissention from the accepted wine ranks in the chapters of the book that lay ahead, I promise.

WHAT WE TALK ABOUT WHEN WE TALK ABOUT WINE QUALITY

....

Any philosophic explanation of Quality is going to be both false and true precisely because it is a philosophic explanation. The process of philosophic explanation is an analytic process, a process of breaking something down into subjects and predicates. What I mean (and everybody else means) by the word 'quality' cannot be broken down into subjects and predicates. This is not because Quality is so mysterious but because Quality is so simple, immediate and direct.

Robert M. Pirsig, Zen and the Art of Motorcycle Maintenance

....

THE ROLES OF wine can be likened to those of a car. Produced ostensibly to be a means to an end, both the transportation device and the beverage offer an array of many experiences on many levels. They may simply satisfy basic needs, taking the passenger on a journey from a-to-b / quenching a thirst, when that's all that's required. Or they can develop into total collecting obsessions. But they are also regularly used as relaxing pastimes and sometimes even as centre pieces for an event or an occasion. Occasionally they are merely toyed with on holidays; often they develop into hobbies. A special example could offer a treasured once in a lifetime opportunity. Both can be multi-tasking: of simple construction and function when that's what is required, yet poised for more erudite pursuits. For fun, nostalgia, culture, historical interest, as a mental challenge, companion piece or even as a badge of wealth, the duties of either consumer good are, in theory, as complex or as simple to understand as the beholder wants them to be. At one end of the job list, wine serves as an easy, refreshing, straightforward alcoholic beverage made from fermented grape juice. Or it can be mentally rewarding in the intellectual challenge it offers. And at the other more lavish, sensually stimulating extreme it can offer a mind-blowingly hedonistic experience. Wine serves many purposes.

Now don't worry, even as a wine professional hanging mainly around that hedonistic camp I'm not about to wax lyrical for pages about how much wine is like a sexy set of wheels. Nor will I endlessly expound in excruciatingly dorkorific details how wine is made or describe the glory of epiphany moments – that's all for you discover if you so choose. You may or may not be interested in knowing that Chablis is made from Chardonnay. Conversations about WILD YEAST, Vosges vs Alliers OAK barrels and post- FERMENTATION MACERATION times could keep you surfing the web all night or send you straight to sleep. Maybe you drank a glass of 1985 Henri Jayer Richebourg and had a vision of Bacchus dancing on the CORK. Or you had a glass of fizzy wine at a party only because your host ran out of beer. Who cares? Your level of wine knowledge, experience and indeed involvement thereof matters little. The only fact that is of concern here is that you drink wine and therefore above and beyond all else, *you want it to be good.* You want quality.

So let's begin by setting basic parameters: What are we talking about when we talk about wine quality? If we put aside most of the tail-chasing philosophic and semantic considerations of the word 'quality', we're really just determining a wine's degree of excellence. "But what is the 'scale' of this degree of excellence?" you may ask, the answer to which may well be a counter enquiry as to the length of a piece of string. Or a more satisfying response is this: as undefinable as the concept "quality" may be, the degree to which a wine fits its purpose will suffice. And as we've already established, wine has many purposes.

With our fit-for-purpose definition as a scale against which to measure wine quality, we're ready to get cracking. Though saying this will have many a philosopher rolling over

Wine has many purposes.

in his or her grave, the defining was the easy part. But to establish the degree to which a wine fits its purpose, whatever that purpose may be, is another matter. In order to do so it is necessary to grasp how quality in wine is constructed or, to borrow the car analogy again, to understand wine quality mechanics. This is the stumbling block for most seekers of this holiest of wine grails. For the vast majority of wine drinkers throughout the world their evaluation of a wine's quality is an opinion on whether they like or dislike the wine. As naive as this may sound to serious winos, this presumption is not so completely off the mark; in fact there are several schools of thought asserting that wine evaluation even by the most uncompromised of experts inevitably incorporates at least an element of such subjectivity, unconscious or not. We're only human after all and wine can be compellingly evocative. But until the day that wine is graded by machines (perish the thought), in order to truly grasp wine quality, the degree to which it fits its purpose, a wine taster needs to put aside his or her own personal preferences, as much as humanly possible, and take an objective view. This involves recognising and assessing the FUNDAMENTAL QUALITY FACTORS or mechanisms of quality and how they relate to one another. As we'll come to see the wine's intrinsic and relative level of excellence at the point of tasting will ultimately result from the vine, its regional / climatic provenance, vineyard site, vineyard management, processing and development of that wine from grape to glass.

Fundamental Wine Quality Factors

To determine the degree of wine quality the experienced taster assesses a number of FUNDAMENTAL QUALITY FACTORS that like the various parts and mechanisms in a car will exist and serve in relationship to one another. Likewise all are vital to a wine's implicit functionality, though some may play more of a critical part than others when we look beyond the role of basic soundness and extend to the pinnacles of the "FINE WINE" experience as achieved through wine excellence.

These FUNDAMENTAL QUALITY FACTORS include:

–   The absence of FAULTS in the wine, although this is sometimes a grey-area
–   Fruit Health & RIPENESS as it manifests itself during tasting
–   The wine's level of CONCENTRATION
–   The BALANCE of the wine's component parts
–   That seemingly intangible concept known as COMPLEXITY
–   And the wine's Length & Nature of FINISH

Additionally there are a few other SUPPORTING QUALITY FACTORS that are less universally embraced, but which sometimes play a role in the final tasting assessment of many wine experts:

– The wine's ability / potential to Age
– Regional typicality
– Value for money
– Drinkability
– Compatibility with Food
– And Uniqueness of grape variety, STYLE and/or region

These somewhat optional indicators will be touched upon in **Chapter 7**.

The Wine Purposes Pyramid

Throughout the course of this book we'll be discussing the meaning and functionality of FUNDAMENTAL QUALITY FACTORS and how to identify their successes and shortcomings across many wine purposes. In other words, we'll be considering wine quality using a sliding wine purpose scale whereby the wine's purpose is a variable, which will necessitate a consideration of its purpose prior to evaluating how well it performs to each quality factor. Therefore it needs highlighting from the get-go that not all wines are designed or indeed expected to perform to every one of the FUNDAMENTAL QUALITY FACTOR standards we'll be discussing, at least not to the highest degree or even so that they're notable. Because by and large not all wine drinkers are looking for that Lamborghini or FINE WINE experience when they buy a bottle of wine; in fact the vast majority are not.

For most folks, those that may be termed as a "low involvement wine drinkers", a great wine experience needn't necessarily be perceptibly complicated by concerns such as relative levels of BALANCE or COMPLEXITY – it is enough that it tastes delicious and isn't for example overtly FAULTY, bitter / unripe, watery or so out of BALANCE that it is not "drinkable". Thus the sense of higher level wine quality concepts such as CONCENTRATION, BALANCE, COMPLEXITY and FINISH will suffice towards the bottom of the pyramid whereas a more tangible awareness of these factors becomes important around the middle and a clearer knowledge of these attributes is sought after and indeed embraced at the pinnacle of purposes. Likewise as we move up that pyramid, drinkers are increasingly interested in nuances such as recognizing variety and/or TERROIR, which are better evaluated with an extensive MENTAL WINE LIBRARY and expressed with clear markers such as CONCENTRATION, BALANCE and COMPLEXITY while accentuated by length and nature of FINISH.

Created to facilitate the discussion of wine quality as it exists across many purposes, to a certain extent the WINE PURPOSES PYRAMID I've constructed for this book is an approximate model demonstrating how individuals' levels of involvement with wine affect their awareness of wine quality factors and personal expectations of what a wine of perceived quality should offer. Based on my own extensive experience of working with consumers in the wine trade (20+ years) and research such as that on perceived wine quality performed by S. Charters, et. al in 2007 and W.V. Parr, et. al. in 2011, quality factors of increasing relevance have been approximately placed amongst the 3 major levels of wine drinker involvement: Low, Medium and High. Irrespective of the precise placement of factors on this hypothetical pyramid, one thing is clear to most wine industry experts – with increased involvement, awareness and indeed knowledge of wine, drinkers develop expectations for wine to extrinsically (grapes, winemaking, marketing, etc.) and intrinsically (taste, COMPLEXITY, drinkability, emotional effect, etc.) do more.

THE WINE PURPOSES PYRAMID

KNOWLEDGE

I want more - the full monty. Let's talk about intensity, balance, complexity and length. Dude, I want my wine's finish to go on and on!

High Involvement Wine Drinker

Wine is exciting & hedonistic.

Extensive mental wine library or reference; History; Terroir; Winemaking

AWARENESS

I'm looking for ripe fruit, decent concentration and balance, but not in so many words. Some complexity wouldn't go amiss either, just don't blabber on about it.

Medium Involvement Wine Drinker

Wine is interesting, cultural, challenging and fun.

Etiquette; Grape Variety; Region; Vintage

SENSE

I just want my wine to taste good, be drinkable, smooth and not give me a headache. I don't want to think about it too much though.

Low Involvement Wine Drinker

Wine is an easy, refreshing, straightforward alcoholic beverage.

Affulence Symbol; Brand; Style; Red, White, Pink...?

More involved wine drinkers want wines that can do more.

Beyond Mechanics

Once we've covered the major parts and mechanisms of wine quality and understood how they work both individually and as a unit, we'll get down to the diagnosis and assessment of the overall state of quality. Now, one thing I'd like to make perfectly clear from this outset: understanding the mechanics of wine quality will not make the wine that you're drinking better or worse. The goal here is to help you isolate the relative benefits and shortcomings in your glass, point the way for you to see wine quality, describe it and perhaps boost your appreciation of the quality more. But to go back to the analogy of wine being like a car – you can have a whole lot of fun and enjoyment with a car without knowing the first thing about how it works. So in the penultimate chapter we'll step back from accepted thought and convention, pause the hard-core mechanics and consider Wine Zen using a somewhat unorthodox parable as an example. The aim here is present a balanced view of all aspects of wine quality appreciation, hopefully showing that both knowledge of the mechanics and an embracement of Zenness can better fulfil your expectations and ultimately enhance your experiences of wines.

Finally the various means of expressing wine quality conclusions will be covered, with an emphasis on expressing your views in a language of wine (WINE-SPEAK) so that they mean something not just to you but to anyone else you may care to share your findings with, either verbally or in the form of written tasting notes. As part and parcel of this I'll broach the contentious topic of evaluating wine by numbers, otherwise known as WINE RATINGS. Up for discussion will be questions such as: How important and indeed valid are RATINGS? Why and when were they developed? What purpose do they serve? And, what are the various RATING systems in common use? We'll also delve into how to assign WINE RATINGS at which stage we will need to commit to a single wine purpose – changing the sliding wine purpose scale to a fixed wine purpose scale – in order to be able to apply the RATINGS with consistency.

But first let's have some fun by popping open the hood / bonnet on wine quality in order to better understand how it's put together.

WINE FAULTS

....

There is nothing either good or bad
but thinking makes it so.

William Shakespeare, Hamlet, Act 2, Scene 2

....

THE FIRST THING TO determine in the assessment of the quality of a wine is if there's anything wrong with the wine. In other words, does it have a FAULT? So here you are, peering into the depths of a wine's colour, sniffing and sipping away, searching, tasting, feeling, swishing the wine all around your palate to find…what? What exactly is a wine FAULT?

Consider for a moment what a wine would be like if it were in that idealistic state of absolute wine faultlessness. It would be a wine that possessed purely desirable grape variety / vine and TERROIR (soil, climate, weather, grower, etc.) derived AROMA and FLAVOUR compounds plus only the winemaking characters that a winemaker intentionally imparted (OAK, desired FERMENTATION derived FLAVOURS, MALOLACTIC by-products, etc.). It is therefore clean of any undesirables. That is not to say the wine is good. On the contrary, once it's past this first test there are a whole bunch of other factors that can render the quality hopelessly wonky. It is simply clean. And clean is always best, right? Oh, if only the topic were that black and white.

Grasping the merits and bummers of that nebulous area between clean and FAULTY needn't be overly daunting. Suffice to say that this whole subject of wine FAULTS could on its own constitute a weighty tome and an onerously technical one at that. But rest assured that wine drinkers don't have to have a PhD in microbiology to determine a wine's relative state of faultlessness in the context of determining wine quality. Most people who have racked-up a reasonable amount of wine-time are already familiar with some of the more likely FAULTS such as CORK TAINT and OXIDATION – unfortunately incidences are just the nature of the beast - or can otherwise detect when an AROMA or FLAVOUR in wine appears 'off' or just *wrong*.

So to start kicking the wine quality tires, let's examine an undisputable wine defect. All FAULTS can occur in greater or lesser degrees but there are some FAULTS that will, at any level, always downgrade the quality of a wine. One of the most prevalent and just plain evil for lovers of wine of these is CORK TAINT or TCA.

Cork Taint resulting from 2,4,6, Trichloroanisole / TCA

A TAINT can be defined as an undesired character that is totally foreign to a beverage or food, normally coming from an exterior source. And indeed CORK TAINT does not arise or originate from grapes or winemaking per se. 2, 4, 6, TRICHLOROANISOLE (or TCA for short) is a chemical compound derived largely from the CORK stopper in a wine bottle and to a lesser extent from other sources such as wood (OAK barrels, roofs, floorboards, etc.) in a winery. There are a few other compounds responsible for "CORK" taint, but this is the major one. TCA is generated by naturally-occurring fungi that often exist in the crevices of wood or CORK (which is the bark of wood) coming in contact with chlorine compounds, which are ubiquitously present in pesticides, cleaning / sterilising / bleaching agents and wood treatments, etc. Chlorine is highly volatile; it disperses easily far from its original source and it's often difficult to keep offending fungi from coming in contact with chlorine. When the fungi meet the chlorine there's an ungodly engendering that occurs, TCA is formed and it ain't pleasant - pernicious in its ability to instantly spoil a wide range of food and beverage items including mineral water, coffee and apple juice.

Naturally produced from the renewable bark of OAK trees (Quercus suber), CORKS have for hundreds of years existed as an excellent closure for wine bottles. However they are far from perfect, giving rise to what many in the wine industry believe to be unacceptably high incidences of TCA. Perhaps the even greater though less measurable risk is "RANDOM OXIDATION" whereby over the course of 15-40 years+ the CORK will gradually lose its elasticity and therefore its airtight seal allowing oxygen into the bottle, which oxidises bottles at varying rates. This means that every single bottle of wine "aged" under CORK will be slightly different in its state of OXIDATION / maturity. For this reason many wine critics will lament over a bottle of older wine gone-bad, exclaiming: "There are no great wines, only great bottles!"

Even if minute concentrations of a few parts per trillion are instilled by TCA generating fungi within the CORK into the wine that it touches, it can be detected by the human nose, imparting an unpleasant mouldy / musty, damp cellar or wet cardboard character. At levels below the DETECTION THRESHOLD TCA can still insidiously damage the wine, muting or otherwise dulling the expression of AROMAS and FLAVOURS in a wine without actually giving the game away that it is CORKED. In my experience, once a CORKED wine is exposed to air the "CORKINESS" does not dissipate; it gets worse. Others claim the wine can recover slightly with air, though this is most likely an effect of becoming accustomed to the smell and/or the TCA odour fading into the background as other wine AROMAS emerge.

Wines can be just a little CORKED or very CORKED – it really depends on how much of the compound is present in the wine and the STYLE of the wine. For example, even the tiniest concentrations will stand out like a sore thumb in Champagne while the same amount may be hardly detectable in a big, red Chateauneuf du Pape.

Recent research performed at Osaka University in Japan suggests that TCA can desensitise the nose, suppressing the nasal sensory cells and causing them to at least partially shut-down. This means it seems likely that when you smell TCA your ability to smell is temporarily dampened. The research also indicates that this dampening effect is accompanied by our brain's conjuring of the tell-tale TCA mouldy smell, which in fact could be a phantom. Regardless of whether the unsightly smell is real or not, one other important TCA fact is that individuals vary significantly in their ability to detect the compound; some are very sensitive to it while others can hardly notice it all. It does take a bit a familiarization to be able to identify the effects but one thing is for certain: even if you can't name that smell, if it's TCA *you're not gonna like it.*

To date, there is no viable cure for a CORKED bottle of wine and the only "quality" solution is to throw the offending bottle away and open another...unless it's the last bottle you have or indeed of that wine on the planet – TCA has no heart for special or expensive CORKS / bottles and makes no exceptions. (Note that wineries can do random testing for TCA on large batches of corks and the best wineries do it on a more representative sample, but it is not practical or practised that a winery tests every CORK.) It is estimated by various sources - everyone from CORK manufacturers to the SYNTHETIC CLOSURE / CORK folks and a whole crowd of agendas in between - that anywhere between 1-7% of all wines bottled under CORK are "CORKED" in some way. So pick a figure somewhere in the middle and that's how likely you are to get a bad bottle. As a final note on this topic and in case there is any doubt, it is highly unlikely that you will encounter a wine with TCA TAINT that has been sealed with a SCREW CAP, SYNTHETIC CORK or a "DIAM", which is a brand of an AGGLOMERATED CORK that is made of tiny cork pieces, treated to get rid of TCA and glued back together into a CORK shape. Wines under these common alternative closures can be

TAINTED before they are bottled from other sources such as wood in the winery but the TCA is usually detected prior to bottling and therefore it should not have been bottled in an unacceptable TCA FAULTY state. That is not to say it doesn't happen; I've had 'CORKED' wines from a bottle with a SCREW CAP. But this is exceedingly rare.

Unequivocal wine defects like CORK TAINT / TCA are uncommon in the big scheme of FAULTS. Most wine professionals who make a business out of assessing quality know that there is a vast grey-area that exists between a) pristine fruit AROMAS accompanied purely by deliberately imparted WINEMAKING DERIVED CHARACTERS and b) totally unacceptable FAULTS like TCA. Truth be told, the overwhelming majority of wines that we drink reside in a grey-area somewhere between the polar absolutes of pristine-clean wines and those possessing so many multiple counts of wine FAULTINESS that they should be classed as hazardous waste. Almost all wines possess a number way more affable rogues - GREY-AREA FAULT characters - that in small doses can contribute a bit of seasoning to wine, though in larger doses constitute a certain level of quality compromise.

Four of the most common of these GREY-AREA FAULTS include:
- OXIDATION
- REDUCTION
- VOLATILE ACIDITY
- BRETTANOMYCES

Oxidation & Reduction

During processing and MATURATION all wines need oxygen but as with any relationship the secret to success here is the degree of exposure and timing. Overexpose a wine to too much and you've got a flat, lifeless case of OXIDATION, too little you can have a stinky dose of REDUCTION… this is basic chemistry.

When we consider the very different AROMAS and FLAVOUR characteristics of OXIDATION and REDUCTION, as FAULTS they would on the sensory surface appear to be completely unrelated. OXIDATION changes the colour, dulls and dries-out the fruitiness in wine, while REDUCTION can instil pungent, sulphurous off-smells or otherwise rather unpleasant SULPHIDE COMPOUNDS or mercaptans. But OXIDATION and REDUCTION are in fact a couple of mischievous paired reactions that go skipping hand in hand in the tank / barrel / bottle / glass throughout a wine's evolution, storage and MATURATION; whenever one does something the other always does something else. Trust me, these two are always up to something and though they're not always good, for sure they are not always bad either.

Now I promised I wouldn't dish out a lot of chemistry in these wine FAULT explanations and I won't go back on that deal by delving into the blah, blah, blahs of redox (the scientific nickname for REDUCTION-OXIDATION) reactions and potentials. So for the purposes of dipping our toes into the most basic understanding the whys and hows of these two GREY-AREA FAULTS, it is enough to know that they are inextricably linked. When an OXIDATION reaction occurs in wine, a REDUCTION action happens simultaneously. Apart from this all you need to be concerned about is the impact that this twosome will have on the AROMAS, FLAVOURS and TANNINS / PHENOLICS (if present) of the wine. So when a wine is exposed / over-exposed to a lot of oxygen, it is likely to develop an "OXIDATIVE" (good ☺) or "OXIDISED" (bad ☹) character. When the wine is protected from / deprived of oxygen it becomes prone to developing "REDUCTIVE" characters, "REDUCTION" or "REDUCED SULPHUR COMPOUNDS" such as SULPHIDES or THIOLS which can be either good ☺ or bad ☹ depending on how they manifest themselves, to what degree they exist and of course however they may appeal or offend in the eye of the beholder.

Oxidation

Let's start with OXIDATIVE ☺ characters vs OXIDATION ☹ . As soon as the skin of a grape is broken, the juice is exposed to oxygen and it is prone to OXIDATION. This is why winemakers generally avoid crushing fruit until just before it's ready to be prepared for FERMENTATION. Chilling grapes and juice can help to slow OXIDATION reactions but not stop the process. Therefore if grapes or juice are to be left for any period of time prior to FERMENTATION, inert storage conditions will be sought (e.g. protecting the grapes / juice in a non-reactive container like stainless steel with a covering of non-reactive gas such as CARBON DIOXIDE / CO_2, Nitrogen or Argon). And an ANTIOXIDANT will usually be sprinkled or sprayed over the grapes in the form of potassium metabisulphite, which is an easily applied / readily available form of SULPHUR DIOXIDE. Once the FERMENTATION starts, the wine is naturally protected from OXIDATION by virtue of CARBON DIOXIDE, which is a by-product of FERMENTATION and is heavier than air so it "blankets" the FERMENTATION vessel. Thus FERMENTATION, occurring in the absence of oxygen, is a mainly REDUCTIVE reaction. BUT, after all the SUGARS in the grape juice are converted into ALCOHOL and the FERMENTATION stops, CO_2 will no longer be created, is at some point dispersed and then the wine is once again prone to OXIDATION. Ok, so there are a lot of ifs-ands-buts-and-maybes to this sequence, but essentially grape juice and nascent wine are protected either actively or by nature from OXIDATION until the MATURATION stage when the opportunity arises to use oxygen as a stylistic tool.

Slow, controlled 'OXYGENATION ☺ ' as opposed to OXIDATION ☹ can be beneficial to wine quality as part of the MATURATION process that occurs after FERMENTATION. What's the difference between OXYGENATION ☺ and OXIDATION ☹ ? Well there's none really apart from the fact that the former alludes to a winemaker being in control of the wine's exposure to oxygen using it to shape the structure and/or building more COMPLEXITY in the wine, while the latter implies the oxygen exposure is swerving dangerously out of control and headed straight for a cliff.

There are a lot of positive quality benefits to controlled OXYGENATION. A great many red wines and some whites such as Chardonnay are barrel aged, which is a process that allows slow, deliberate exposure to small amounts of oxygen. RACKING (moving the wine from

Why do some of my great and expensive white wines, particularly white Burgundies, sometimes oxidise prematurely in the bottle for no apparent reason?

Ah, that'll be a wine FAULT spectre that's commonly referred to nowadays as "PREMOX", short for PREMATURE OXIDATION. Once dismissed as an urban wine legend, this very real heinous FAULT does what its moniker suggests: oxidises a wine before its time or at least renders bottles dried-out and "dead" ahead of many critics' best-before estimates and that the track-records for a wine's aging potential would suggest. Recent research by Denis Dubourdieu and Valerie Lavigne at the UNIVERSITY OF BORDEAUX suggests PREMOX is the very real prodigal son spawned of wine's ever-present OXIDATION tendencies and, those paving stones to damnation, winemakers' good intentions. The trends to sew cover crops and avoid nutrient additions in the vineyard are partly at FAULT because it seems as these can starve vines and grapes of nitrogen, which is important for the grapes' production of the natural anti-ageing compound glutathione and for ensuring a smooth and complete FERMENTATION and ultimately a more stable wine. Harvesting riper / higher-SUGAR grapes with lower ACID levels and increased pHs combined with a tendency to add less SO^2 and MATURE more wines for longer in barrel may have played to recent consumer preference trends but in doing so have further upset the delicate ageing balance. The use of CORK probably doesn't help either. Other research also performed by Dubourdieu and Lavigne identifies the lactone SOTOLON, a defining feature of many BOTRYTISED wines and RANCIO STYLES, as one of the major offending PREMOX AROMA compounds, its precursor produced in significant quantities by the OXIDATIVE degradation of ASCORBIC ACID as well as a by-product of certain YEAST strains. Now for the really scary part: continued research also by Dubourdieu seems to suggest that this is not just a blight affecting whites and that many red wines, especially from warmer / riper years like 2009 Bordeaux, could also be affected.

one container to another) and micro-OXYGENATION (pumping tiny amounts of oxygen into the wine) are means of exposing the wine to even more oxygen. Slow OXYGENATION can change the fruity or PRIMARY AROMAS in wine into less vibrant yet more COMPLEX AROMAS and FLAVOURS including ESTERS, which are formed of ACIDS and ALCOHOLS combined in the presence of oxygen. The TANNIN compounds in red wines are encouraged by oxygen to combine or "POLYMERISE", becoming larger units that appear softer in the mouth and eventually fall out of solution as sediment, resulting in a suppler / less TANNIC wine. Prolonged exposure to oxygen can further result in OXIDATIVE or "RANCIO" characters arising from the evolution of fruit AROMAS and formation of ALDEHYDES such as ACETALDEHYDE (the OXIDATION of the primary ALCOHOL in wine, ETHANOL). Some of these desirable DESCRIPTORS include: nutty, dried fruit / berry, bruised apple, caramelised, RANCIO and raisin, characters that define distinctive wine STYLES such as Tawny Port, Vin Santo, Tokaji, Oloroso Sherry, Vin Jaune, Rutherglen Muscat, Madeira and Banyuls.

OXIDATION in wine refers to a FAULT resulting from oxygen exposure / dosing gone too far and/or happening at the wrong time. One of the initial and most obvious signs of OXIDATION is the premature deepening and browning in colour of a white wine (i.e. the wine goes from a pale lemon yellow to an increasingly deeper straw, golden and then brown colour) or a red wine that begins to go orange or brown in the rim at an unusually early stage. However be aware that these occurrences can be natural consequences of the grape variety or winemaking. For example, the red grape Nebbiolo is notorious for going orange / brown early-on in its bottle development and OAK barrel ageing of a white wine often deepens the colour. The confirmation of the deleterious impact of OXIDATION is in the smelling and tasting. When PRIMARY AROMA / fruit characters in wine are exposed to oxygen either during wine processing or storage (e.g. once the bottle is opened or when a bottle's closure is compromised and air is allowed inside) they become dulled and / or faded. Examples of the aromatic profile of an OXIDISED wine may include the smells of old apple core, straw, leather, dried berries / fruits, raisins or nuts when clearly these are not part of the wine's intended STYLE. Furthermore the palate will lack freshness and vibrancy. In more advanced stages of OXIDATION the wine is likely to develop VOLATILE ACIDITY (see right) and/or an ALDEHYDIC character from the formation ACETALDEHYDE caused by the aforementioned OXIDATION of the ALCOHOL. ACETALDEHYDE has a somewhat bruised / old apple and nutty smell. If you're interested to know what precisely what ACETALDEHYDE smells of, get a bottle of fino or manzanilla sherry, as the flor YEAST that produce this distinctive wine generate large amounts of ACETALDEHYDE and in this case the ALDEHYDIC character is part of its STYLE.

Apart from those wines that are deliberately made to an OXIDATIVE STYLE, another grey-area with OXIDATION is that many of the characters just mentioned will naturally develop over time during bottle ageing and as part of the way a wine may MATURE into a more COMPLEX, EVOLVED, or MATURE nose, commonly referred to in our somewhat

OUTDATED WINE JARGON as a "BOUQUET". But certainly when present on a young wine, particularly one destined for early drinking such as most Beaujolais wines, Pinot Grigios or Sauvignon Blancs, OXIDATION is likely to dull and flatten the character of the wine, detracting from the wine's quality and constituting a FAULT.

Reduction

REDUCTION is the opposite of OXIDATION; it's a chemical reaction within the wine that happens in the absence of oxygen. The main concern is the REDUCTION of sulphur, an element common in wine (both naturally present and added), and sulphur compounds resulting for example in the formation of the foul smelling FERMENTATION by-product HYDROGEN SULPHIDE (H_2S).

So let's back up a second. What business does sulphur have being in wine anyway? Sulphur (sulphate) is naturally found in grapes albeit in very small amounts. During the process of fermentation it gets converted into a very effective ANTIOXIDANT known as SULPHUR DIOXIDE or SO_2 for short. An ANTIOXIDANT does just what it says on the tin. It protects wine from oxygen and therefore OXIDATION by binding with it - kind of like a policeman cuffing him/herself to a prisoner – and therefore the oxygen can no longer do its damage. This works great for keeping wine from oxidising. The problem is that wines

OXIDISED or well-aged? It's hard to judge if a wine is suffering from OXIDATION just by looking at the colour. If this amber coloured wine was a glass of a young, dry Sauvignon Blanc, it would most certainly be OXIDISED. It was however a beautifully mature glass of 1957 Chateau d'Yquem Sauternes, drinking at its peak. So the verification of this GREY-AREA FAULT is ultimately in the taste!

naturally have very little "free" SO₂ available to handle a potential OXIDATION situation and this free SO₂ can get "bound" to rogue oxygen molecules very quickly so that it is no longer effective in tackling the rest of the oxygen gang that may be lingering in the wine and indeed any potentially hazardous newcomers. That's why winemakers commonly send in the supports: added SO₂.

I've already mentioned that FERMENTATION is a REDUCTIVE process, meaning that it occurs in the absence of oxygen. It is very common during FERMENTATION, particularly if there is a low level of YEAST nutrients (namely nitrogen) available in the juice, for some of the sulphur present in the wine to be converted into a simple but very stinky REDUCED SULPHUR COMPOUND known as HYDROGEN SULPHIDE or H₂S. This is a foul, 'rotten egg' or pronounced sulphurous smelling molecule that is thankfully a highly unstable / VOLATILE FAULT and can usually be dispersed simply with aeration (e.g. RACKING the wine, decanting the bottle or swirling the glass), though this method does of course carry with it the risk of OXIDATION. It's formation can also be controlled by winemakers by adding nitrogen to the fermenting wine, usually in the form of diammonium phosphate or DAP. However, if H₂S is allowed to form and left untreated in a REDUCTIVE environment (in the absence of air such as in a closed tank or sealed bottle), it may combine with other elements in the wine to form more stable odorous "REDUCTION" compounds such as other SULPHIDE COMPOUNDS (inc. DIMETHYL SULPHIDE / DMS and dimethyl disulphide), MERCAPTANS / THIOLS, METHYL MERCAPTAN or ETHYL MERCAPTAN. These compounds are incredibly varied, commonly manifesting themselves in a struck-match, rubber or burnt tire character but also sometimes giving notes of garlic, canned corn, olives, onions, truffles, dirty drains and sewage. Once these are formed in the wine they can be much more difficult to get rid of than simple H₂S.

How common is REDUCTION and when are you likely to see it? Generally speaking, thanks to the science of modern winemaking the malodourous side of REDUCTION is fairly uncommon but it does rear its ugly head sometimes in wines that have been produced with very little air contact and very occasionally with those sealed under SCREW CAP, which is more REDUCTIVE than most CORKS. Also worth noting it that some grape varieties such as Syrah / Shiraz appear to be particularly prone to REDUCTION, which in the case of this cultivar tends to manifest itself as the aforementioned rubbery, burnt rubber or struck match characters especially in a young / recently bottled wine. Or it can appear as an earthy / truffle and sometimes lifted raspberry fruit character - perhaps through the influence of DIMETHYL SULPHIDE (DMS) on its glycosidic AROMA PRECURSOR. REDUCTION in such incidences may or may not be appealing depending on how complimentary and pronounced it is. Another example is certain Chardonnays, especially those that are aged on LEES (which create a REDUCTIVE environment), can similarly have a struck-match or "SULPHIDE" character that may be considered remarkably pleasant in small doses, otherwise an overpowering detraction. AROMATIC VOLATILE THIOLS (as they are sometimes termed) are a set of REDUCTION compounds that are sometimes actively sought-after by winemakers who may even choose specialised CULTURED YEAST that are targeted specifically to generate AROMATIC VOLATILE THIOLS from previously odourless AROMA PRECURSORS in grapes. For example, 3-mercaptohexanol is the REDUCTION (and sulphur containing) thiol of a grape-derived AROMA PRECURSOR in Sauvignon Blanc that lends an appealing grapefruit or passion fruit like smell to the finished wine. 2-Furanmethanethiol is another AROMATIC VOLATILE THIOL thought to be generated from AROMA PRECURSORS found in Petit Manseng, Cabernet Sauvignon, Cabernet Franc and Merlot lending the AROMA of roast coffee to some wines produced from these grapes.

Volatile Acidity (VA)

VOLATILE ACIDITY may well sound like a diabolical chemical warfare agent but I can assure you it is completely harmless. In fact volatile ACIDS are naturally occurring components that are present in all wines. ACETIC ACID is the most abundant of the volatile ACIDS in wine, existing in very small concentrations as a by-product of FERMENTATION. It is also a major component in vinegar, lending its distinctive AROMA and taste. Now wine doesn't ordinarily smell or taste of vinegar, and indeed it shouldn't if its level of ACETIC ACID is within the range that is naturally generated even with careful handling and production methods and is in BALANCE with the other components in the wine.

Here's the dark side of this "FAULT": ACETIC ACID is produced in unpleasantly high concentrations when the wine is exposed to omnipresent ACETIC ACID generating bacteria (called ACETOBACTER) in the presence of oxygen, usually as a consequence of OXIDATION. So as a wine oxidises it is increasingly likely that its level of ACETIC ACID will dramatically increase over time and usually within a few days of exposure during winemaking or a bottle being open / exposed to oxygen you will be able to detect the distinctive "vinegar" smell and taste. When the vinegar character becomes notable, overpowering and/or uncomplimentary to the STYLE of wine, VA can certainly be a FAULT and in extreme cases render the wine undrinkable.

But at the more acceptable end of this GREY-AREA FAULT, some wines and indeed STYLES possessing relatively high and even detectable levels of VA may not call-for a negative tick against quality and this can even be a positive. Such is the case with some older / MATURE red wines and STYLES like a very old Bordeaux red or an Amarone. Another STYLE exception worth considering is BOTRYTISED sweet wine (where the grapes are infected with BOTRYTIS CINEREA or NOBLE ROT in the vineyard) within which it is natural for a much higher level of ACETIC ACID to be present than in a table wine and in this incidence a very slight whiff on the nose and tang on the palate can contribute to COMPLEXITY. If this sounds crazy then consider this foodie example: think about how much better a rich, oily beurre blanc or butter sauce is with the added and notable freshness of a little vinegar. Now imagine great Sauternes where the INTENSITY and richness of the wine is complimented by the "lift" from an elevated yet harmonious level of VA. Not so bad after all, eh?

Brettanomyces (Brett)

Infamous for the last 20 or so years as the YEAST responsible for a lot of stylistic changes and/or malingering damage (depending how you look at it), affecting even some of the most venerable wine names produced throughout the world, nowadays wineries everywhere are on high alert for public YEAST enemy No 1: BRETTANOMYCES, AKA "BRETT". This common YEAST genus generally works differently from the beloved SACCARAMYCES CEREVISIAE wine YEAST whose main job is to convert the SUGARS in grape juice into the ALCOHOL in wine, though BRETT can produce ALCOHOL. In fact BRETTANOMYCES was first discovered by ale breweries in the UK just over a century ago doing just this and yielding a very *different* tasting beer. Today it is embraced by a small clutch of brewers for the unique character it instils, but elsewhere in the alcoholic beverage world it mainly viewed as no-good-dirty-rotten spoilage YEAST. In sectors of the modern wine world the faintest whiff of BRETT is enough to stir-up an angry lynch mob of FAULT-busters, but taking into account consumer perception, acceptance and indeed preferences, in a practical sense it is well within the grey-area.

Grey-area or not, given BRETT's tendency to get out-of-control it is never a welcome guest in wineries. BRETT is a consummate gate-crasher. Throughout the wine FERMENTATION process, if BRETTANOMYCES is around it's generally not a problem as SACCHARAMYCES CEREVISIAE tends to dominate the microbial population in burgeoning wine as the life and soul of the SUGAR party, converting all that's possible for this YEAST into ALCOHOL. The trouble begins 'the morning after' FERMENTATION finishes, particularly for wines that are not STABILISED straight away with FILTRATION (which strips out any unwanted YEAST cells) and

The Barrel Cellar - A Potential Party Venue for Brett

SULPHUR DIOXIDE additions. (Apart from being an ANTIOXIDANT, SO_2 is also anti-microbial, inhibiting the activity of BRETT. It's also worth mentioning at this stage that SO_2 is even more effective at lower pH levels and BRETT less so, which is why a lot of white wines with higher ACID levels have increased natural protection against BRETT.) There is a growing trend these days for many FINE WINES to have minimal STABILISATION in an effort to preserve as much of their original character as possible as they enter a period of MATURATION, often occurring in wooden barrels. Herein lays BRETT's golden opportunity. BRETTANOMYCES has the ability to party-on with types of RESIDUAL SUGAR that are not fermentable by wine YEAST, as well as OAK imparted SUGARS (e.g cellulose and hemicellulose) that come from new (not previously used) barrels. And even if up to the point of MATURATION the wine had remained BRETT-free, sources of infection can come from BRETT lying dormant in the receiving OAK barrels, having the ability to survive on the smallest traces of substrates and hide deep into the wood's crevices. BRETT can furthermore lurk on all kinds of winery surfaces or find its way in on grapes or equipment brought in from another winery and without too much effort finds its way into the stash: maturing wine. Therefore winery hygiene has increasingly become an essential tool in recent years for controlling BRETT infiltration.

Although BRETT has the ability to survive on and metabolise SUGARS and make ALCOHOL like its rival SACCHARAMYCES CEREVISIAE, the big grief with this interloper is the mess it leaves behind: a range of imparted odorous by-products. The two by-products of major concern to winemakers are: 4-ETHYLPHENOL (4EP), giving rise to sweaty saddles, barnyard, earthy and sometimes medicinal, Band-Aid or iodine notes, and 4-ETHYLGUAIACOL (4EG), producing smoky, charred, menthol or somewhat spicy aromas of cinnamon stick and cloves. These by-products are mainly synthesised from AROMA precursors existing in grapes: coumaric ACID for 4EP and ferulic ACID for 4EG. These precursors are most abundant in the POLYPHENOLS found in grape skins. Since some grape varieties, particularly reds such as Mourvedre, Syrah, Cabernet Sauvignon and Pinotage, naturally contain more POLYPHENOLS and therefore more of these precursors, they are by nature predisposed to "BRETTINESS" if they come in contact with the yeast.

Now – don't panic straight away if you smell spices, earth, leather or smoky characters in your prized glass of wine. Not all wines demonstrating some of the DESCRIPTORS common to BRETT will necessarily have BRETT or its by-products. It is important to know that there are a good many grape and/or OAK derived AROMAS and FLAVOURS that can appear very similar to 4EP and 4EG, so some condemnations by the BRETT police could be overly hasty. But with experience you can learn to lock-on to the very specific BRETT smells and, for the most part, separate them from competing grape, OAK and bottle age smells. If the presence of these compounds is not glaringly obvious, the only failsafe way to sort the contribution of other wine characters vs the BRETT is to measure the concentration of the offending by-products by isolating the main compounds using gas chromatography and a mass spectrometer (GC-MS).

Nearly all wine industry laboratories that conduct such tests and advise on "FAULTS" have a tolerance range for acceptable, virtually undetectable levels of 4EP and 4EG and can otherwise offer services to deal with out-of-control situations.

If a winemaker detects a BRETT infected barrel either through smell/taste or more scientifically through testing the wine for the tell-tale by-products, BRETT growth and its formation of by-products can be halted before the bottling stage by removing the wine from the barrel, sterile FILTERING it to get rid of the YEAST (but not the by-products), and returning the wine to a clean barrel or tank. Furthermore 4EP and 4EG in wine can, in extreme cases, be removed using REVERSE OSMOSIS, essentially an even more stringent form of FILTERING. It is not a good idea to bottle a wine that contains any BRETT YEAST cells as they can and often do continue their activity in the bottle so long as there are nutrients in the wine upon which to survive, and as we've already established BRETT doesn't need much, so the impact of BRETT in the bottle can be unpredictable and more often than not detrimental. FILTERING – sterile FILTERING to get rid of YEAST and/or REVERSE OSMOSIS to remove the by-products - is the best means to control the spread and damage of BRETT... however the TRADE-OFF is that FILTERING to these levels is also likely to remove some of the good elements / COMPLEXITY in the wine too. By far the best way to deal with Brett is prevention: a strict winery hygiene policy and sufficiently deterrent SO$_2$ levels...but unfortunately not all wineries are all that vigilant when the vintage party is in full swing.

How common is it to come across a BRETT contaminated wine? Well, hate to say it but even with all recent, easily accessible scientific knowledge of this pesky intruder and how to control it, it still manages to get around a lot and at least in small doses remains fairly common in certain wine STYLES. Since its main contamination opportunity is during the MATURATION process and because OAK barrels are by nature notorious back doors for contamination (being nearly impossible to sterilize completely), BRETT infection particularly tends to affect the character of barrel aged wines, which usually includes these STYLES of red wines and a few similarly handled whites, especially if they are not STABILISED, contain any traces of any SUGARS (ergo riper STYLES are more vulnerable) and fall within higher pH ranges. Another point already mentioned is that thick skinned red grape varieties (high in polyphenol levels) contain more of the AROMA PRECURSORS for 4EP and 4EG, and as previously mentioned this renders them more predisposed to BRETT forming increased levels of these compounds. Wines bearing the hallmarks of BRETT have emerged from just about every major wine region of the world, most famously affecting even some of the finest red wines from Bordeaux, the Rhone, Napa Valley, Chile, Australia, Italy, South Africa... and the list goes on and on!

Although in larger doses it is generally considered a FAULT in wine, there is a grey-area as to the impact or even contribution of BRETT in small to medium doses. UC DAVIS research performed by Lucy Joseph and Dr Linda Bisson has uncovered evidence to suggest that BRETT DNA mutates easily and therefore may be vineyard specific, adding support to arguments that it contributes to TERROIR expression in as much as WILD or NATURAL YEAST used to conduct the primary alcoholic FERMENTATION do. Plus when you consider that the majority of BRETT AROMAS are not unpleasant per se, unless someone is utterly BRETT-intolerant (and there are a good many *look-at-me-I-can-spot*-BRETT wine experts in this camp) it is understandable how a little BRETT can be considered as seasoning. In fact recent research has been conducted by the AWRI in Australia, UC DAVIS in California and Stellenbosch University in South Africa on the consumer acceptance of BRETT by-product containing wines, all of which indicated that a small to moderate amount BRETT associated with certain wine types (e.g. red, OAK aged wines) is actually considered very palatable. Dr. Linda Bisson of UC DAVIS has gone so far as to compare BRETT to "a color in an artist's palette" while unveiling her "BRETTANOMYCES Aroma Wheel" in 2013. For sure if the BRETT characters in a wine are appealing, complimentary and in balance with other elements in the wine, it does seem "a foolish consistency" to damn its contribution to COMPLEXITY altogether. However levels of 4EP and 4EG significantly above the DETECTION THRESHOLDS can, apart from being generally considered unpleasant in nature, more importantly dominate the delicate nuances of the GRAPE DERIVED AROMAS and, arguably, TERROIR or "sense of place" (if this is one of its purposes as a quality indicator) in wine, unquestionably constituting a FAULT.

Superficial Faults

Before we sign-off on this topic of wine FAULTS and GREY-AREA FAULTS, it's worth mentioning a few of the more common SUPERFICIAL FAULTS that can occur in wines. "SUPERFICIAL FAULTS" is a term I use for occurrences that can mar the look / appearance of wine but not the smell or taste. A perfectly faultless, flawless wine appearance dictates that wine should be crystal clear. While the insistence of clarity may sound overly fussy, there is some method to this madness. Not only can a cloudy wine just plain look unappetising, but the lack of wine clarity can suggest real but relatively rare FAULTS such as post-bottling microbial spoilage. Such incidences are usually due to the winemaker's choice to use little or no anti-microbial additives (e.g. SO_2) and/or FILTRATION at bottling. Nowadays many FINE WINE producers and NATURAL WINE makers try to use little or no SO_2 additions and/or FILTRATION. The exclusion of such treatments is a complicated and contentious issue that has as much to do with philosophical pursuits as it does with minimising additives and preserving all of the naturally imparted characters in wines that ultimately contribute to COMPLEXITY. But without these treatments there is always the chance, however careful the winemaker may be in terms of hygiene and minimising opportunities for microbial contamination, that some rogue YEASTS and/or bacteria are bottled with the wine. If so, microbial activity such as a second FERMENTATION or MALOLACTIC FERMENTATION could occur in the bottle, resulting in a cloudy wine and sometimes instilling notable bubbles or even fizziness to the wine plus unappealing changes to the AROMA and FLAVOUR profile. And if this or similar microbial activity (there are a wide range of possible microbial contaminants) happens, while the affected wine poses no health threat, it is unquestionably ruined, constituting a full-blown wine FAULT. Therefore when winemakers avoid SO_2 additions and/or FILTRATION they always run a risk of spoilage of which consumers should be aware.

More commonly a wine may simply be cloudy or contain bubbles (if a still / non-sparkling wine) due to harmless suspended sediment (especially if it has some bottle age and hasn't been properly settled and decanted) or some largely inoffensive residual CO_2 from protective bottling, which either preserves / makes use of the naturally instilled CO_2 left in the wine after FERMENTATION or injects some in the head space between the wine and closure to replace the ambient oxygen and therefore opportunities for OXIDATION.

PROTEIN HAZE is another SUPERFICIAL FAULT that doesn't affect the smell / taste of the wine but can render it with a distinctly cloudy appearance. This can happen when residual protein molecules - that are so small they are not visible in wine - POLYMERISE (combine), particularly when exposed to warmer storage conditions, to form larger visible particles, which give wine a cloudy appearance that is usually not advisable to rectify through FILTRATION once it occurs. Red grapes generally contain far less heat unstable proteins than white grapes. Also the POLYPHENOLS in red wines usually precipitate protein molecules out of red wines during FERMENTATION as they combine with TANNINS to form part of the sediment (LEES) that can be separated from the wine after FERMENTATION and/or LEES AGEING have completed. Therefore PROTEIN HAZE is far less common in red wines. Most white wines are STABILISED against PROTEIN HAZE by FINING them with bentonite. Some grape varieties such as Sauvignon Blanc are particularly prone to high levels of unstable proteins and therefore bentonite FINING is pretty much a requirement. However some FINE WINE white winemakers avoid or at least minimise such FINING if at all possible as it is felt that that over-FINING with bentonite can strip some of the nuances from the wine that give it COMPLEXITY. Most quality conscious winemakers nowadays test wines for protein instability prior to bentonite additions to minimise over-FINING...but that is not to say that routine use and occasional overuse does not exist. In drastic cases it is possible to FILTER out protein particles using ultrafiltration (an extreme form of CROSS-FLOW FILTRATION) but this is mainly used as a cure rather than prevention as this level of FILTRATION also strips out some PHENOLIC and AROMA compounds.

TARTRATE CRYSTALS or wine diamonds at the bottom of the bottle are other harmless, SUPERFICIAL FAULTS that may detract from the look but not the palate. They are naturally formed during winemaking when TARTARIC ACID combines with elements in wine, mainly potassium, to form insoluble salts such as potassium bitartrate. They are more common in white wines than red wines for two principle reasons: 1) the high levels of POLYPHENOLS in red wines inhibit the formation of TARTRATE CRYSTALS and 2) the crystals are less soluble at cooler temperatures and white wines are generally kept at colder temperatures than reds. Because they can look unappealing and sometimes alarming to unaware consumers, many wines are now COLD STABILISED prior to bottling in order to force any unstable TARTRATE CRYSTALS out of solution and avoid incidences of their occurrence during bottle storage / ageing. A few FINE WINE white winemakers feel however that COLD STABILISATION is an overly harsh treatment that can strip wines of nuances and they therefore avoid the practice.

Since SUPERFICIAL FAULTS like sediment, minor CO_2 bubbles, PROTEIN HAZE and TARTRATE CRYSTALS don't affect the nose or palate of the wine, it's up to the taster to decide if they are quality detractions. PROTEIN HAZE is generally considered a FAULT as is it particularly unappealing but professionals and consumers are far more tolerant of sediment, minor CO_2 bubbles caused by protective handling at bottling and TARTRATE CRYSTALS. Certainly a wine critic should in the very least comment on such occurrences in an assessment, though they may leave damning marks / remarks out of their assessment. Ultimately the choice to accept or reject a wine with superficial FAULTS is up to the consumer. The one possible exception is in the case of very old bottles (e.g. 30 years+), where it can be rare to find an example that is crystal clear and bereft of any suspended sediment and therefore minor cloudiness as a matter of course for old bottles should be accepted by consumers as part and parcel of drinking old wines.

Final Word – Detection Thresholds and Subjectivity

As a final word on FAULTS, it needs mentioning that an individual's DETECTION THRESHOLDS (levels at which various AROMA compounds are detectable) can convolute the whole clean or FAULTY discussion. Even the greatest wine critics in the world differ in their ability to detect lower levels of compounds such as TCA or 4EP. Furthermore subjectivity (personal preference / tolerance) and can lead to divergent views about GREY-AREA FAULTS. One taster might consider the level of a GREY-AREA FAULT in a wine to be an unacceptable detraction from the fruit and will downgrade the wine's quality while another taster might find that the same character does not degrade and may even enhance the wine. In my book, while life is too short (and livers are too valuable) to drink bad or FAULTY wines, there is also nothing more boring than a wine that is so clean and sterile that the 'life' has been stripped out of it. More to the point, it is another vital quality factor – BALANCE (covered in **Chapter 4**) – that will always play the deciding role in this grey-area debate.

FRUIT HEALTH & RIPENESS

....

Before everything else, getting ready
is the secret of success.

Henry Ford

....

YOU'VE PROBABLY ALL heard the familiar phrase: You can't make a silk purse from a sow's ear. Well, it is likewise impossible to make great wine from terrible grapes (though, as you'll soon discover in **Chapter 3** and **Chapter 4**, quite easy to make a terrible wine from great grapes). Great quality wine must first and foremost be inherent in the grapes from whence it comes. As suggested in the previous chapter on wine FAULTS, this begins with healthy grapes free from undesirable FAULTS. Not all FAULTS happen in the winery though; there are a few that can arise in the vineyard, damaging potential quality prospects even before the grapes make it to the cellar. These are usually caused by fungal diseases such as mildews, undesirable BOTRYTIS / 'GREY MOULD' or a related microbial metabolite known as GEOSMIN, all of which can infect grape bunches during the growing season. Pests, small (e.g. bugs, moths or insects such as PHYLLOXERA) and large (e.g. birds or even kangaroos), can damage grapes and/or reduce vine productivity and the vine's ability to ripen grapes. Viral diseases such as leafroll and bacterial infections of the vine like Pierce's disease are slightly more insidious, infecting vines almost without exception incurably, stunting growth and berry ripening until the disease eventually consumes the vine. In extreme cases an entire crop can be wiped-out by disease or pests.

Fortunately a better understanding of the causes and control of such potential blights as well as increasingly sophisticated fruit sorting in the vineyard and winery have kept detectable vineyard FAULT AROMAS and FLAVOURS in wine - including mouldy, earthy, beet / turnip, VOLATILE, vegetal or just plain dirty characters - to a minimum in recent years, though they still rear their ugly heads from time to time.

Apart from healthy fruit, a concern of major quality importance is GRAPE MATURITY otherwise known as the RIPENESS of the grapes at the time of harvest. Now if wine faults were something of a grey-area, well the concept of "RIPENESS" is an even murkier topic because like the nature of quality itself, it is to a certain extent subjective. What may be considered an ideal level of RIPENESS by one winemaker might be over-ripe to another and under-ripe to still another.

Furthermore, optimal RIPENESS greatly depends upon the STYLE of wine being produced. For example the RIPENESS of grapes used for high quality sparkling wines would in most cases be considered far too under-ripe to make a still wine. The best sweet wine grapes conversely are generally ripened to SUGAR levels that would equate to ALCOHOL levels too high for balanced dry styles.

To understand how RIPENESS can impact STYLE, BALANCE, CONCENTRATION, COMPLEXITY and ultimately quality, it's important to have a basic grasp of what chemical changes occur both within the berry's flesh and in its protective outer layer, the skin, as the berry approaches maturity. The fundamental changes relating to RIPENESS are followed by the

Grape Sorting at Jasper Hill Winery, Heathcote, Australia

grower and/or winemaker particularly after VÉRAISON - when grapes just begin to change colour - and in the run-up to harvest by monitoring and often measuring the ripening progress of key maturity indicator grape components including: acids, sugars, TANNINS and aroma / flavour compounds.

In many viticultural regions of the world birds are a major pest capable of consuming or damaging the quality of an entire vineyard in a matter of hours. Although costly and labour intensive, one widely used solution is to cover the entire vineyard in netting when the grapes approach maturity and are at their most vulnerable. Pictured here are nets being applied at one of Vasse Felix's vineyards in Margaret River, Australia, where birds are an annual disaster waiting to happen!

How can I spot a wine made from disease or pest damaged grapes?

It can be very difficult to know for sure from tasting alone if wine quality has been directly or indirectly impacted by pests and diseases. Under-ripe characters such as vegetal / herbal AROMAS, lack of AROMAS / FLAVOURS and bitter TANNINS can be a clue to a struggling, disease ridden vineyard or vintage. There are a number of microbial or pest disorders in vineyards around the world that can devastate crops or, in lesser doses, noticeably impact the colour, smells, FLAVOURS, STABILITY and therefore quality of wine. Some of the more prevalent examples include:

Name	What is it?	Look / Smell / Taste?
BOTRYTIS CINEREA or GREY MOULD	A ubiquitous fungal disease that infects grape bunches. It is particularly detrimental to red wine quality, directly impacting the colour of wines. However "good" BOTRYTIS, sometimes known as "NOBLE ROT", produces some of the greatest sweet white wines in the world by concentrating SUGARS and ACIDS in the berries.	Negative effects (i.e. not including wines made from intentional "NOBLE ROT" infected grapes) include diminished fruitiness, lessened / dulled colour, increase in VA, increase in tendency to oxidise, lends a 'sweet & sour' character, can impart a phenolic or iodine-like character and in extreme cases can appear "mouldy".
POWDERY MILDEW (OIDIUM)	A fungal disease that starts in the green tissues of the vine and therefore affects ripening and YIELDS. In worst cases POWDERY MILDEW can spread to grape bunches.	POWDERY MILDEW mainly affects the vine's ability to ripen bunches possibly rendering under-ripe characters in wines although in severe cases it can cause bunch rot with similar effects as BOTRYTIS CINEREA.
GEOSMIN	A metabolite / organic compound produced by various moulds (fungi) and bacteria. Detectable in wine at very low concentrations, it can contaminate just a few bunches of grapes and still have a significant impact.	Imparts an earthy (i.e. like wet dirt or PETRICHOR), beets, turnips and/or sometimes musty/ mouldy smell in wine. It used to be (and often still is) attributed as a "TERROIR" character. Sometimes it is considered to contribute to COMPLEXITY and therefore could be included as a GREY-AREA FAULT. This compound is thought to degrade over time and be barely detectable in wines after a few years of bottle ageing.
Mealybug (family Pseudococcidae)	An insect that feeds on plant fluids and reproduces in ripening grape clusters, excreting a sweet, gooey substance called honeydew, which seems mainly to pose a risk to resulting wine quality by encouraging the growth of moulds.	Makes wines more prone to OXIDATION and reduces PHENOLIC content in red wines.
Asian ladybird (Harmonia axyridis) / European ladybird (coccinellidae) / ladybug / lady beetle /	Harmonia axyridis is a type of ladybird / ladybug indigenous to eastern Asia and now present in Europe and North America. It feeds on damaged grapes in the run-up to harvest time and, if present, can be harvested and processed with the grapes. During crushing and pressing the bug releases hemolymph – a circulatory fluid containing foul-smelling defensive compounds, most notably a METHOXYPYRAZINE (IPMP). It is now believed the common European ladybird species (coccinellidae) can also be responsible for the TAINT.	"LADYBIRD TAINT" (LBT) is caused by the release of 2-ISOPROPYL-3-METHOXYPYRAZINE (IPMP) into MUST (grape juice) imparting a distinctive green, leafy, herbal or bell pepper character reminiscent of under-ripe fruit. Fruit sorting, lighter pressing and MUST heating can minimise the impact but once a significant amount is in the wine (above DETECTION THRESHOLD) it is difficult if not impossible to remove and does not appear to degrade with time. Some believe many 2004 Red Burgundies are afflicted with LBT.

Ripening: ACIDS & SUGARS

Throughout the growing season the most fundamental change within the berry is directly related to the photosynthesis process we all learned about as kids: ultraviolet light falling on chlorophyll in the leaves converts CARBON DIOXIDE from the atmosphere into carbohydrates in the form of SUGAR (sucrose) within the leaves, which is then transferred to the berries and converted (hydrolysed) into grape sugars (mainly glucose and fructose). Thus sustained periods of sunlight over the growing season result in a correlating increase in SUGAR levels in the berries as they "ripen". SUGAR accumulation is critical to wine grapes because the amount of SUGAR in grape juice directly impacts the amount of ALCOHOL by volume and RESIDUAL SUGAR, in some cases, in the finished wine as well as the BODY or appearance of relative weight that a wine gives. As you can guess, SUGAR is directly impacted by the amount of sunshine and to a certain extent heat that the vine receives. Therefore a sunny and consequently dry (but not drought affected) climate or vintage will equate to an increase in grape SUGARS in the berry more rapidly and often to a higher concentration at harvest than a cloudy or rainy and therefore cooler climate or vintage.

Throughout ripening as the SUGAR level increases in a grape so do the levels of ACIDS but not proportionately so. The two major ACIDS in wine grapes are TARTARIC, an ACID unique to grapes, and MALIC, an ACID common to other fruits such as apples. Although TARTARIC ACID continues to be manufactured in the berry throughout ripening, the overall CONCENTRATION of ACID decreases relative to that of other components such as SUGAR and water. And in fact the more sour MALIC ACID is respired or consumed by the berry during ripening, generally resulting in grapes that are higher in the less tart TARTARIC ACID at the time of harvest. Therefore a better BALANCED grape is naturally achieved as "RIPENESS" approaches in the run-up to harvest. This relationship between SUGAR and ACID is often expressed by winemakers as a ratio as they monitor the ripening process and eventually choose a harvest date based on optimal fruit RIPENESS for the vintage's conditions.

Because they're such fundamental WINE COMPONENTS, minimum CONCENTRATIONS of SUGARS and ACIDS have traditionally been considered important indicators for calling a harvest date. In the relative sense of modern winemaking however, the achievement of acceptably high enough levels during ripening have become of lesser concern. Nowadays SUGAR and ACID additions can easily be fudged in the winery and if done judiciously and at the right time the AMELIORATION is more or less undetectable. CHAPTALIZATION, the adding of sucrose (SUGAR) to grape juice prior to FERMENTATION to increase the final level of ALCOHOL, has been practiced in cooler climates for centuries, since Roman times in fact, is still legally permitted in some major regions of the world and commonly performed in those today. In certain cases such as some German Rieslings sweet grape juice, called SÜSSRESERVE, can be added after FERMENTATION to BALANCE the higher levels of ACIDITY. ACIDIFICATION, usually involving the addition of TARTARIC ACID (and less often MALIC or citric ACIDS), is commonly practised in warmer climates and vintages where legally permitted and where SUGAR levels can be sufficiently high but ACIDITY may be lacking or the PH is too high to the extent of producing a potentially unbalanced (e.g. flat, flabby, cloying or dull) and unstable wine.

Adding SUGAR or ACID to forge a better BALANCED wine may be relatively easy-peasy for winemakers these days but it is still way more difficult to take them away from the juice without affecting other components. DEACIDIFICATION, the lowering of ACIDITY with correlating increase in PH in grape MUST or wine, is performed occasionally where permitted in some of the cooler areas of Europe such as Germany and in cooler vintages in New Zealand. It is a chemical process that involves adding a harmless compound, normally calcium carbonate, potassium carbonate or potassium bicarbonate, which will encourage some of the TARTARIC ACID in wine to crystallize and come out of solution as TARTRATES, after which it can be removed. Another far more common, ubiquitously legal and arguably 'natural' means of lowering the appearance of ACID in wines is MALOLACTIC conversation more commonly known as MALOLACTIC FERMENTATION or MLF. In truth, it is not a 'FERMENTATION' but a conversion of the tarter, more sour MALIC ACID in wines into the softer, less edgy LACTIC ACID, performed by the action of LACTIC BACTERIA that are either naturally present in the winery or added. This is done on almost all red wines around the world since they pretty much universally benefit qualitatively from the 'roundness' that LACTIC ACID lends. There is only really one white grape that ubiquitously gets the malolactic treatment: Chardonnay, especially cooler climate / higher ACID examples such as wines from Champagne, Chablis and the Cotes de Beaune. Why just red wines and Chardonnay but no other white grapes? Well apart from the fact that most white wines actually benefit from more apparent ACIDITY or "freshness" than reds, another effect of MALOLACTIC conversion is a subtle to pronounced change to the FLAVOUR profile of the wine, depending on the strain of LACTIC BACTERIA used and the amount of MALIC ACID that is converted. The converted wine's PRIMARY AROMAS will be degraded and new by-product compounds of the conversion will be instilled, including the distinctly buttery smelling / tasting DIACETYL. The AROMA / FLAVOUR changes of MLF are far less noticeable on red wines, and can particularly compliment Chardonnay but this is much less true of other white varietals such as Riesling or Sauvignon Blanc. If it compliments and plays a BALANCED role in the wine, MLF changes can contribute to COMPLEXITY, but if wrongly used it can mar the purity and/or overpower the fruit, so care needs to be taken.

Too much SUGAR in grapes is the bane of many warm climate growing regions. If the SUGAR level is too high (e.g. > 20 baume or 15% potential ALCOHOL) the winemaker runs the risk of not achieving a smooth (and more likely FAULTless) and complete FERMENTATION (i.e. only trace amounts of RESIDUAL SUGARS) as the YEAST struggle at such high SUGAR and ALCOHOL CONCENTRATIONS. Apart from this, too much SUGAR is also likely to equate to an excessive level of ALCOHOL in the wine and heaviness to the BODY, which could both render the wine difficult to pleasantly drink (see comments on "drinkability" in **Chapter 7**) and out of BALANCE. A few inventions in recent years have made it possible to remove some or all of the ALCOHOL in finished wines – notably REVERSE OSMOSIS and Spinning Cone devices. While these are reasonably effective at what they do, they are generally considered harsh treatments that can also strip some of the desirable compounds, concentrate the less desirable components and/or otherwise alter wines, therefore are not considered ideal solutions and will often be dismissed as an option by FINE WINE makers.

All this talk of lowering ALCOHOL begs the question - if a winemaker is so busy monitoring sugar levels in the run-up to harvest, why might he/she allow SUGAR to accumulate more and sometimes a lot more than is ideally desired? The answer lies within the complex ripening puzzle of wine grapes that consists of many changes occurring within the berry, each triggered by differing mechanisms. Continual researchers' gradual connecting of the pieces to this ripening puzzle has led to the recent revolutionary change of primary focus in grape-growing, switching the emphasis on SUGAR accumulation to far more important pursuits: getting the TANNINS and FLAVOUR compounds ripe.

Ripening: TANNINS & FLAVOUR Compounds

Winemakers are intensely aware that nowadays the trickiest part of berry ripening - critical to wine quality - is achieving RIPENESS of TANNINS and AROMA (FLAVOUR) compounds / AROMA PRECURSOR compounds. Known somewhat imprecisely as achieving PHYSIOLOGICAL RIPENESS or otherwise referred to more specifically as PHENOLIC RIPENESS, these quality factors beyond achieving basic SUGARS and ACIDS levels are very difficult if not illegal (in the case of adding non-GRAPE DERIVED AROMA compounds to wine in many wine producing nations) to manipulate in the winery and even then the results will not be a quality-compensation but a compromise.

TANNINS play an important textural role wines, as well as contribute to the BODY and STRUCTURE of mainly red wines. Their ANTIOXIDANT properties are critical factors in the ability of red wines to age. But unresolved or "unripe" TANNINS can be deeply unpleasant. Not only can they make a red wine hard, seemingly "rough" or coarse in the mouth with an overly ASTRINGENT TEXTURE and generally lacking finesse but they're bitter – the one taste that wine shouldn't have.

Unripe / undeveloped FLAVOURS are equally bad. These can result in a relatively flavourless wine, lacking in CONCENTRATION or one that at the very least is simple in nature, robbed of its true potential for COMPLEXITY achievable for a given grape variety and/or vineyard.

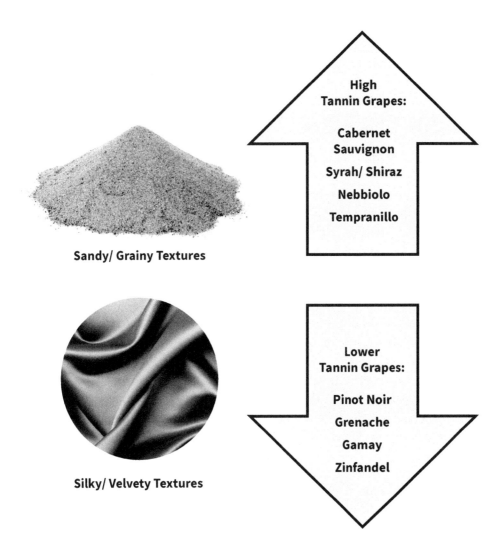

Sandy/ Grainy Textures

High Tannin Grapes:

Cabernet Sauvignon

Syrah/ Shiraz

Nebbiolo

Tempranillo

Silky/ Velvety Textures

Lower Tannin Grapes:

Pinot Noir

Grenache

Gamay

Zinfandel

And occasionally under-ripe FLAVOURS can be manifested in wines as mild to pronounced leafy, herbal, green pepper and/or vegetal streaks caused by the presence of unresolved METHOXYPYRAZINES, which can be particularly unappealing if too pronounced in red wines.

To understand how such unripe travesties against wine quality and hedonic nature could happen, first let's consider TANNINS. TANNINS are types of POLYPHENOLIC COMPOUNDS (POLYPHENOLS or PHENOLIC groupings) produced in plants, characterized by their ability to interact with and precipitate proteins. (In fact their ability to "tan" leather was how they got their name.) Part of the sensual effect TANNINS produce on the palate is their interaction with the proteins on the tongue and sides of the mouth, producing a drying feeling or sensation of ASTRINGENCY that is commonly described by wine experts as anything from sandy / grainy (more ASTRINGENT) in TEXTURE to silky / velvety (less ASTRINGENT).

TANNINS play important sensory roles on the palate of wines, contributing to the MOUTH-FEEL, BODY and to a lesser extent the FLAVOURS of almost without exception red wines. Why not white wines? Because apart from the ASTRINGENCY of TANNINS not suiting the STYLE of most white wines, it's the skins of red grapes, integral to the red winemaking process, which contain far more TANNINS than white grapes. That said, some white grapes such as Chardonnay and Gewurztraminer do contain relatively high levels of TANNINS for white varieties, which winemakers can either work with to build textural character (MOUTH-FEEL) or not, depending on the wine STYLE they envisage. Red or black skinned grape varieties vary in the levels and types of TANNINS they produce in the skins. Generally speaking, the thicker the grape skin, the more TANNINS the variety tends to produce. The size of berries is also a factor in determining the amount of TANNINS a grape can give relative to volume of juice. Smaller berried grapes offer lower skin to flesh ratios and therefore potentially more TANNINS. So the smallest berried, thickest skinned black grapes tend to offer the most TANNINS, a good example being Cabernet Sauvignon, while varieties with larger berries and thinner skins such as Grenache produce less TANNINS relative to the amount of juice.

Another point to consider is that while wines and especially reds mainly get TANNINS from their grape skins, a small amount of "lower grade" TANNINS (generally more bitter and harsh because they consist of smaller / seemingly harder subunits such as CATECHINS rather than larger / more ASTRINGENT compounds) can come from SEEDS and STEMS, to the extent that these are used.

TANNINS in wine can also come from sources other than grape skins, SEEDS and STEMS, such as new OAK barrels, OAK staves, OAK chips and/or they can be commercially bought and incorporated with the fermenting MUST as "ADDED TANNINS", though these TANNIN sources mostly (but again not always) play supporting roles to the wine's natural skin derived TANNINS.

Can I detect the difference between TANNIN types in wine?

With practice experienced tasters can usually spot subtle textural and taste differences between the specific TANNIN contributions from the major sources although this would not be an overly precise assessment because wines almost always contain TANNINS from more than one source and each source contains more than one type of TANNIN with some sources sharing some of the same types of TANNINS. For interest's sake, here are some generalizations:

TANNIN source	TANNIN type(s) & contribution to wine
Grape Skins	Grape skin TANNINS are highly varied in nature and range from smaller CATECHIN and epicatechin units, which tend to be the "unripe", bitter sort with a low degree of polymerization, to "ripe" or highly POLYMERISED compounds. Ideally skins should mainly contain larger / highly POLYMERISED molecules such as procyanidins and prodelphinidins resulting in TANNIN-protein or TANNIN-polysaccharide complexes, which offer greater ASTRINGENCY but less bitterness to wines. The nature and composition of skin TANNINS can differ significantly according to grape variety and growing conditions. Fully ripe grape skins should have low or undetectable levels of CATECHINS. The lack of bitterness in wines with fully ripe TANNINS is occasionally noted as "sweet" TANNINS by critics, though in fact they contain no SUGARS.
Grape STEMS	Grape STEMS contain high levels of TANNINS consisting mainly of proanthocyanidins and CATECHINS and these are generally of a much lesser degree of polymerization than ripe grape skin TANNINS. They are occasionally used in red winemaking (especially with Pinot Noir and Syrah wines) to boost TANNIN levels, but should be used judiciously as they are generally more bitter and can give a harsher effect than grape skin TANNINS. Note that like grape skins, STEMS ripen with HANG TIME, becoming browner / less green and less bitter to a degree. Therefore as with grape skins, it is important to aim to use ripe STEMS if STEMS are to be utilized. For more information beyond TANNIC contribution see the **Glossary of Wine Quality Terms** entry on "STEMS".
Grape SEEDS	Seed TANNINS largely consist of CATECHINS and epicatechins with relatively very low degrees of POLYMERISATION compared to grape skin or even STEM TANNINS. They tend to be overly bitter and harsh and are therefore generally avoided by winemakers by minimising contact during MACERATION and level of pressing. Like grape STEMS, SEEDS ripen from a green colour / harsher tannin sensation (largely due to their more extractable nature) to a less extractable nature and brown colour / apparently softer feel with HANG TIME.
OAK **Barrels, Staves and Chips**	OAK derived TANNINS tend to consist of hydrolysable (soluble) ELLAGITANNINS with TANNIN levels imparted in wine depending on the species of OAK (e.g. AMERICAN OAK or FRENCH OAK), where it is grown, how it is seasoned and TOASTED, the amount of wine surface area in contact with the OAK (e.g. size of the barrel) and the period of time that wine spends in contact with the OAK. For the most part only new / first use OAK gives any significant level of TANNINS. ELLAGITANNINS can be broken down into 2 major groups: 1) monomers, which are relatively ASTRINGENT and 2) dimers, which are relatively bitter. This bitterness and ASTRINGENCY imparted by OAK TANNINS, while generally approachable compared to unripe grape skin, seed or STEM TANNINS, can be a marker for OAK TANNINS and can therefore render them ORGANOLEPTICALLY distinctive from ripe grape skin TANNINS.
ADDED TANNINS	Ok so adding store-bought TANNINS to create or boost existing TANNIC TEXTURE and STRUCTURE levels probably sounds like a bit of a swizz but it is actually very common practice and many of the greatest wines of the world contain "ADDED TANNINS", including some fine red wines from Australia, California, Bordeaux and Burgundy. ADDED TANNINS are commercially produced from a variety of sources, though winemakers can purchase types that only contain grape skin TANNINS or skin, seed and OAK tannin cocktails. Some TANNIN additions contain TANNINS from more exotic sources such as other types of woods and nuts. I tend to find the uniformity of ADDED TANNINS a little boring in younger wines but what these concoctions rob of wine in terms of individuality and sense of place, they make up for in control and consistency. They are sometimes apparent in their overly powdery TEXTURE. If the main reason that they're added is to increase the wine's ageing potential, then as the wine ages and TANNINS polymerise and eventually precipitate out of solution their contribution becomes less relevant anyway. How can you detect commercially produced TANNINS simply by tasting? Well, it is hard to point a finger at any particular characteristic, but if the TANNINS in a wine just appear too uniformly similar, soft and cuddly to be true, they're probably added!

TANNIN production and ripening in the grape's skin differs in means, rate and timing from formations of the SUGARS and ACIDS in the flesh. For a start, grape TANNIN ripening unlike SUGAR ripening is not merely a matter of accumulation; it also involves the development or POLYMERISATION of TANNINS from smaller subunits such as aforementioned CATECHINS into larger, more ASTRINGENT and less bitter 'POLYMERISED' compounds. CATECHIN (as opposed to POLYMERISED or "ripe" TANNINS) content in wines is generally avoided and therefore lower CATECHIN / TANNIN ratios in grapes are generally sought and occasionally analytically monitored by winemakers. Lower CATECHIN content naturally occurs as the berry and its SEEDS ripen and can be monitored by laboratory testing (e.g. ETS Laboratories in California performs such testing) or more commonly by tasting the berry skins and SEEDS for tell-tale CATECHIN associated bitterness and harsh impression. Like many FLAVOUR compounds, which we'll consider in a moment, TANNIN synthesis and ripening happen mainly within a narrower temperature band and at a different pace to SUGAR accumulation. So in an ideal grape-growing world, the weather throughout the growing season will be relatively dry with temperatures and sunlight exposure that are moderate enough to slow the SUGAR accumulation while allowing TANNINS (and FLAVOURS) to progress at steady pace that will eventually become fully manifested and resolved, meeting neatly with optimal (desired) SUGAR RIPENESS within a seemingly magic "harvest window" *at the same time.*

Is it true that lower YIELDS make better wines?

YIELD figures are often used as an indicators of wine quality but, as with so many things when it comes to wine quality, the devil is in the details. The most common means of reporting YIELDS in Europe is tonnes (of grapes harvested) per hectare (of vineyard land) or hectolitres (of wine produced) per hectare. Elsewhere "tons per acre" is the popular means of measurement. YIELDS are often touted as a marker for quality whereby the assumption is that the lower the YIELDS, the better. This premise is the basis for the INAO's (Institut National de l'Origine et de la Qualité - the organisational body that regulates the production of French agricultural products within a region) and similar bodies elsewhere in Europe, which imposed rules on maximum YIELDS allowed within delimited AOC (Appellation d'Origine Contrôlée) regions in France and elsewhere. The presumption is that with lower crop loads to ripen, vines have more opportunity to ripen those loads and produce more CONCENTRATED, fully ripe berries, which make better wine. In fact the "lower-is-better" marketing mantra is often a good rule of thumb but it isn't always the case.

There are a number of variables such as regularly permitted changes to the INAO's "strict" YIELD limits, inaccurate ways of reporting YIELDS and, most importantly, other ripening factors for a given vineyard and vintage that are also crucial to anticipating the calibre of fruit and therefore potential wine quality. For instance, although France's INAO has seemingly draconian rules regarding maximum permitted YIELDS within regions, they also allow for quite a lot of wiggle room on their stipulated figures with the "plafond limité de classement" (PLC) allowance, which can allow for AOC YIELD limits to be adjusted up considerably depending on the vintage. Also the permitted ways of reporting YIELDS aren't always an accurate reflection of what was really produced in the vineyard for that vintage. Often when reporting YIELDS French wineries need only declare the amount of wine they made or potentially made from the harvest *based on the grapes that came into the winery*. But of course this sometimes doesn't include all the grapes that were left unharvested and hanging on the vines – a common practice even in some of the "finest" regions such as Burgundy. Another critical factor not taken into account by those commonly touted, neat-and-tidy YIELD figures is that they don't address what is perhaps the more important figure when it comes to fruit quality: average YIELD per vine. Nor do YIELD figures address key ripening factors such as sunshine hours, soil fertility, water availability, vine health, HANG TIME and the vine vigor or leaves per bunch – all being vital to determining how much fruit a vine can ripen for a given vintage. As examples that the lower-is-better rule doesn't always work largely because of some or all of these other crucial variables, some of the lower yielding vintages in Bordeaux such as 1984 and 1991 have produced predominately lousy wines across the region whereas relatively high yielding vintages like 1982 and 1990 have produced many extraordinary wines. So to suggest that a stand-alone low YIELD figure such as 30 hectoliters per hectare is a direct indicator of fruit quality is to over-simplify what is a very complex equation consisting of many important variables. Often it is best to take commonly quoted YIELD numbers with pinches of salt and recognize that the proof of quality is not necessarily in a direct correlation with a YIELD figure; the proof is in the fruit and ultimately the wines.

TANNIN levels and RIPENESS are quantitatively and qualitatively impacted by a number of vintage and vineyard management parameters. We know, for example, that under-ripe TANNINS can result from excessive YIELDS or cooler vintages lacking sufficient sunshine and heat hours or even overly dense / shaded vine canopies (the vine's cover of leaves and shoots) since under these circumstances the vine simply can't generate enough energy to fully ripen its load. Likewise, in warm climates where rapidly rising SUGAR levels and plummeting ACIDITY force the winemaker's harvest hand, TANNINS may not be sufficiently ripe due to limited HANG TIME.

The most critical period of ripening for TANNINS and generally speaking FLAVOUR compounds, which we'll consider next, occurs after VÉRAISON. The period between VÉRAISON and harvest is of vital importance to grape growers as it is make or break time for quality. The beginning of the VÉRAISON stage is visually characterised when red / black berries will begin to synthesise ANTHOCYANINS (colour compounds) though even white grapes will soften and change from a pale vibrant green colour to more of a deep green, yellow or gold colour. But colour is not the only change occurring in the berry - significantly MALIC ACID is metabolised through respiration, SUGARS accumulate, herbal FLAVOURS degrade and fruity or PRIMARY AROMAS / FLAVOURS synthesise while TANNINS POLYMERISE and become less bitter. All of this of course happens in order to make the "ripe" grapes more attractive to animals, which by nature's design are intended to eat the berries once the SEEDS are ready and deposit these SEEDS far and wide. For grape growers this colour change at VÉRAISON is a visual marker that ripening is about to begin and for those that are more technically inclined ANTHOCYANIN accumulation in skins can be used as an indication of TANNIN and to a certain extent FLAVOUR RIPENESS.

Volatile AROMA and AROMA PRECURSOR compounds are more complicated to discuss because there are so many differing sources involved in the great matrix that constitutes a wine's "BOUQUET". It is estimated that there are more than 800 volatile AROMA compounds contributing to the AROMAS / FLAVOURS of wine in total and not all of them have been isolated yet. The source of wine AROMAS can be broken down into 3 major groups: 1) those that are GRAPE DERIVED 2) the ones that are synthesised through winemaking and 3) others that evolve through the aging process(es).

VÉRAISON marks the beginning of the most critical ripening period.

With regards to the ripening of GRAPE DERIVED AROMA compounds, it is important to note that the CONCENTRATION of some AROMA (FLAVOUR) compounds and AROMA PRECURSOR compounds increase as the grape approaches desired SUGAR accumulation levels while others can degrade, necessitating that the winemaker has a very specific knowledge of his/her grape variety and a clear idea of the wine STYLE plus the AROMA compounds that he/she wants to produce / preserve. Furthermore not all naturally-occurring AROMA compounds are particularly embraced by winemakers, a common case in point being pyrazines or, more specifically, METHOXYPYRAZINES, molecules that can start forming in the berry at an early stage before VÉRAISON and that degrade as the berry ripens.

Known for the green / leafy / herbal characters they lend to wines, METHOXYPYRAZINES are more common in some grapes than others, especially prevalent in Sauvignon Blanc, where the characters are often valued, and its close relatives Cabernet Sauvignon and Cabernet Franc, where they are best avoided. Research indicates that the easiest way

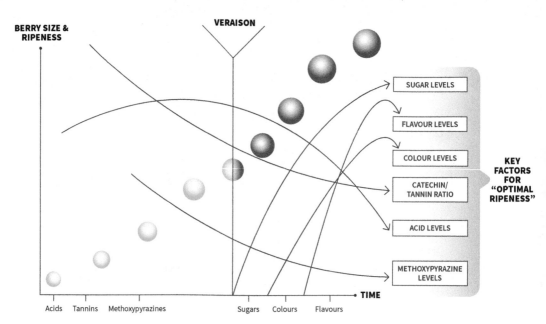

STAGES OF GRAPE BERRY RIPENING

Key Ripening Compounds & their Accumulation Stages

to avoid the formation of the herbaceous METHOXYPYRAZINE characters in grape skins and therefore minimise its presence in wines is to ripen the compounds out with plenty of sunshine on grapes (which can be aided by early shoot and leaf removal) and HANG TIME… but this is not always possible in all climates and/or vintages. Both under-cropping and over-cropping in the vineyard have been shown to exacerbate the METHOXYPYRAZINE problem.

What is also detectable by the wine taster/drinker is that at the extremes of RIPENESS AROMA (FLAVOUR) compounds can either be severely diminished and under-developed or overblown, simple and lacking finesse. If a winemaker harvests too early in an attempt to force an elegant, crisp, lighter bodied / lower ALCOHOL STYLE of wine, the FLAVOUR compounds may be green, lacking or both. If the winemaker harvests too late, aiming for a big, full-bodied, CONCENTRATED STYLE that the vine / vintage / site combination doesn't necessarily want to give, some of the finer FLAVOURS may have started to degrade, giving way to a relatively simple and sometimes a jammy or cooked fruit character, particularly if the grape has started berry SHRIVEL or to "raisin" on the vine.

Another important piece in this ripening puzzle is that at temperature extremes – temperatures above around 35 degrees C or below 15 degrees C – and during extreme drought conditions grape vines go into survival mode and "shut down". Essentially the leaves of the vines will close their pores on the underside, known as stomata, in an effort to minimise water loss through evaporation. This means that the exchange of CARBON DIOXIDE also stops and so until water is administered (via rain or irrigation) or the temperature hits the "growing range" again vines will not continue to conduct metabolic changes in the berries. In fact even short bouts of excessively cold or hot temperatures can be deceptive in their impacts on ripening as it is often difficult to get the vine started again after such a phase, by which time the viable growing season may have been significantly diminished. Heat-waves at temperatures much above 35 degrees C for periods of more than a few days can further produce an unpleasant under-ripe / over-ripe character particularly in red grapes. In other words they can have a green / ASTRINGENT streak from the unripe FLAVOURS (e.g. PYRAZINES) and unresolved TANNINS, but also a baked berry or raisin-like character from the literal raisining (BERRY SHRIVEL) caused by accompanying sunburn and/or dehydration. This can further result in red wines of a paler colour. As a slight aside, OLD VINES (more mature vines, say 20-25 years+) may have an advantage here with their deeper root systems that are better able to source water during drought conditions plus have more stored carbohydrates in their larger root systems and thicker "cordons" (arms) to help stabilise the vine through temperature extremes, minimise incidences of shut down and get them restarted quicker after shut down. (Although note that this hypothesis is purely based on anecdotal evidence from my discussions with growers.)

The inconvenient truth about getting TANNINS and AROMA (FLAVOUR) compounds exactly right is there is a very small moving-target window of ideal harvest date(s) – a culmination of the ideal number of "sunshine days" and temperature ranges during the growing season - that will allow the SUGARS in the berries to accumulate at a steady rate and that gives the TANNINS and AROMA (FLAVOUR) compounds a chance to fully ripen so that they all come together for the desired results *at precisely the same time*.

To intensify this menacing migraine for winemakers...the target window for each grape variety is different. This is why it is so important to marry the right grape variety to a supportive climate and complimentary site for reliable ripening. Otherwise, if the unpredictability of the growing season weather for an area is a known variable, planting a number of different varieties (as is common in Bordeaux) can act as an insurance policy. But any way you slice it, that in all but the world's very best vineyards and vintages the conditions are not going to be ideal for simultaneous SUGAR / ACID RIPENESS and TANNIN / FLAVOUR RIPENESS (termed nowadays as "PHYSIOLOGICAL RIPENESS" or sometimes more specifically as "PHENOLIC RIPENESS") - and they oh-so-rarely are - the winemaker will inevitably be forced to make some sort of a quality TRADE-OFF. This is agriculture after all and far more often than not the results are less than perfect.

A very OLD VINE planted in the 1860s at Henschke Hill of Grace, Eden Valley, Australia

Can "green" or "vegetal" AROMAS / FLAVOURS be minimised with winemaking methods or bottle age?

Usually the "green" aromas / flavours – leafy, grassy, vegetal or herbal characters that sometimes occur in wine – are a result of METHOXYPYRAZINES, either natural to the grape or contaminating the must as is the case with LADYBIRD TAINT. Research indicates that grapes harvested with high levels of MP are pretty much destined to make wines with notably high levels too, as MP is present in both the flesh and skin of berries. SETTLING the juice (in the case of white wines) and thermovinification (heating crushed grapes to very high temperatures prior to fermentation) during the winemaking process have been shown to lower levels of MP but are not always viable or desired methods. Recent studies into the effect of wine ageing on the presence of MP in wines (especially Cabernet Sauvignon, Cabernet Franc and Merlot) using GC-MS have revealed that the level does not decrease with time in bottle nor does the character appear to fade. This supports my own experience following the development of vegetal characters in wines as they age. In the worst cases MP can transform from a somewhat pleasant freshly mown grass, Mediterranean herb or bay leaf character in the wine's youth into a distinctly rotten vegetable odour, which is particularly unappealing in Sauvignon Blanc and one reason why many of the "greener" Sauvignon Blancs are considered not to age well.

In this chapter we've discussed how the ripening process is a diddly of a conundrum. Even getting down the edges of the puzzle here should've helped shed a little light on how the combo of vine, site and climate/weather plus a skilled grower or two has the potential to produce the holy grail of wines...albeit once in a blue moon. Healthy / clean and fully ripe berries – however the grower or winemaker interprets the concept of RIPENESS - though critically important to wine quality, are just another part of the mechanisms contributing to wine quality and one that can easily be let down without winemaker vision and skill. Even pristine fruit harvested at the peak of RIPENESS cannot a great wine make without careful handling to avoid winemaking related FAULTS, which were already covered in the first chapter. But equally essential to wine quality is the measured coaxing by the winemaker to achieve the "right" types and amount of CONCENTRATION for the expression of that vision.

Chapter 3

CONCENTRATION

....

An artist is not paid for his labor but for his vision.

James Whistler

....

THIS MAY COME as a shock to some of the "NATURAL WINE" bunnies out there, but great wine doesn't make itself. And if you've ever heard a winemaker modestly reply to a compliment about his/her wine that, "It's made in the vineyard", well that's just a marketing line full of NATURAL WINE bunny poo.

In the last chapter we established, "Great quality must first and foremost be inherent in the grapes," demonstrating how this potential for greatness is achieved through the health and RIPENESS of the grapes. To put it bluntly though, grapes are simply the raw materials. Just like you can't make an Aston Martin out of tin cans or create the Mona Lisa with finger paints, 1961 Petrus could not be made out of my Italian grandfather's back garden grapes grown in New Haven, Connecticut. But by the same token, if someone had handed my grandfather Petrus' 1961 harvest with which to make wine (as he always had in his bathtub), I guarantee you it wouldn't have tasted too different from the other run-of-the-mill batches of his homebrew.

Winemaking is on the one hand a technical skill. There is a lot of science and chemistry involved in getting to the quality endgame nowadays. Although I will probably get lambasted by techies for romanticising this somewhat science-generated product thus: *great quality wine is also an art*. It's not simply that great wine can be appreciated like art (as one of its purposes if you will); the highest quality wines can only be made by

artists because these wines require vision. Max Schubert (Penfolds Grange), Jean-Claude Berrouet (Petrus), Helen Turley, Henri Jayer, Richard Geoffrey (Dom Perignon), Egon Muller – these are all winemakers that have or had the vision to create. And just as with a car or a painting, by using the same or very similar raw materials the Aston Martin or Mona Lisa can be more or less reproduced, a wine can too. This is how BRANDED WINES aiming at consistency year in and year out, such as Non-Vintage Champagnes, work. But unlike cars, paintings and wines forged for stylistic consistency, the highest quality FINE WINES require constant, continual vision because they rely on agriculture, meaning each year the health and RIPENESS of grapes - the raw materials - will be markedly different. And so a winemaker will need a certain amount of creative brilliance to forge a different masterpiece for each year. (Or not at all in some years, because, let's face it, no one is always brilliant and I'm sure even da Vinci had a few screw-ups.)

OK, so what the heck does artist's vision have to do with this chapter's topic: CONCENTRATION? Well, _everything_, in fact.

CONCENTRATION refers to the relative density of a WINE COMPONENT or collection of components, with particular importance placed on how dilute vs CONCENTRATED it is relative to the grape's major component: water. CONCENTRATION is a wine term largely interchangeable with the concept of INTENSITY, which more often specifically refers to the colour, AROMAS and FLAVOURS rather than other WINE COMPONENTS.

Champagne Dom Perignon's Richard Geoffroy, Chef de Cave (cellar master) since 1990

The components for achieving CONCENTRATION and INTENSITY are ripened in the grape throughout the growing season in the vineyard (see **Chapter 2**) and extracted or rejected to a degree of winemaker vision in the winery. So essentially winemaking is philosophically a bit like Johnny Mercer crooned in the old song, "You've got to accentuate the positive / eliminate the negative." In wines of high quality, CONCENTRATION is mainly constructed from naturally produced grape parts and to a lesser extent from winemaking factors / additions.

A little like colours of paint that can be separated out into different bases, hues and textures / thicknesses to be used to different effects by an artist, grapes can be broken into component parts, collectively contributing in varying degrees to the overall experience and therefore quality that a wine offers.

The GRAPE COMPONENTS of major significance include:

- SUGARS (mainly glucose and fructose)
- Organic ACIDS (tartaric and malic account for around 90% of these acids)
- POLYPHENOLIC COMPOUNDS, inc.:
    - Colour pigments (ANTHOCYANINS)
    - TANNINS (ranging from small sub-units that are more bitter to large or POLYMERISED compounds, which are more ASTRINGENT)
- AROMA and AROMA PRECURSOR compounds
- Nitrogenous compounds (important for YEAST nutrition and can be a nuisance if too much protein renders the wine cloudy) including: amino ACIDS, ammonia, nitrates, proteins, etc.
- Minerals / Cations (mainly potassium, which can affect pH and TARTRATE STABILITY, but grapes also contain trace amounts of sodium, iron, calcium, etc.)
- Water (a whopping 70-80% of the grape's volume)

The next chapter will demonstrate how WINE COMPONENTS are slightly different from GRAPE COMPONENTS because the FERMENTATION, MATURATION and storage processes not only create the ALCOHOL in wine but dramatically change the GRAPE COMPONENTS while instilling new by-products / compounds. The components that are exclusively WINEMAKING DERIVED CHARACTERS will also contribute to the overall CONCENTRATION of a wine but because they should play merely supporting roles in great wines, they will be discussed as part of the chapter on BALANCE and again when we look at COMPLEXITY.

In most but not all wine producing countries of the world there are strict laws regarding what can and can't be added to wines to supplement the naturally derived GRAPE COMPONENTS during winemaking. Winemakers in the highest quality and well established regions are extremely limited when it comes to bolstering the raw materials. So the trickiest part of being a winemaker / artist looking to achieve the BEST POSSIBLE WINE from a particular vintage and single vineyard is that the BEST POSSIBLE WINE will be detectably different every year because the raw materials will be different.

Annual growing season weather is one of the major influencing factors towards grape health and RIPENESS, varying the levels and indeed the quality of the components in grapes (for more info on health and RIPENESS see **Chapter 2**). During the run-up to harvest, it is usually the winemaker that calls the picking date(s), because the winemaker is the buck-stops-here guy or gal that studies and envisages how the burgeoning components will come together to make their wine. And just in case you

IMPORTANT GRAPE COMPONENTS

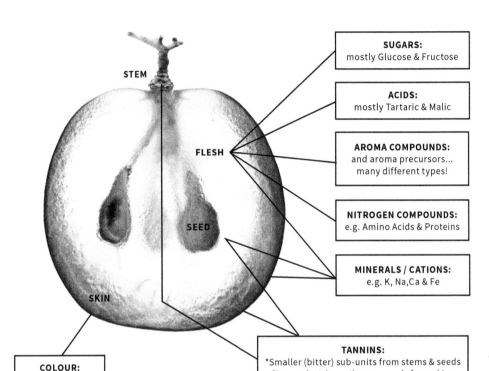

SUGARS:
mostly Glucose & Fructose

ACIDS:
mostly Tartaric & Malic

AROMA COMPOUNDS:
and aroma precursors...
many different types!

NITROGEN COMPOUNDS:
e.g. Amino Acids & Proteins

MINERALS / CATIONS:
e.g. K, Na,Ca & Fe

TANNINS:
*Smaller (bitter) sub-units from stems & seeds
*Larger (astringent) compounds from skins

COLOUR:
Anthocyanins

STEM

FLESH

SEED

SKIN

were wondering - it is not practical, often legal or desirable (!) to grow wine grapes hydroponically, so this unpredictable nature of weather necessitates more often than not that there will be winemaker TRADE-OFFS throughout the creation process.

A winemaker TRADE-OFF is an important decision made throughout the winemaking process that will be a compromise between that which is practical/possible/affordable and that which is qualitatively desired. Once grapes are in the winery the raw materials for making the wine are no longer variables in the winemaking equation, though how they are employed and to what extent the extractable components are used still are. The vision of a winemaker is in understanding what it he or she has to work with and how it can be used to make the best possible wine that is fit for its purpose.

In order to achieve CONCENTRATION at whatever level, the winemaker's test of skill is in the extraction of the right amounts of desirable components in the grapes that will best suit the purposes of the wine. Implicit in this statement are the other critical tasks – leaving behind or separating out to a degree any undesirable components and

Is it just me or did someone put black pepper into my wine?

No, it's not just you and no, it is highly unlikely that anyone put anything but grapes and permitted additives into your wine, which certainly does not include black pepper! Most major wine producing countries of the world have very strict production regulations prohibiting foreign FLAVOUR additives in products that are labelled as "wine". Wine is legally defined in the EU thus: "the alcoholic beverage obtained from the FERMENTATION of the juice of freshly gathered grapes, the FERMENTATION taking place in the district of origin according to local tradition and practice". There's very little wiggle room beyond this definition for adding FLAVOURS. But wine can for sure appear to have an extraordinary array of seemingly alien aromas / FLAVOURS that aren't in fact foreign at all; they're naturally imparted by grapes, TERROIR and winemaking. Black pepper is just one example. The spice, black peppercorn, gets much of its distinctive scent from a compound it possesses known as ROTUNDONE, which also naturally exists in Syrah / Shiraz grapes and accounts for that unmistakable smell in some examples of wines made from this varietal. So whether your wine whiffs of limes, apples, violets, cloves, butter or honey – and a whole range of other very un-grape-like scents – what you're smelling is in fact purely that beguiling transformation of grapes into wine, in all its COMPLEX and mysterious glory!

---

addressing component inadequacies, sometimes necessitating permitted AMELIORATIONS. Undesirables might include unhealthy / rotten fruit (best left in the vineyard or on the sorting table!), bitter / under-ripe TANNINS, green or herbal characters in red grapes, excessive ACID, excessive water that could cause dilution, deleterious nitrogenous content and proteins that could cause off-FLAVOURS and / or cloudiness and excess minerals that could lead to TARTRATE instability.

Once the GRAPE DERIVED COMPONENTS are weighed-up, CONCENTRATION inadequacies are also assessed and, where possible and legal, AMELIORATIONS may be applied. In the USA the term AMELIORATION (meaning "to make better") usually refers to the practice of adding water to must or burgeoning wine. Further afield the definition of AMELIORATIONS could include a larger range of permitted MUST adjustment practices such as CHAPTALIZATION, ACID additions (ACIDIFICATION), TANNIN additions (ADDED TANNINS) and added SWEETNESS (e.g. SÜSSRESERVE or dosage). It's only under very rare circumstances that water may lawfully be applied to the fermenting grape juice in some countries (e.g. California, USA) if there is an immediate risk of a "stuck FERMENTATION" (an arrested FERMENTATION) due to SUGAR content so excessive that the YEAST can't cope (i.e. potential ALCOHOLS of around 15.5% and above). However it is legally forbidden in most wine regions to add water to juice or wine, which is not to say the euphemistically called "black snake" (water hose) of AMELIORATION never finds its way into the tanks of warmer areas / vintages!

The major difference between red and white winemaking are in desired components to be extracted and how this extraction is achieved. Most fundamentally, in red winemaking a certain amount of colour (ANTHOCYANIN compounds) and TANNINS will be sought. Thus

This photo demonstrates whole / uncrushed white and pink-skinned berries (in this incidence, Koshu grapes from Japan) being loaded into a pneumatic or bladder press to make white wine. The extraction of GRAPE COMPONENTS – the building blocks for wine – is fairly straightforward for white wines in that it is mainly achieved by crushing the berries and pressing them to release the juice from the skins. Often grapes are crushed prior to pressing but in this photo grapes are being "WHOLE BUNCH" pressed, meaning that they are crushed and pressed at the same time in an extra effort to minimise skin contact. This is also how many sparkling wines are made, whereby a white wine can be produced from red grapes (e.g. Pinot Noir and Pinot Meunier) because the separation of the juice off the skins is so swift. The amount of "press juice", juice from the final stages of pressing that will contain more skin components such as TANNINS, retained and used is a stylistic and quality decision made by the winemaker.

Red wine is produced by allowing the grape juice to spend time in contact with the grape skins to extract colour compounds and TANNINS. *This can be done before, during and/or after the* FERMENTATION *process, with varying stylistic results. For example, the* ETHANOL *(*ALCOHOL*) in wine acts as a solvent and can draw even more* POLYPHENOLIC COMPOUNDS *from the skins after* FERMENTATION, *if so desired. As with making a cup of tea with* TANNIC *tea leaves or bags, other key variables in red winemaking apart from the presence of* ETHANOL *include time, temperature and method of mixing skins with juice, otherwise known as* MACERATION. *This method of* MACERATION *in the photo above is an unusual* BIODYNAMICALLY *employed "pumping over" technique, whereby the juice from the bottom of the tank is pumped over the skins floating on top to extract more from them and it is "dynamised" in the process or swirled into a vortex, which* BIODYNAMIC *producers believe activates the energy in liquids. It is just one of many, many techniques to extract varying skin components at varying levels to achieve varying* CONCENTRATION *results.*

red winemaking will use and extract much more from the skins and so the extents of contact with crushed berries (MACERATION) before, during and after FERMENTATION are important factors. White winemaking will generally minimise skin contact and focus mainly on extracting desired compounds from the flesh and its juice.

When it comes to the extraction of GRAPE COMPONENTS, innovations in modern winemaking have completely changed the game. New gadgets, gizmos, techniques and tools aimed at pulling more of the beauteous stuff out of grapes or getting rid of the ugly-warts enter the scene with every vintage. Winemakers have a lot more options than ever before and although this has not directly resulted in wine being intrinsically better, some winery installations such as pneumatic / bladder presses and inert temperature controlled storage tanks have meant that wines produced today are more consistently better.

A starter culture of YEAST *burbles and froths into activity as it is prepared for addition to a much larger tank of unfermented grape juice. This* CULTURED YEAST *(Laffort VL3) has been specially selected for its ability to make citrus and passion fruit scented* THIOLS *(REDUCED SULPHUR CONTAINING COMPOUNDS) from* AROMA PRECURSORS *present in Sauvignon Blanc juice with an aim to boost the "fruity"* AROMAS / FLAVOURS *in the wine.*

But the road to bad wine is often paved with good intensions. Nowadays winemakers have all these cellar options and contraptions at their disposal - perhaps too many for their own good. Marketing demands, bottom-line considerations, consumer preferences and even the tastes of influential critics sometimes pressure winemakers into cobbling together expressions of the grapes that just aren't qualitatively compatible with their site, climate, vintage and/or variety. Settling on a tactic for ultimately achieving the desired CONCENTRATION of GRAPE DERIVED and WINEMAKING DERIVED CHARACTERS all boils down to soul-searching questions of authenticity and integrity for our artists / winemakers such as: "Should I do a pre-FERMENTATION cold soak?" "How much do I crush?", "What do I do with the skins, stems and seeds?", "How much SO$_2$ should I use and when?", "Should I CHAPTALIZE?", "Should I artificially concentrate the juice with REVERSE OSMOSIS or cryo-extraction?", "What kind of FERMENTATION vessel do I use?",

"Do I use WILD YEAST or add a CULTURED YEAST and, if so, which one?" "How much do I mix-up the grape skins with the fermenting wine and what tools do I use (e.g. punch down / pigeage, rotary fermenter, pump over, delestage or submerged cap, etc.)?", "How long do I macerate on skins?", "What temperature do I maintain for the soaking grapes / fermenting wine and how do I maintain it?", "What kind of press do I use and how much press juice shall I retain and add back?", "What do I do with the LEES?", "Do I BLEND with other batches, parcels and/or grape varieties?", "How do I store or MATURE the finished wine?", "What's the right proportion of new OAK?", "Should I micro-oxygenate?", "Should I decrease the final ALCOHOL with spinning cones?" "What tools do I buy, what tools do I use, what tools don't I use?", etc., etc., etc.

All these winemaking variables (and more) directly or indirectly impact the quantity and quality and/or type of CONCENTRATION components...and, once again, the devil is in the details.

That's enough about the winemaker...what about you? How can a taster recognize and evaluate CONCENTRATION in a wine?

The CONCENTRATION and INTENSITY of a wine's component parts are vital quality indicators that can readily be seen, smelled, tasted and/or felt by a taster of any level. You can see the CONCENTRATION of colour, particularly in red wines. You can smell the INTENSITY of grass / herbal scented compounds (e.g. METHOXYPYRAZINES) in a Sauvignon Blanc, floral notes in Riesling (e.g. TERPENES) or of black pepper smelling ones (e.g. ROTUNDONE) in Syrah. You can taste SUGARS / SWEETNESS towards the front of your tongue or ACIDITY generally towards the sides. You can feel the coarseness and ASTRINGENCY of TANNINS as they interact with the proteins on the surfaces of your mouth.

Some common WINE-SPEAK terms that are used to make reference to a wine's (or component thereof) relative state of CONCENTRATION or INTENSITY include:

Lacks CONCENTRATION **(quality detractor)**	weak, insipid, watery, skeletal, dilute, lacks AROMA / FLAVOUR, shallow, slight, attenuated, lean, weedy, light, empty, HOLLOW
Possesses Sufficient to Generous CONCENTRATION **(quality enhancer)**	rich, CONCENTRATED, INTENSE, generous, ample, just enough, delicate, subtle, elegant, profound, pronounced, robust, voluptuous, muscular
Too CONCENTRATED **(quality detractor)**	overpowering, pungent, overblown, blousy, powerful, overwhelming, heavy, OVER-EXTRACTED

Why are some wines SO INTENSELY **fruity while others don't appear very fruity at all?**

Wines with more apparent fruit were once thought to be purely the result of sunnier / warmer climates. In fact many wines from warmer "New World" (an example of OUTDATED WINE JARGON – see **Chapter 9**) regions have often been stereotyped as "fruit-forward" or "fruit-driven", even though the relative warmth of the climate is sometimes coincidental. It is true that a certain amount of sunshine and heat during the growing season are important factors in dialling-up the fruit element because these directly impact the synthesis and ripening of the AROMA PRECURSORS and compounds that yield wine AROMAS. However, perhaps more important are how these elements are manifested or revealed through the winemaking process. Winemakers can actually kick it up a notch on the fruit, in other words intensify fruit expression / fruitiness for a given CONCENTRATION of AROMA compounds, without actually extracting more from the wine or even artificially concentrating it. There are several modern means of achieving more seemingly "fruity" character, namely through cool FERMENTATIONS, REDUCTIVE HANDLING, enzyme additions, CULTURED YEASTS and/or YEAST nutrient e.g. DAP (di-ammonium phosphate) additions. If this all sounds a bit like wine sleight of hand, yeah, well, it is…and it isn't. Ubiquitous uses of modern tools-of-the-trade have made it more a matter of stylistic choice. "Traditional" approaches that do not involve artificial cooling, meticulous protection from OXIDATION, added YEASTS or YEAST nutrients – for a long time the only means available to "Old World" winemakers before modern science stepped in – generally produce a more "restrained fruit" STYLES and characters. Apart from Luddite attitude, why would any 21st Century winemaker shy away from more fruit? Many shun INTENSELY fruity STYLES in an effort to reveal more subtle nuances that can be masked by those somewhat in-your-face fruit elements, others bandy "NATURAL WINE" and TERROIR claims, while a few just love that traditional retro-charm of making wine by practicing the methods of their forefathers.

While it's all well and good to have the wine lingo to address the topic of CONCENTRATION, you may well be wondering how you can possibly judge how much or how little the impact of the CONCENTRATION is. How do you put CONCENTRATION into context and ultimately evaluate it?

I can recall the first few times that I ever tasted wine, when asked what I thought I could only shrug and mumble, "It tastes like wine." Although when pressed I could probably describe the hue of colour and pick out a few specific AROMAS and FLAVOURS, I couldn't possibly comment upon how CONCENTRATED or INTENSE any of these aspects were...because I had no significant MENTAL WINE LIBRARY with which to compare the levels of components or collection thereof.

And it's here, in the midst of our CONCENTRATION discussion, that we arrive at a major schism between levels of wine criticism experience: novice tasters vs experienced tasters. The compounds associated with wine FAULTS, fruit health and RIPENESS (subjects of the first two chapters) including all the GRAPE COMPONENTS discussed thus far – once locked, loaded and retrievable in a taster's brain - are factors that any novice with a fully functioning nose and palate can detect and comment upon. But our evaluation of wine CONCENTRATION is largely relative to our experience of other similar wines. Thus to make a judgement call, to comment beyond, "It tastes like wine", a taster needs experience.

The novice taster and the experienced taster may in fact have the same "natural abilities" to smell and taste. A novice can indeed have more natural talent; perhaps they have a more sensitive nose or more taste buds per square centimetre than the experienced taster. Be that as it may, natural talent will only get a taster so far towards being an experienced taster because that requires, well, experience. You gotta go through the process of tasting a lot of different wines. Throughout this process an experienced taster's MENTAL WINE LIBRARY, *his/her stored memories of many other wines and the ability to recall the memories of relevant wines when tasting,* develops into a skill that is equally as important as her/his natural abilities to smell and taste in order to produce a wine evaluation that takes on a whole new level, which is based upon contextual relevance.

OK, novice or experienced – whatever - even for newbies of very limited experience, one of the surest indicators of substandard quality is an apparently watery or dilute wine. Bottom line here: sufficient colour, AROMAS, FLAVOURS, ACIDITY, SWEETNESS and TANNIN CONCENTRATIONS / intensities can individually and/or collectively play very important roles in anyone's pleasure of wine and therefore its perceived quality. Conversely, too much of a good thing can also be detrimental. For example an overly sweet wine without sufficient ACIDITY to freshen can appear sickly or cloying. Likewise too much ACIDITY, TANNINS or ALCOHOL can make a wine unpleasant to drink. Therefore, looking beyond this somewhat multifaceted concept, you can rest assured that even if you have a limited MENTAL WINE LIBRARY the overriding quality determinant when it comes to CONCENTRATION is always going to be BALANCE.

An experienced taster must go through the process of tasting many wines often over many years and be able to recall those wines when tasting in order to reap the benefits of a significant MENTAL WINE LIBRARY. This knowledge and ability offers contextual relevance, which is all the difference compared to the mainly natural abilities of a novice taster.

BALANCE

....

That any compound, however made,
which lacks measure and proportion, must
necessarily destroy its components and first of
all itself; for it is in truth no compound, but
an uncompounded jumble, and is always a
misfortune to those who possess it.

Plato

....

WHILE CONCENTRATION IS an important quality factor, it is vital that the CONCENTRATION of any component is not considered in isolation but in proportion. One of the most common rookie mistakes when it comes to assessing wine quality is thinking that the biggest, most powerful, monolithic and CONCENTRATED wine must be the best. So if you come away from this read taking just one teensy pearl of wine wisdom with you, let it be this:

When it comes to wine - bigger isn't necessarily better.

Indeed, as with so many facets of life, the golden mean is an ideal median point that lies between that which is too much and that which is not enough.

BALANCE in wine specifically refers to a WINE'S COMPONENTS all existing in harmonious proportions that complement one another so that no single aspect negatively dominates on the palate.

These WINE COMPONENTS include:
- SWEETNESS (SUGARS)
- ACIDITY
- BODY
- GRAPE DERIVED AROMAS / FLAVOURS
- TANNINS, which mainly come from grape skins but can also come from STEMS, and OAK barrels, staves or chips or can simply be ADDED TANNINS
- ALCOHOL
- WINEMAKING DERIVED AROMAS / FLAVOURS, e.g. characters formed or derived from YEAST(s), MLF, LEES, OAK, SULPHUR DIOXIDE (SO_2), etc.
- Winemaking GREY-AREA FAULTS: VA, REDUCTION, BRETTANOMYCES, OXIDATION, etc.

You'll note from the above list that winemakers have way more to consider than just the GRAPE'S COMPONENTS when it comes to shaping a BALANCED wine. When transformed from juice to wine, the resulting product is very different from the raw materials and this change in components goes far beyond the basic creation of ALCOHOL by YEAST. So for example, were you to take a glass of ordinary grape juice that you buy from the supermarket and BLEND it with a neutral tasting spirit such as vodka, you would notice that the resulting cocktail doesn't taste at all like wine.

Achieving BALANCE in a wine is a skill and an art that goes hand-in-hand with the extracting of GRAPE COMPONENTS to build CONCENTRATION – an essential part of the vision and artistry required of a great winemaker. This part of the craft all boils down

What exactly do you mean when you talk about a wine's "BODY"?

BODY is the sensation of the wine's weight on the palate. In common WINE-SPEAK wines that seem lighter in the mouth are referred to as light-bodied while ones that feel heaviest are full-bodied.

The weight of wine in the mouth is mainly due to its VISCOSITY, which is detected by a textural thickening of the wine in correlation to increased levels of SUGAR, extract and/or alcoholic strength. VISCOSITY is sensed on the palate in the form of resistance as the wine coats the mouth and passes over the tongue. Think of the difference between sipping tomato soup and water – the tomato soup is way more viscous. In wine terms a sweet, SUGAR-rich wine will be more viscous than a DRY one, even if they have the same alcoholic strength. ALCOHOL (ETHANOL – the ALCOHOL in "alcoholic" beverages) is more viscous than water, so it is closely related to BODY. And the dissolved solids in wine - its "extract" – also make wine more viscous and therefore fuller-bodied. In wine it is TANNINS, SUGARS, proteins, non-VOLATILE ACIDS (such as TARTARIC), colour compounds (ANTHOCYANINS) and trace minerals (e.g. calcium and potassium) that usually make up the DRY EXTRACT in wine. The TANNIN and ANTHOCYANIN extract in DRY red wines therefore render reds slightly fuller-bodied than DRY whites for the same alcoholic strength. To check it out, simply leave a glass with a small amount of remaining red wine overnight for the fluid to evaporate and in the morning the colour stained, dry extract will remain in the bottom of the glass.

GLYCEROL occasionally makes a minor contribution to BODY. This is a relatively thick, colourless, odourless, sweet liquid and a minor by-product of ALCOHOL FERMENTATION. It is normally present in most wines in un- or barely detectable concentrations, although BOTRYTISED wines sometimes have concentrations that can exceed the DETECTION THRESHOLD. Only when it rarely exceeds levels above the textural DETECTION THRESHOLD (i.e. 28 g/L) is it really of any significance when considering the major components of BODY.

to controlling the levels of extraction, BLENDING, additions and/or omissions with the foresight to anticipate how all the pieces of the puzzle will eventually come together to hopefully form the harmonious wine masterpiece that the winemaker envisaged.

The Winemaker's Balancing Act: The Art of Blending

In an ideal world the labours of harvest would deliver into the winery picking bins laden with pristine, flawless grapes possessing just the right amount of GRAPE COMPONENTS in just the right proportions that, without any winemaker manipulation, would produce a perfectly harmonious, BALANCED wine. Yeah, right. I can say with a good degree of certainty that never in the long history of winemaking has this happened. I'm not saying that you can't make a wine without employing any manipulation to address potential BALANCE inadequacies. Many of those "NATURAL WINE" proponents that I mentioned at the beginning of the previous chapter on CONCENTRATION in fact claim to do so. What I am saying is that it is highly uncommon if not impossible to achieve a perfectly BALANCED wine without some sort of winemaker manipulation or intervention at some point throughout the winemaking process.

The commonest, simplest, perhaps most "traditional" way for a winemaker to achieve BALANCE in a wine is through the act or art of BLENDING. Practiced by winemakers for centuries, BLENDING – the process of mixing two or more grape varieties, fruit sources and/or wines - can be carried out in many ways, on many levels to achieve many different results. In truth virtually all wines produced around the world are now BLENDED in some way, at some point prior to bottling. This is not always done to achieve a better BALANCED wine; it is also widely used to achieve a certain STYLE of wine (e.g. a NV Champagne, Port or Sherry) and/or to standardise a product (e.g. a wine where the BRAND expression is deemed more important than that of the grape and/or TERROIR). Most

Considered one of the greatest "master blenders" of our time, winemaker / oenologist Michel Rolland has worked as a BLENDING consultant for hundreds of wineries across 14 countries throughout the wine world.

often it is used or also used to improve the overall quality of the various individual wines by creating a sum that is better BALANCED and in some cases more COMPLEX than the individual parts.

In modern winemaking, the production of wine and especially a BRANDED wine often involves incredibly complex BLENDING operations, incorporating components that can come from many different sources (e.g. various clones, parcels, blocks, vineyards and/ or regions) and from a wide variety of other variables, such as: different grape varieties, juice from different pressings, juice possessing higher / lower ACID, SUGAR or TANNINS, wines fermented at different temperatures, fermented with different YEASTS, fermented in different vessels, various percentages of MLF, different OAK and other MATURATION treatments, wines from different vintages, etc. Apart from winemaker vision, the only limitations on the extent of BLENDING lots are local labelling laws that restrict for examples the use of different vintages within a vintage labelled wine, or non-permitted grape varieties within a wine that is from a variety restrictive region, or the percentage of other grapes in a wine that mentions a particular grape on the label, or the percentage of extra-regional fruit within a wine that mentions a legally recognized, delimited region.

The Winemaker's Balancing Act: Bordeaux, the Quintessential Wine Blend

Perhaps the best illustration of achieving BALANCE and other wine STYLE and quality goals through BLENDING is a peek into Bordeaux's philosophy of winemaking. One of the crucial need-to-know facts about Bordeaux is that all the wines - both whites and reds - are blends of some kind. Fundamentally the wines are almost exclusively blends of different varieties, most famously giving rise to the globally popular "Bordeaux Blend" mix of red grapes. Traditionally and continually, the exact blends of grapes used in the wines each vintage are determined by which grapes have succeeded best in terms of health and ripening in that year. Most notably for instance, the BLENDING of predominately Cabernet Sauvignon and Merlot in the Medoc and Graves sub-regions can act as an insurance policy in marginal vintages of inclement weather, frost, rains, etc. Cabernet Sauvignon is a late budding, late ripening variety that needs the heat advantages of gravel in the Medoc to coax the grape to RIPENESS, which in lesser vintages may not happen. Merlot buds and ripens up to two weeks earlier than Cabernet Sauvignon sometimes making it less susceptible to frost and at times it has the advantage of being harvested before the rains. Apart from weather and RIPENESS issues, Merlot often provides the wine with generosity and more approachable TEXTURE in the MID-PALATE, which Cabernet Sauvignon often lacks. Cabernet Sauvignon provides structure with higher levels of TANNINS and ACIDS, which are necessary for long aging. So it is easy to see how the opportunities for achieving better BALANCED wines with greater consistency are improved with this classic "Bordeaux Blend", simply by adjusting the amounts of

Cabernet Sauvignon and Merlot in the final ASSEMBLAGE each year.

In Bordeaux, apart from the different grape varieties, different parcels of fruit will also commonly be vinified and MATURED separately then BLENDED prior to bottling. The "Grand Vin" of a classified growth Bordeaux chateau will be BLENDED from the grape varieties of optimal ripeness, best parcels, best vines, best barrels, etc. After the first RACKING (off the gross LEES) the first round of tastings occurs, with a view to the ultimate blend that will make up the finished wine. Then after cask ageing (normally 12-24 months for a Bordeaux red wine) the wine is BLENDED and tasted again. Heavily-oaked lots aged in new OAK barrels may be muted by BLENDING with less oaky (those aged in older OAK) lots of the same wine. This blend is usually stored for a period to allow the components to marry and STABILISE prior to bottling.

The BLENDING operation, or ASSEMBLAGE as it is known in France, is far from a witches-brew type scenario with a bucket of this and a smidgeon of that thrown wantonly into a vat. It is an incredibly meticulous operation, which is carried out initially in a laboratory with a range of possible component wines, measuring cylinders

A typical "Bordeaux Blend" wine is usually not just a blend of different "Bordeaux varietals" but of different parcels, vineyards, winemaking methods and OAKS. The various components of the blend are often MATURED separately in barrels in temperature controlled cellars or caves, such as the one pictured, and BLENDED in very large, stainless steel blending tanks to a carefully created "formula" - which is usually different every vintage - just prior to bottling. Pictured here: Almaviva Winery in Maipo, Chile, producer of a well-known Chilean "Bordeaux Blend".

and tasting glasses. This experimenting session results in a trial blend or a number of trial blends, which is/are compared to the components to ensure that the tentative result is first and foremost well BALANCED and then ultimately meets any other possible requirements of the blend such as BRAND signature, TERROIR expression / regional STYLE and/or utmost COMPLEXITY. There will also be financial considerations such as if the desired blend can be produced in large enough volumes to meet the owner's profit expectations. If not, the blender(s) may have to go back to the BLENDING bench and try, try again…!

The Winemaker's Balancing Act: GRAPE DERIVED vs WINEMAKING DERIVED CHARACTERS

The winemaking contributions to wine - FERMENTATION, MATURATION and storage processes - instil distinctive winemaking characters that will contribute to quality factors such as the final CONCENTRATION, BALANCE and COMPLEXITY in wine. However it is widely felt that these winemaking contributions should play supporting roles in a wine at the peak of its DRINKING WINDOW, and certainly not dominate the GRAPE DERIVED COMPONENTS. In other words, WINEMAKING DERIVED AROMAS should provide seasoning rather than constitute the main ingredient in the wine. This is because the expressions of grape and/or time and place (vineyard, TERROIR or region, call it what you will) are key purposes of wine that make it extraordinary amongst beverages and, as we move up the aforementioned WINE PURPOSES PYRAMID, sit near the pinnacle. So an <u>awareness</u> of the BALANCE between GRAPE DERIVED and WINEMAKING DERIVED CHARACTERS followed by the <u>knowledge</u> to recognize / appreciate this in wines can be considered steps up the WINE PURPOSES PYRAMID towards becoming more involved with the process, journey and product and ultimately looking for a wine to do *more*.

Getting the BALANCE right between the GRAPE DERIVED AROMAS and the winemaking instilled ones is a tricky job. It can be tempting for a winemaker to get carried-away in the winery, after all it is their job to *make* the wine, but extremely important that they maintain a sense of proportion when it comes to the winemaking contributions within the overall effect. The greatest wines of the world will scarcely if at all reveal the seams of how they were stitched together and they will likewise "marry" winemaking contributions more or less imperceptibly in with the fruit. In a great wine the winemaking imparted components should ideally enhance, compliment and ultimately better express the grape variety(s) and/or region(s) or vineyard(s).

There are a number of winemaking techniques that are detectable when tasting the finished wine. Some are more ubiquitously practiced and much discussed in wine tasting

How do Bordeaux winemakers manage to speed-up their BLENDING process to produce barrel tasting wines for en primeur week evaluation?

En primeur, futures or simply primeurs and consumers buying wines "en primeur" is a somewhat modern phenomenon that has really rocketed in practice and popularity since the 1980s. It begins with a designated week in early April during which the major Chateaux / wineries offer barrel tastings for the assessment of professional wine buyers and critics of their pre-release wines from the previous year. After "En Primeur Week", the Chateaux begin releasing initial en primeur or pre-release prices as a means of procuring early financing for their harvests. Consumers can therefore buy the wines 1-2 years before they are even bottled based largely of the assessments of those participating buyers and critics. Now, assuming the previous year's grapes were harvested in September and the new wines went into OAK barrels for cask ageing (ÉLEVAGE) in October that means by April they will only have been in barrel for around 6 months maximum. Geeks with a little winemaking knowledge will probably spot that's hardly enough time for most of the barrels to have even "naturally" completed their MALOLACTIC FERMENTATIONS (MLF) and not nearly enough time in barrel to complete the typical period of Bordeaux ÉLEVAGE. Assuming the final blend will not take place until after ÉLEVAGE - as is the normal practice in Bordeaux - you may rightfully ask, how do the winemakers produce finished wines to present for assessment to professional wine buyers and journalists during En Primeur Week? The cynical (and perhaps most honest) answer is: They fudge it. In fact at the en primeur week stage of the game it is impossible for a Bordeaux Chateau to present a "finished", final wine blend for assessment so early. So what they show is a possible / probable blend to offer an indication of what the finished wine will be like. To do so they will usually rush the wines through MLF by inoculating them with LACTIC BACTERIA in tanks just after FERMENTATION or heating a barrel room containing the young wines to speed-up the MLF process. What happens next is really down to the integrity of the winemaker and / or Chateau owner in terms of how representative the actual barrel sample presented for tasting will be of the probable finished blend. While it would obviously be quite tempting to produce a blend of only the very best, most FORWARD wines that represent a tiny proportion of the wines destined to produce the final blend, winemakers know full well that they will eventually get caught-out trying to deceive buyers and critics with a completely different wine when the wine is eventually bottled. So while it is highly likely that the winemaker will to a certain extent aim to put the vintage's best-foot-forward, the en primeur blend has to offer a reasonable approximation in terms of STYLE and quality to what will eventually be bottled. Still it is down to the taster to see through the possible shenanigans and accept the validity of the en primeur blend with a grain of salt, so to speak.

such as the use of OAK, the major types and characteristics to be related in detail in the next chapter on COMPLEXITY. However, many other winemaking techniques and tools are less common and/or obvious but certainly detectable by the trained taster. This is where good background knowledge of winemaking processes can come in handy though for the most part is not essential for isolating and evaluating winemaking contributions to the overall BALANCE of wine.

When it comes to the <u>Key Winemaking Techniques detectable through Tasting Analysis</u>, there are 2 major Categories:

A) Those that are used to manipulate the expression of GRAPE DERIVED CHARACTERS, e.g.
- REDUCTIVE HANDLING
- OXIDATIVE HANDLING
- FERMENTATION and MATURATION Temperature
- YEASTS: WILD YEASTS or CULTURED YEASTS

B) Those that contribute new, non-grape associated characters to the wine, e.g.:
- YEASTS: WILD YEASTS or CULTURED YEASTS
- Use of SULPHUR DIOXIDE (SO$_2$)
- MALOLACTIC FERMENTATION
- LEES CONTACT
- OAK
- GREY-AREA FAULT microbial organisms such as BRETTANOMYCES and ACETOBACTER (see **Chapter 1 – Wine** FAULTS) that produce AROMA / FLAVOUR instilling by-products

These winemaking characters, sometimes known as SECONDARY AROMAS / FLAVOURS, are either an expression of or wholly distinctive from the PRIMARY / GRAPE DERIVED AROMAS / FLAVOURS and can generally be picked out by even an inexperienced wine taster when shown what to look for.

The Winemaker's Balancing Act: Oxygen & Temperature as Stylistic Winemaking Tools

There are all sorts of winemaking techniques that, apart from achieving CONCENTRATION in wines mould, manipulate or otherwise express GRAPE DERIVED CHARACTERS. The use of oxygen and temperature are powerful winemaker's tools towards crafting desired STYLES.

OXYGENATION and OXIDATION and the effects of these were largely covered in **Chapter 1**. The exclusion of oxygen as a stylistic tool is known as REDUCTIVE HANDLING. In **Chapter 1** we discussed REDUCTION as a GREY-AREA FAULT, but the meaning of "REDUCTIVE HANDLING" is different in that it does not refer specifically to the REDUCTION of sulphur compounds in the absence of oxygen in wine but the preservation of PRIMARY AROMAS or GRAPE DERIVED CHARACTERS by avoiding contact with oxygen. This can be achieved most commonly through the protective uses of inert gases (e.g. CO_2, Nitrogen and Argon), inert / stainless steel tanks and cooler handling and storage temperatures. REDUCTIVE HANDLING is mostly practiced on aromatic white grape varieties such as Riesling or Muscat or those where INTENSE fruitiness is desired, such as Sauvignon Blanc. And it is precisely this INTENSITY of AROMAS / FLAVOURS that give REDUCTIVE HANDLING away on the nose and palate when you're tasting.

The temperature(s) of grape juice and wine that is/are maintained throughout the wine's processing can significantly impact the expression of GRAPE DERIVED CHARACTERS as detectable by tasting. On a most basic level, temperature can be used to speed up chemical reactions or slow them down. And let's face it – winemaking, MATURATION and bottle development mainly boil down to chemical reactions within the wine, whether it be FERMENTATION, OXIDATION, REDUCTION, MLF or the formation of ESTERS during MATURATION and development, for examples. Therefore at higher or lower temperatures all these reactions will happen at a faster or slower rate with different aromatic and taste results. Generally speaking, cooler temperatures (16-20 degrees Celsius) tend to preserve delicate aromatics and in the case of very cool FERMENTATIONS (those performed at 15 degrees C or less) result in particular ESTERS that lend a "lifted" character or intensified aromatics, which give distinctively "fruity" STYLES though sometimes perhaps speak more of the cool FERMENTATION rather than grape variety or region. (But of course for wine MATURATION and storage, less than 15 degrees C, but not much cooler than 10 degrees C, is perfect for preserving the wine's PRIMARY AROMAS / characters and encouraging slow development.) Warmer temperatures particularly for FERMENTATIONS equate to broader, less INTENSELY fruity STYLES. At very warm FERMENTATION temperatures (e.g. at around 30 degrees C or above) problems can occur such as a stuck FERMENTATION and VOLATILE ACIDITY as a consequence. At very warm temperatures for FERMENTATION and storage / MATURATION, wines can take on an unpleasant cooked berry, jammy, MADERIZED, RANCIO or caramelised characters, which can be detrimental to the GRAPE DERIVED expressions in most STYLES but of course defines the character of particular STYLES including well-known examples like Madeira and certain Australian FORTIFIED wines.

The Winemaker's Balancing Act: Non-Grape Associated Characters

Non-grape associated characters include the detectable use of MALOLACTIC FERMENTATION (MLF -resulting in a "softer" ACID profile as well as degraded fruit and sometimes a buttery character), LEES CONTACT (toasty, bread-like, yeasty notes) and OAK (woody, cedar, baking spices and/or a roasted coffee characters and a more prominent TANNIC contribution than GRAPE DERIVED TANNINS), for incidences. You'll note that YEASTS (I've used the plural here in reference to the several species and many strains used in winemaking) fall within both categories A & B because they both manipulate the expression of grape derived characters, including revealing previously mute AROMA PRECURSORS, and they impart new elements / characters such as ETHANOL, higher ALCOHOLS, fatty ACIDS, VOLATILE ACIDS and ESTERS while breaking down / converting some grape aromatics. As part and parcel of the winemaking, these SECONDARY CHARACTERS can be considered to include those GREY-AREA FAULTS such as VOLATILE ACIDITY, BRETTANOMYCES and REDUCTION (see **Chapter 1** for DESCRIPTORS).

All of these the non-grape associated winemaking characters can enhance quality if they are in BALANCE with the other GRAPE DERIVED COMPONENTS in the wine and do not take centre stage.

The Winemaker's Balancing Act: Fine-Tuning with FINING

One of the final fine-tuning procedures commonly used for creating a better BALANCED red wine is FINING. FINING is performed for a range of very different purposes and therefore there are a variety of methods and means of achieving these purposes. The common aspect of all FINING techniques is that they involve adding a substance or "FINING agent" to wine which will bond with the target component in the wine that the winemaker wishes to remove and precipitates both as solid sediment, which can then easily be removed by RACKING and/or FILTRATION. FINING is different from FILTRATION because it has the ability to isolate and take-out specific soluble components in the wine according to their chemical make-up, whereas FILTRATION strips out components by nature of their size and is therefore much less specific in what is removed. The two major components that are commonly fined from wines are proteins (see "PROTEIN HAZE" in the **Glossary of Wine Quality Terms**) and TANNINS. TANNIN FINING is in fact a very old and common technique for "fine-tuning" red wines, practiced traditionally on the red wines of Bordeaux and Burgundy and now throughout the world. And even today the old-school, traditional FINING agent regularly employed to "soften" the ASTRINGENCY / TANNIC impact of red wines is egg whites. When mixed in red wines the proteins in egg whites combine with TANNINS via an electrostatic interaction to form large protein-TANNIN complexes that settle to the bottom of the barrel, off which the wine can be racked. Egg white FINING is usually done towards the end of barrel ageing. Anywhere between 1-6 egg whites per 225 litre barrique is used, depending how much TANNIN the winemaker wishes to remove. Sometimes the egg whites are whisked with a little salt prior to use to increase their solubility. Generally employed with the best intensions to help forge a better BALANCED wine, FINING is however not practiced by all winemakers. Like FILTRATION (discussed in the next chapter on COMPLEXITY), FINING is considered by some winemakers as an unnecessary stripping of natural WINE COMPONENTS and is therefore avoided.

How do I spot non-grape associated winemaking AROMAS / FLAVOURS **in my wine?**

It can be a bit difficult separating the WINEMAKING DERIVED AROMAS in wine from the GRAPE DERIVED AROMAS, particularly if these contributions are well married or intertwined within the wine. At the most basic level, YEAST – the very organism that makes wine, well, wine – contributes significantly to non-GRAPE DERIVED CHARACTERS, most importantly perhaps being the creation of ALCOHOL from SUGAR. At the same time YEASTS create a wide range of aromatic by-products and, as you can probably guess, different types (species as well as strains) of YEASTS create different AROMAS and FLAVOURS. WILD YEASTS (naturally occurring ambient YEASTS that exist in vineyards and wineries and of which there are many types) contribute their own characters and while the results are less predictable than those of CULTURED YEASTS (usually of the SACCHARAMYCES CEREVISIAE species), a growing number of winemakers consider "wild ferments" to express their unique site and contribute to TERROIR. (For more information see the "CULTURED YEAST" and "WILD YEAST" entries in the "**Glossary of Wine Quality Terms**".

Apart from yeast, some of the major non-GRAPE DERIVED winemaking AROMAS include:

Name	What is it?	Look / Smell / Taste?
SULPHUR DIOXIDE (SO₂)	SO₂ is an ANTIOXIDANT and antimicrobial compound added to wine to prevent it from oxidising and STABILISE it against microbial activity. DRY red wines that contain higher levels of POLYPHENOLS / TANNINS – natural ANTIOXIDANTS – usually do not need much added SO₂ and it is therefore rare for it to be used at detectable levels in this STYLE. White wines are bereft of the protection of TANNINS and tend to contain more added SO₂ to preserve their freshness. Aromatic varietals whites usually have even more, which is sometimes detectable on newly bottled wines (e.g. at levels greater than 100 mg/l). Sweet wines have the highest levels of SO₂ in order to help prevent re-FERMENTATION of the SUGARS in them. Examples include most German Rieslings, Sauternes and late harvested sweet wines.	SO₂ smells most notably of sulphur, which can whiff unpleasantly and sometimes acridly of struck match or rotten eggs. A high amount of "free" SO₂ (unbound to oxygen, the binding of which naturally occurs with bottle age) can not only smell distinctly of sulphur, but it can mute or dull the aromatics of wines, especially young / newly bottled wines. On the palate it can render a mild burning sensation at the back of the throat and the effect also tends to linger in the sinuses through RETRONASAL action, particularly if you've tasted many wines with high levels of free SO₂ within a single session. As the sulphur becomes "bound" to oxygen with aging, it becomes less prominent and the aromatics are often revealed. This is a major reason why it can be very difficult to drink great examples of German Rieslings or Sauternes when they are very young (within first year or two of bottling) and why they appear markedly more INTENSE and COMPLEX with bottle age.

Name	What is it?	Look / Smell / Taste?
MALOLACTIC FERMENTATION (MLF)	LACTIC BACTERIA (primarily OENOCOCCUS OENI) are either added or naturally instilled in wines in order to convert the very tart MALIC ACID present into softer, less sour LACTIC ACID. This is commonly performed for most red wines and some varieties / STYLES of white wines, particularly Chardonnay, and sparkling wines such as Champagne.	Although MLF is mainly performed to soften the impression of ACIDITY and increase the pH in wines, it also generates new FLAVOUR compounds and alters the aromatic and FLAVOUR profiles of wines. Different strains of bacteria produce different results but generally speaking the major by-product produced by OENOCOCCUS OENI is DIACETYL, lending a distinctive buttery or caramel character especially to more delicate white wines. MLF also results in a slight loss of fruitiness to wines, which some winemakers embrace while others shun.
LEES CONTACT, BÂTONNAGE, SUR LIES and AUTOLYSIS	In this context, LEES are the dormant YEAST cells that remain in wine after the YEAST have converted all the SUGARS they can or are permitted to convert in the wine. A good many wines across all colours and most STYLES can and often do involve at least some time spent on LEES. Which LEES are employed (gross or fine lees), how long they left in contact with the wine and how they are used (e.g. simply left at the bottom of the tank / barrel or regularly "stirred" up with the wine, known as BÂTONNAGE, etc.) can dramatically change the effect it has on wines.	One of the most often touted benefits of LEES CONTACT for both still and sparkling wines is the building of TEXTURE or "MOUTH-FEEL" in wines. This can be detected as a boost to the wine's perceived "creaminess" with the effect of an apparent slight increase to wine VISCOSITY and BODY. Apart from this, contact with LEES can degrade grape aromatics and the impact of MLF generated DIACETYL. So wines that have had significant LEES contact can appear less overtly fruity and, if MLF has occurred, less buttery. Extended contact with LEES (12 months+), as is the case with many sparkling wines undergoing second FERMENTATION in the bottle, lends a distinctly toasty or bread-like character to wines, most apparent after 18 months+ on LEES.
Wood / OAK: Barrels, Staves or Chips	Apart from imparting TANNINS (see **Chapter 2** on tasting TANNINS), OAK allows for slow OXYGENATION of wines and new(er) OAK imparts FLAVOURS that are leached from the contact between the wine and the surface of the wood. "New" OAK means barrels that have never previously been used before, although "one year" OAK (used for one vintage) can also give some FLAVOURS.	Different types of wood, species of OAK and means of seasoning and TOASTING the wood will give markedly different FLAVOURS. Generally speaking, these can include woody, cedar, baking spices, vanilla, coconut and/or roasted coffee characters. A more detailed account of OAK types with various COOPERAGE treatments and the particular nuances they impart is available in "**Chapter 5 –** COMPLEXITY".

Knowing the Winemaking Rules for Achieving Balance

Certain STYLES, regions and philosophies of winemaking are downright draconian with the rules of how BALANCE can be achieved in the winery whereas others are fairly liberal. For example, a winemaker of Grand Cru level Red Burgundy is not legally allowed TO BLEND vintages, grape varieties or vineyards but they can CHAPTALIZE within limits (add SUGAR to increase the ALCOHOL and therefore weight / BODY and enhance MOUTH-FEEL). In Champagne, winemakers can do all those things just mentioned and more in order to produce better BALANCED, non-vintage sparkling wines. Many lovers of wines that have little or virtually no winemaker manipulation (whether by local edict or personal philosophy) claim that less winemaking intervention equates to a wine that better reveals its grape and TERROIR, while appreciating that any inadequacies of the time (vintage) and place (vineyard) have no place to hide. Also it may be the case that part of the fun of drinking a wine is, for some, in the understanding of the local or self-imposed rules that were involved in creating that wine and marvelling at what was achieved more "naturally" given the lack of permitted winemaking adulteration hardships. This is perhaps why the great wines of Burgundy are an appreciation that experienced tasters "mature" into, whereby a good dollop of knowledge perhaps martyrs the wines and *sympathises* the palate.

Balance: STRUCTURE & Ageing

The wine's STRUCTURE – predominately the levels and types of ACIDS and TANNINS (if present) - is another important aspect in BALANCE and/or preparing a wine to become BALANCED and ultimately *better* (more COMPLEX) after bottle age. STRUCTURE can be seen to provide a backbone, foundation or a frame to support the wine's "flesh" or fruit characters. STRUCTURE further creates textural / MOUTH-FEEL and/or taste layers that contribute to the overall COMPLEXITY effect.

Bottle ageing in a temperature controlled cellar (ideally between 10-15 degrees C) can render some wine STYLES better BALANCED and more COMPLEX after a period of years or even decades.

If creating the most COMPLEX wine is the ultimate goal, this begs the question as to why aspirational winemakers don't always make highly STRUCTURED STYLES with lashings of mouth-puckering TANNINS and rasping ACIDITY when initially bottled. The answer lies in **Chapter 2** on "Fruit Health & RIPENESS". Firstly, if the FLAVOUR compounds aren't fully manifested and abundant enough in the grapes, then there won't enough flesh or fruit characters to match the STRUCTURE - now or ever. Secondly, if the TANNINS are not "ripe", in other words they are bitter and overly ASTRINGENT (hard), then no degree of polymerization or softening through bottle ageing is ever going to change that character. In short, an overly STRUCTURED, under-ripe wine in youth is not likely to get any better with bottle age.

So as a yes-but-not-always cautionary note on BALANCE presumptions, it is important to remember that many high quality wines destined for long aging may begin their life in bottle "out of BALANCE". When assessing such a wine it is important to evaluate the ripeness of tannins (if present) and the CONCENTRATION of fruit relative to the amount of ACID. Some awareness of the grape variety and TERROIR and their ability to develop COMPLEX characters with age will also help such assessments (see **Chapter 5 –** COMPLEXITY). If all these elements appear in order it is worth mentioning in an evaluation of the BALANCE of a young wine that, for example, while the TANNINS and appearance of ACIDITY, OAK, etc. may currently seem out of BALANCE, the other quality indicators (e.g. RIPENESS, grape variety and TERROIR) lead you to believe that this wine has the ability to age and over time to eventually result in a BALANCED wine. Or this assessment can in common cases like barrel tastings or newly bottled grand vins go without saying and simply be reflected in your quality conclusion in the tasting note and RATING (if used).

How do some wines become better BALANCED after "ageing"?

Many great wines can begin their lives in bottle poorly BALANCED and they are sometimes intentionally produced thus because the winemaker is aiming to create a STYLE that will be revered for the COMPLEXITY that it can achieve with evolution / maturity. Usually this will equate to an overly STRUCTURED wine when young, with high levels of TANNINS (though they must be "ripe" – see **Chapter 2 – Fruit Health &** RIPENESS) and ACIDITY, which can stand-out or otherwise appear unpleasant in the wine's youth but can develop that sought-after "seamlessness" with bottle age.

The effects of MATURATION on the TEXTURE of red wine are mainly determined by the PHENOLIC changes that occur within the wine, which are time and temperature dependent. These PHENOLICS include TANNINS, ANTHOCYANINS and some FLAVOUR compounds. During barrel MATURATION and bottle ageing the PHENOLICS react with each other under the influence of small amounts of oxygen, which have dissolved in the wine during processes such as RACKING, topping up and later on, bottling.

A fine red wine ready for bottling may contain TANNINS and ANTHOCYANINS as well as POLYMERISED complexes derived through barrel ageing such as TANNIN salts, TANNIN-ANTHOCYANIN compounds and more elaborate colloids such as TANNIN-polysaccharides. Polymerization continues in the bottle. When these polymers reach a certain size they become too heavy to be held in solution and precipitate as dark reddish-brown sediment, leaving a wine that is progressively less ASTRINGENT and paler in colour. But while these TANNINS are "softening" they are also preserving the aromatic compounds wine with ANTIOXIDANT properties. This further allows the wine to measuredly develop more COMPLEX characters such as ESTERS (see **Chapter 5 – "How do some wines become more** COMPLEX **after ageing"**).

ACIDITY, generally considered an important component in in great red and white wines destined for long ageing, can render wines overly tart in youth and while the level of ACIDITY does not change with bottle age, it can *appear* less prominent. This is because the AROMAS and FLAVOURS in the wine can be "MUTE" when it is first bottled, either by the action of added ANTIOXIDANTS such as SULPHUR DIOXIDE, CARBON DIOXIDE or nitrogen or by nature of their composition. With time, the PRIMARY AROMAS and SECONDARY AROMAS and FLAVOURS may blossom into COMPLEX TERTIARY / MATURE characters that help to modify the impact of ACIDITY, with a similar but not nearly so dramatic effect as SUGAR has on modifying ACIDITY. The formation of COMPLEX ESTERS will further modify this appearance of ACIDITY (see **Chapter 6 -**). Likewise sweet wines can appear drier with bottle age as the SWEETNESS is similarly modified by the blossoming FLAVOURS in the wine.

Tasting Balance

So how do you, the wine taster, determine the relative state of BALANCE in a wine you taste? Well, one of the clearest examples of how to understand the harmonious or balanced interplay of WINE COMPONENTS is by looking purely at the relationship between ACIDITY and SWEETNESS for a moment. When you consider the difference between drinking straight lemon juice and lemonade, the secret behind creating a BALANCED perception of ACIDS and SUGARS is obvious. SWEETNESS modifies the taste of sourness and vice versa. When any beverage (including wine) tastes not so sweet that it's sickly and not so sour that it's uncomfortably tart, then it is demonstrating BALANCE. Cooler climates such as in the Mosel in Germany or Champagne in France often produce grapes with relatively high ACID levels. By leaving a judicious amount

The modern winery has more equipment and options available than ever before for making great wine. Knowing what to use (and what not to use), when to apply it, how and to what degree are all part of the winemaker's vision towards assembling a BALANCED wine in the winery. Pictured here: Staglin Winery in Napa California.

of RESIDUAL SUGAR in the wines, either in the form of grape SUGARS (glucose and fructose) or added SUGAR (sucrose) known as dosage in Champagne, the wines of these regions can seem more palatable and better BALANCED. Conversely, in very sweet wines such as those from Sauternes in Bordeaux the SUGARS would (and sometimes do in lesser examples) appear sickly-sweet or cloying were it not for the high levels of GRAPE DERIVED ACIDS and VOLATILE ACIDS rendered largely by the action of BOTRYTIS CINEREA – making for a better BALANCED and infinitely more drinkable sweet wine.

Now take that example of the relationship between the tastes of ACIDITY and SWEETNESS and factor in all the other WINE COMPONENTS: GRAPE DERIVED AROMAS / FLAVOURS, BODY, MOUTH-FEEL, WINEMAKING DERIVED AROMAS / FLAVOURS, ALCOHOL and any GREY-AREA FAULTS that may exist in the wine. As mentioned, in a very well BALANCED wine the taster should not be able to see the stitching of the winemaker's handiwork. It is in fact common to refer to a wonderfully BALANCED wine as "seamless". Other widely used references to great BALANCE are "harmonious" and possessing "poise". In such wines a taster should not easily be distracted or certainly discomforted by basic parts standing apart from the overall experience of the wine. Thus major components such as SWEETNESS, ACID, TANNINS or ALCOHOL should not stand-out over the fruit (GRAPE DERIVED AROMAS and FLAVOURS). Nor should the OAK, DIACETYL (buttery character from MALOLACTIC FERMENTATION) or toasty / bready character (from YEAST contact / BÂTONNAGE) overwhelm the fruit. While a little VOLATILE ACIDITY, REDUCTION, BRETTANOMYCES or OXIDATIVE HANDLING can give seasoning, when the seasoning overwhelms the fruit these GREY-AREA FAULTS become full-blown flaws (see **Chapter 1**).

The taster's assessment of BALANCE seems deceptively simple but it actually incorporates an intimate knowledge of all those formerly discussed building blocks (components) of wine and how they relate. Once this is understood the taster can accurately describe why the wine is out of BALANCE. But, going back to our discussion on CONCENTRATION, what separates the novice from the experienced taster is the breadth and depth of their MENTAL WINE LIBRARY in order to instil contextual relevance.

For describing wines that are out of BALANCE, the world's wine drinking community has developed its own WINE-SPEAK jargon. Some general terms for an unbalanced wine include: clumsy, angular, insipid, rough, incongruous, monolithic or simply unbalanced. The following chart lists some of the more common words that specifically address the state of unbalance of the various WINE COMPONENTS:

DESCRIPTORS **for Unbalanced** WINE COMPONENTS

Component	DESCRIPTORS **when Too High**	DESCRIPTORS **when Lacking**
ACIDITY	Sour, tart, ACIDIC, austere, very crisp, aggressive, sharp	Flabby, flat, dull
SWEETNESS	Cloying, sickly, flaccid, heavy	ACID stands out, sour, tart, ACIDIC
ALCOHOL	Hot or warm (particularly in the FINISH), fat, heady, powerful	Watery, dilute, thin
BODY	Heavy, monolithic, fat, massive, oily	Thin, watery, dilute, lean, angular, HOLLOW, empty, narrow, stringy, sinewy
Fruit CONCENTRATION	Monolithic, fruit-bomb, blowsy	Watery, dilute, lacks expression, lean, austere, HOLLOW, attenuated
TANNINS	Hard, ASTRINGENT, unresolved, chewy, aggressive, puckering, drying	Attenuated, soft
STRUCTURE	Angular, firm, austere, disjointed, tight, skeletal	Lacks STRUCTURE / backbone, flat, formless, spineless

COMPLEXITY

....

"Everything must be made
as simple as possible. But not simpler."

Albert Einstein

....

LET'S CLIMB BACK into the front seat of our car analogy from the **Introduction**. You drive. We'll imagine that you've driven a car before, so you're familiar with the basics: ignition, steering wheel, brakes, gear shift, clutch, indicators, lights, mirrors and wind screen wipers, etc. But this car is new to you, so it takes a few moments to work out where everything you need is located and exactly what you've got. Of course the more experience you have of lots of different cars, the easier it is to quickly suss everything out and appreciate from the get-go any extra features, enhancements, gizmos and exceptional crafting. We'll assume nothing is so completely foreign or off-putting in this car that you can't possibly drive it. Off we go. Soon we arrive at our destination and park-up.

How was your drive?

You can imagine there are a lot of variables involved in answering that question. There are the major, most basic issues of comfort, safety, ease of handling, speed, performance and mileage. Beyond all these fundamental boxes that need ticking there are higher-level emotional aspects such as pleasure, enjoyment, evocation, challenge, intellectual stimulation, the profoundness of the situation and the thrill. No, none of these latter elements are essential for getting from a-to-b. But they make your perception of the journey a whole lot more COMPLEX and ultimately rewarding. And it almost goes without mentioning that your experience of these emotional aspects with any given car would most likely be different from that of your mother or your partner.

I think you can see where I'm headed here. If there are a lot of possible cars in the world for you to experience, trust me, there are way more wines. And this whole question of "What is a COMPLEX wine?" can be subjective. What is perhaps quite a weird, disconcertingly strange and overly complicated experience for one person is unique, exciting and intellectually stimulating to another or staid, commonplace and boringly straightforward to someone else. One thing's for sure though: as your interest, knowledge and experience of wine grow, the result is usually a correlating increase in your desire for a wine to do MORE. And as we rise to the higher realms of what a wine can intrinsically offer – its purpose – we begin to enter the upper stratosphere of wine's roles, which should ultimately elicit one or more positive emotional responses. To do so the wine needs to appear COMPLEX, at least to you.

COMPLEXITY is generally deemed as an element in all great quality wines and many very good ones. Lesser quality wines will often have simple FLAVOURS which are easily described, succinctly listed and always fall short of satisfying our emotional and intellectual expectations of a wine (if we have any). When a wine offers too little to satiate *your* intellectual thirst for wine, then it is too simple. I can't put it any simpler than this ☺.

COMPLEXITY: the Major Components (Grapes & TERROIR)

In the last chapter on BALANCE we touched upon the point that in wines of great quality the GRAPE DERIVED CHARACTERS will account for the major AROMA / FLAVOUR features or components while the winemaking contributions should sit in the background like nuts, bolts and accessories holding it all together plus enhancing the experience. Why? Well, to put it bluntly, the grapes and their expression of where they come from are precisely what make a wine quintessentially a wine. This being the case, some wines are predisposed to being more COMPLEX because the grape varieties that produce them, by nature of their species and cultivars (varieties), have the potential to yield more COMPLEX wines. Thousands of years of viniculture have taught mankind this major truism: all grape vines are NOT created equal. It would have saved the wine world a lot of time, money and effort if a PHYLLOXERA (a vineyard-devastating insect) resistant species of vine were the most palatable and COMPLEX in the world. But, sigh, it just so *happens* that one of the frailest rooted, most PHYLLOXERA susceptible species in the world – Vitis vinifera - makes the best wine, and that's that. Even within this vinifera species there is what can be considered a *Varietal Class System of Greatness* with Kings and Queens, e.g. Cabernet Sauvignon and Chardonnay, Princes and Princesses, for example Pinot Noir and Riesling, Knights like Syrah and Grenache, Ladies in Waiting such as Sauvignon Blanc and Semillon and, er, Serfs like Ugni Blanc and Airen. What makes some grapes innately more COMPLEX than others? Not to be facetious, but this is a complex question.

Some cultivars by nature simply give more than others: more AROMAS / FLAVOURS, more CONCENTRATION / INTENSITY, more SUGARS, more ACIDS, more TANNINS (and of a better quality), etc. Cabernet Sauvignon, Grenache, Sauvignon Blanc and Syrah / Shiraz are good examples here as they tend to race past the starting line at full throttle. Some grapes can be a bit reticent to begin but possess the ability to age and develop COMPLEX TERTIARY AROMAS / FLAVOURS over time. Nebbiolo and Semillon are typical examples of this. Others have a beguiling propensity to express a sense of place and this is a forte of varieties like Pinot Noir and Riesling. While there are also lower quality work-horse grapes that are easy to farm and produce a lot of wine for the grower's buck but don't really give an awful lot in terms of, well, any of these COMPLEXITY factors we're discussing. Ugni Blanc (known as Trebbiano in Italy) and Spain's Airen are examples.

In **Chapter 2**, I mentioned in reference to Fruit Health and RIPENESS, "how the combo of vine, site and climate/weather plus a skilled grower or two has the potential to produce the holy grail of wines". The collective term, TERROIR, which is so important to achieving optimal grape RIPENESS, is considered by many to be equally essential to contributing to COMPLEXITY. How? Once again not to be facetious, but God only knows. There have been a number of technical articles and even books written on the subject of TERROIR and its scientifically provable contribution to COMPLEXITY, which has proven, well, not a lot that is universally accepted. Ultimately it appears in fact that God only knows why the Romanee Conti vineyard in Burgundy is capable of producing such awe-inspiring, heart-thumpingly great Pinot Noir, which other similar Pinot vines of a similar age planted / managed in the same way to other similar soils / climates around the world or even right next door to Romanee Conti cannot. Clones, the individual traits of those precise Romanee Conti planted Pinot vines and the intricate mix thereof, can perhaps partially account for some differences, but not all.

One of my more controversial theories on the matter of the reality behind the TERROIR question mark is that it is partially

Grape Variety Royalty

Cabernet Sauvignon
Chardonnay
Pinot Noir
Riesling

Grape Variety Nobility

Syrah
Grenache
Sauvignon Blanc
Sémillon

Grape Variety Serfs

Ugni Blanc
Airén

a phantom - an imagined character in an urban wine legend of our own making. Our willingness to buy into the legends of a vineyard or a name encourages us to suspend our disbelief. Were we wine lovers to be less accepting of such stories and truer to our palates, we might be more inclined to disengage the pause button on our disbelieving objectivity and see that the question mark in the TERROIR equation is just a fantasy quality marker created merely because we want to believe in this magic otherness of particular names or TERROIRS. Even for some experienced tasters the phantom question mark can turn into a black beast that consumes their better judgement. Why? Often it is insecurity when it comes to tasting "expertise" along with that dastardly duo of wine tasting deadly sins – pride & ego – that lead even experienced tasters into supporting a vineyard's label that isn't always all it's cracked up to be. Funny thing is, we wine experts know about our black beast and it is one of the reasons why so many of us insist that BLIND TASTINGS (with the label / identity concealed) are the only true way to accurately assess wine quality. But surely if one maintains one's ability to disbelieve and is otherwise not compromised (e.g. by financial agendas) in any way, BLIND TASTING as a matter of course is not necessary.

Grape variety and indeed <u>real</u> TERROIR instilled characters can be highly emotive and intellectually stimulating all on their own, without any suspension of disbelief or phantom question marks.

That all said I do truly believe that in great vintages, when all the angels are singing if you will, Romanee Conti can be one of the greatest Pinots on the planet bar none. One of my most orgasmic wine experiences ever was with a bottle of this wine. And you'll forgive me for playing devil's advocate again in order to offer a balanced view, but another vintage of this very same wine has also been one of the most disappointing bottles of my wine career. How can the same vineyard inspire such thrill and disappointment? Because I refuse to suspend my disbelief and buy into the story that wines from such a hallowed turf can never be anything other than hallelujah-glorious.

But the ability for a wine to express a sense of place – to display its TERROIR – is most certainly NOT all a pile of cow's dung shoved into a cow's horn and buried in the winter's dirt (as perhaps the ultimate terroiristes, BIODYNAMIC proponents, are inclined to do in good faith). On the contrary. The combined effects of Soil, Climate, Weather and Topography, the major intrinsic elements of TERROIR, often contribute COMPLEX attributes to wines that expert tasters can detect even when a wine is served BLIND. For instance, in the MASTER OF WINE BLIND practical (tasting) exam students are expected to be able to name with a high degree of accuracy not just the grape variety but the country, region and vintage. And they do. We wouldn't be able to do that if, for example, the 2002 vintage in Barossa, South Australia did not impart particular TERROIR characters in the glass that extend beyond the variety, viticulture management techniques and winemaking factors.

TERROIR: Perhaps manifested most clearly in Burgundy, France

TERROIR FAQs

Q: Isn't TERROIR really just the French word for dirt?

Yes and no. TERROIR can literally be translated from French into "soil" or "dirt", but in the context of wine it encompasses much more than this. It can be defined as the interaction of the unique elements of the vineyard habitat - Climate, Topography, Weather and Soil plus in some cases the ways and means of Managing the Vineyard – and their influence on wine STYLE, character and quality. All vineyards have a TERROIR but not all wines convey their terroir, nor are they necessarily made this way.

Q: If God only knows how TERROIR contributes to a wine's characters and therefore quality, then how do we know its contribution even exists?

A: Amongst of the clearest and most often cited examples we have that TERROIR'S contributions to wine characters and therefore potentially the quality are real are the wines of long-since established and clearly delineated regions such as Burgundy. Here, where it's almost exclusively a one grape (Pinot Noir or Chardonnay) wine and when vineyards are not BLENDED, we can typically find that neighbouring vineyards owned by the same grower and produced identically – whereby every known variable in the grape-derived-COMPLEXITY-equation are precisely the same except for minor differences in the TERROIR - will produce notably and sometimes remarkably different wines. One wine may have more perfume, INTENSITY and finer TANNINS, indeed be beguilingly more COMPLEX, whilst the other might be thin, weedy and positively dull by comparison. This could and may well largely be due to minor meso- and micro-climate variations in berry ripening brought about differing aspect, slope and altitude. But the full story is likely to be even more complicated and, for example, partially due to the varying textures and compositions of the soils which can affect the availability of water and nutrients to the vine as well as soil temperature, equating somehow to discernible differences that go beyond RIPENESS alone.

Q: So, does this "MINERAL" character in wine that I've heard about come from TERROIR?

A: That some of the vine's surrounding dirt or components thereof might actually make it into the grapes and therefore wines, imparting what many critics refer to as MINERALITY, is highly doubtful and has not been scientifically proven. What's more, some common "MINERAL" DESCRIPTORS have actually been identified as winemaking generated. For example, it has been suggested that the "gun flint" character in some wines comes from the production of benezenemethanethiol from the breakdown of an amino ACID during FERMENTATION. Those chalky or crushed stone AROMAS in certain wines have been suggested to be due to low pH / high ACIDITY. Earthiness could be due to microbial activity from GEOSMIN or BRETTANOMYCES. But (and with wine there's always at least one 'but') there are some soil borne elements such as potassium and sodium ions which have been found to transmigrate to the grapes and profoundly affect the wine STYLE / character. They don't quite give wines that COMPLEX "MINERALLY" character everyone loves, in fact the former increases the pH of wine while that latter can make it detectably salty, but at least we can't say nothing at all comes from soils.

Q: If not "MINERALITY", then what exactly does TERROIR bring to the wine quality party beyond the obvious fruit health & RIPENESS?
A: It's hard to pinpoint any discernible AROMA compound that TERROIR specifically gives to wine, but you could say that it <u>uniquely</u> contributes to all the amounts and qualities of all the GRAPE DERIVED COMPONENTS in wine, imparting and distributing them in a way that is for every wine, well, <u>unique</u>. That TERROIR has a definitive and measurable impact on Fruit Health & Ripening (**Chapter 2**) and that this directly relates to wine quality is really not in question. How it contributes to the unique STYLE, COMPLEXITY and therefore other quality benefits is the less well understood…in short, God-only-knows. But we do know that different TERROIRS impart differences in the wines they produce that we can smell and taste and that some TERROIRS give MORE. This more-ness may simply manifest itself as more AROMAS, or more different AROMAS, or more CONCENTRATED AROMAS, or AROMAS in a more appealing ratio / proportion, with a corresponding (or not) effect on other GRAPE COMPONENTS. Bottom line though, we simply know that the wine from this vineyard is more or less COMPLEX than that vineyard and the production difference in some cases is solely down to TERROIR.

Not all wines aim first and foremost to express the place from which they come and therefore the TERROIR attributes may be minimised by the winemaker in an effort to maximise upon varietal expression and other FUNDAMENTAL QUALITY FACTORS such as BALANCE and/or emphasise BRAND or stylistic expression. It is up to the winemaker as to whether her or his vision of the wine being forged will look to maximise the expression of terroir as the major COMPLEX features of the wine or minimise it to focus more on other characteristics such as the grape variety(s), fruit RIPENESS, CONCENTRATION and BALANCE. It's important to note that either approach does not necessarily make the wine more or less COMPLEX and therefore does not automatically affect quality. But it's also worth noting that these differing winemaking pursuits can account for a schism between otherwise like-minded wine critics as to what should constitute the heart of a great quality wine; a topic to be discussed under the heading of "**Regional Typicality**" in **Chapter 7** – SUPPORTING QUALITY FACTORS.

COMPLEXITY – The Minor 'Nuts, Bolts & Accessories' Components (Winemaking & Aging)

Apart from the grapes and the somewhat spiritually begotten yet tangibly real contributions of TERROIR, which collectively should account for the main COMPLEXITY components in a wine of greatness, other factors that can contribute the minor "nuts, bolts & accessories" to COMPLEXITY include:

- FERMENTATION and MLF (if employed) derived characters (see **Chapter 5**)

- MATURATION / Storage derived characters (see **Chapter 5** and this chapter)

- GREY-AREA FAULTS - We learned in the first and second chapters that wine AROMAS and FLAVOURS can come from FAULTS, both those arising from the vineyard (see **Chapter 2**) and those that are a result of winemaking and/or aging (see **Chapter 1**). It was also mentioned in both chapters that some winemaking / MATURATION and vineyard related "FAULTS" exist in a grey-area, whereby in certain circumstances these can be considered as part of the STYLE and/or contribute to COMPLEXITY.

To the extent that the grape / TERROIR derived characters with time change considerably into less discernable features, bottle age derived characters such as ALDEHYDES and ESTERS (see this Chapter, ***"How do some wines become more COMPLEX after "ageing"?"***) can, in proportion, also contribute to complexity.

So in summary COMPLEXITY implies an individually satisfying amount of pleasant / interesting / stimulating wine characters that will have developed mainly from the grape (variety) and/or TERROIR with supporting contributions from winemaking and/or bottle ageing. One final finer detail is what I call, *The Layered Effect*. COMPLEXITY shouldn't hit you all at once like Mack truck full of smell / FLAVOUR; it should develop in stages or layers. This is certainly true of many great wines, which are inclined to transform in aromatics over a period of time – ranging from a few minutes to hours – in the opened bottle, decanter or glass. Equally important is what occurs on the palate where different FLAVOURS may manifest themselves in the first impressions, on the "MID-PALATE" (FLAVOURS that develop while the wine is in the mouth) and in the FINISH.

Types of OAK, Coopering Techniques and the Aromatic, FLAVOUR & Textural Contributions of OAK Barrel Ageing

OAK is used in both the FERMENTATION and ageing or MATURATION of wine. OAK vat or barrel FERMENTATION and especially MATURATION allows for the slow OXYGENATION of wines and new(er) OAK imparts TANNINS (see **Chapter 2** on "Tasting TANNINS"), and FLAVOURS that are leached from the contact between the wine and the surface of the wood. The type of OAK used, the COOPERAGE techniques employed to produce the barrel and how the barrel is used all play a role in the FLAVOURS, texture and STYLE of a barrel MATURED wine.

The Extraction Level and Types of OAK FLAVOURS and TANNINS in wine are influenced by the following factors:
1) Type of OAK (species, grain, texture)
2) COOPERAGE techniques and Seasoning
3) TOAST Level
4) Age of the Barrel
5) Size of the Barrel
6) Time in Barrel

Around 600 different species of OAK tree with the genus "Quercus" exist in the world. Dozens are thought to be used in winemaking, although there are three species that are mainly used and therefore of major importance: Quercus robur, Quercus sessilus (A.K.A. Quercus petraea and Quercus sessiliflora) and Quercus alba. More commonly wine professionals refer simply to FRENCH OAK, which includes the first two species just mentioned, and AMERICAN OAK, mainly consisting of Quercus alba. Each of these OAK species possesses different characters and attributes directly related to variations in the wood, all of which play a part in the interaction between the wood and the wine. Specifically, it is the differences between the varying textures and the grains that the species offer that determine their suitability to winemakers seeking a specific contribution from OAK ageing.

As you can probably guess, the various OAK forests around the world are wooded with indigenous species. In France, oak from the Limousin forest is mostly of the species Quercus robur - a "robust" FLAVOURED, TANNIC OAK best suited to nearby Cognac production. Other French forests are wooded with several species most notably Quercus sessilus / petraea, which is more commonly used to make wine barrels as it tends to be less TANNIC than robur and offer more desirable aromatic compounds such as EUGENOL and various lactones. The most significant forests for the production of OAK suitable for wine production are in the Vosges, Sarthe, Nevers and Alliers departments or communes of France. Other localised forests in Burgundy, the Loire, Alsace, parts of Eastern Europe and Champagne sometimes produce wood for the use of neighbouring regions. Of significance are the origin and climate in which the tree has grown as these will influence the quality of the grain, texture and suitability (as well as price) of the wood. European or FRENCH OAK tends to have more TANNINS and ASTRINGENCY than AMERICAN OAK and the FLAVOURS are much more subtle, usually imparting suggestions of coconut and baking spices. The increased TANNINS available from European / FRENCH OAKS can be useful in aiding colour formation, STRUCTURE and aging potential of many wines destined for long cellaring.

The major species of AMERICAN OAK is Quercus alba, coming predominantly from forests in the Eastern states, Minnesota, Wisconsin, Missouri and Ohio. AMERICAN OAK has a wider grain and is less porous than FRENCH OAK and therefore can be sawn into staves, rather that requiring that they be hand-split lengthwise as in France. This ability to saw rather than split the wood intensifies the already more prominent lactone laden, vanilla-laced FLAVOURS that AMERICAN OAK tends to instil in wine. It also makes AMERICAN OAK significantly less expensive than FRENCH OAK, almost half the price, since sawing causes less wastage. As well as the obvious markets of North and South America, AMERICAN OAK has a history of use in Spain and Australia. It usually gives less ASTRINGENT TANNINS to wine that, along with the stand-out spicy vanillin FLAVOURS it lends, are considered complimentary to generous, bold FLAVOURED and softly textured red wines such as Rioja and ripe Australian Shiraz.

After cutting the wood (splitting or sawing), the first stage of COOPERAGE that will have a major impact on the characters that the barrel will impart is seasoning. Seasoning the OAK planks or staves - leaving them to rest and dry outside usually for a period of 12-36 months or drying them artificially in a kiln to speed-up the process - is a stylistic tool used by coopers to mellow the impact of the wood and significantly soften/lower the TANNINS prior to barrel making. The period of time spent seasoning the wood, method (kiln or outdoors) and ambient climate all play a role in the quality of the wood.

TOASTING

To "TOAST" an OAK barrel is to literally cook the inner walls of the barrel with a special burner that is usually lowered into the barrel (see photo) and left for a period of time depending on the desired TOASTING level. TOASTING happens during the construction of the barrel and has two purposes: 1) to stress-relieve the wood after it has been bent into the barrel shape and 2) to affect the type and amount of TANNINS and FLAVOURS that will be imparted into the wine once newly filled. The heating causes many changes in the wood's internal structure, creating different compounds and texture / FLAVOUR expressions at different TOASTING levels. TOAST levels are usually classified as light, medium or heavy and the heads – top and bottom of the barrel – may or may not be TOASTED exclusively or included. Generally speaking, the green, woody FLAVOURS of untoasted OAK develop into characters of vanilla, bread, nut, clove, cinnamon and/or coconut with light to medium TOASTING. Heavy TOASTING can instil a distinct "smoky" and often espresso / roasted coffee character. Furthermore, increasing the TOAST level softens the texture of OAK TANNINS and tends to yield less TANNIC influence on the wine.

Barrel Age, Size and Length of Time in Barrel

The age and size of barrels used to MATURE wine have a significant impact on the amount of FLAVOURS and TANNINS the wine will pick-up. First consideration is the age of the barrel since only new OAK barrels (those that have never been filled with wine before) and to a lesser extent second fill / use barrels (those that only been filled with wine only once before) will lend a notable amount of FLAVOURS and TANNINS to wine. Size counts when it comes to barrels – the more surface area of the wine that comes in contact with the OAK barrel, the more FLAVOURS and TANNINS it can extract. Thus the smaller the barrel, the more it will potentially give. To offer winemakers a wide range of stylistic options, barrels are available in a wide range of sizes, generally ranging from ubiquitously used barriques (225 litres) to foudres (very large barrels of up to 10,000 litres or more). The amount of time that the wine spends in a new or second fill barrel will also be a factor in how much FLAVOUR and TANNINS the wine leaches from the wood. More time equals more EXTRACT...up to the point of course when the OAK may have little left to give (e.g. after 24-36 months).

How do some wines become more COMPLEX after "ageing"?

As mentioned in **Chapter 4** in the section "**How do some wines become better BALANCED after ageing?**" with certain wines over time the TANNINS can lessen and soften in appearance while ACIDITY can seem less impactful. Additionally as wines age important changes occur affecting the AROMA / FLAVOUR compounds, rendering some wines more COMPLEX. This is a result of the compounds responsible for the initial PRIMARY AROMAS of the grape, some AROMA PRECURSOR compounds and those resulting from FERMENTATION (SECONDARY AROMAS) interacting with each other, the dissolved oxygen in wine and with other PHENOLICS so that over time the AROMAS may be transformed into a more profoundly COMPLEX, MATURE or EVOLVED nose (what sentimentalists might refer to as a "BOUQUET") of TERTIARY CHARACTERS.

A frequently occurring example of COMPLEX compounds forming over time is the formation of ALDEHYDES by the OXIDATION of various ALCOHOLS in wine (primarily ETHANOL). ACETALDEHYDE, a defining feature of Fino Sherry, is a created by the partial OXIDATION of ETHANOL. Other examples of specific ALDEHYDES found in wines include phenylacetaldehyde, propionaldehyde, glycolaldehyde, isobutyraldehyde, butyraldehyde and even formaldehyde (in trace, legally permitted amounts), which in proportion can all contribute to the COMPLEX array of wine AROMAS.

Another common reaction contributing to COMPLEXITY during MATURATION and bottle ageing is ESTERIFICATION. With the formation of ESTERS from various combinations of ALCOHOLS and ACIDS the range of AROMAS in wines increases. For example, the ETHANOL may combine with ACETIC ACID to form the ESTER ETHYL ACETATE, which in small concentrations can contribute a COMPLEX lift to wine but in higher concentrations lends an unpleasant nail varnish/polish remover character (being an actual component of some such solvents). Other ACIDS such as MALIC, TARTARIC and succinic ACID combine with ETHANOL and other higher ALCOHOLS to form a wide range of aromatic combinations. More than 160 different ESTERS have thus far been identified in wines. The "fruity" ESTERS in wine are said to contribute its distinctly vinous character. Examples include ethyl butyrate (pineapple scented), benzyl acetate (apple scented) and isoamyl acetate (banana scented). ESTERIFICATION can make a wine taste less apparently ACIDIC with age because the ACIDS that become combined take on more COMPLEX FLAVOURS drawing the drinker's attention away from simple ACIDITY. When eventually the wine's PRIMARY AROMAS / fruity FLAVOURS and TANNINS have all but diminished, the ACID (which never actually disappeared) may begin to dominate the palate since its level remains almost constant throughout the bottle's life. The rate at which ESTERIFICATION and other bottle age related changes occur is influenced by a host of factors such as the wine's pH and level of ANTIOXIDANTS, both natural (such as POLYPHENOLS) and added (such as SO_2 and ASCORBIC ACID).

Storage conditions, particularly temperature, will have a significant impact on a wine's rate of aging (see **Chapter 7**) as well as the proportions and types of COMPLEX compounds that are formed. Other factors include the type and quality of bottle closure (e.g. CORK, SCREW CAP, etc.) and the amount and composition of headspace between the closure and wine when the wine is bottled, all of which can inhibit or encourage the influence of oxygen. Although experts understand much about the evolution of age-worthy wines, they are as yet unable to predict with any degree of certainty when wines are likely to reach that COMPLEX stage known as "MATURE", when a wine has reached its optimal levels of BALANCE and FLAVOUR COMPLEXITY and just before the "fruit" begins to fade. A certain amount of experience following young wines through to maturity and a considerable MENTAL WINE LIBRARY can bestow upon better critics the ability to offer a reasonably accurate DRINKING WINDOW of when a wine is likely to be at its peak of BALANCE and COMPLEXITY. But ultimately the perfect time to drink a wine is up to the drinker and her/his personal preference. Some drinkers love wines while they're young, firm and fruity while others prefer older, softer, more COMPLEX expressions that come with age. The beauty of wine is truly in the eye of the beholder!

"TOASTING" the insides of OAK barrels can dramatically impact the FLAVOURS and TANNINS that barrel aging imparts.

Tasting COMPLEXITY

Knowing what COMPLEXITY is and where it comes from is all well and good, but how does it taste? How can it be perceived and evaluated?

To assess the COMPLEXITY of a wine involves taking account of all the AROMAS and ultimately the FLAVOURS in the wine. Simply put, FLAVOUR is the combined effect of taste and smell in the mouth. Smelling strongly INFLUENCES flavour largely through the function of RETRONASAL OLFACTION, discussed in the "**Prologue, Part 1**". In the context of wine, the terms AROMA and FLAVOUR are often used interchangeably since the FLAVOURS of wines predominately consist of AROMA compounds as sensed via RETRONASAL OLFACTION. The brain combines the effects of the two senses into one, resulting in what wine tasters have come to recognize as FLAVOUR...itself a rather complex concept.

As previously discussed, the amount of AROMAS and FLAVOURS in wine as well as where they come from (e.g. grape variety, TERROIR, winemaking and bottle ageing), how they interrelate and ultimately their relative appeal all play important roles in the perceived COMPLEXITY of a wine.

Another important element of COMPLEXITY is MOUTH-FEEL – a wine term for the textural sensation that a wine creates in the mouth. It is essentially a consideration of major tactile components such as TANNINS and VISCOSITY. Intrinsic levels and grades of VISCOSITY and TANNIC TEXTURES often offer vital contributions to the interest and therefore COMPLEXITY of a palate profile.

It's also worth noting that there is evidence to suggest that MOUTH-FEEL / TEXTURE largely impacts our perception of FLAVOURS, although it does not change the FLAVOURS per se. For example, from the results of a 2003 study of the perception of identical tastes and taste levels at varying degrees of VISCOSITY conducted by David Cook, et. al., it was determined that the perception of FLAVOURS decreased as the substances tasted were made thicker. While texture may modify the intensity of FLAVOUR to a certain extent, it does however provide yet another layer to COMPLEXITY.

Finally, some common terms wine professionals use to describe a wine's relative state of COMPLEXITY include:

Simple: straightforward, uncomplicated, monolithic, one dimensional, plain, obscure, vague, poorly defined, boring, predictable, innocuous

COMPLEX: intricate, sophisticated, multi-layered, fine, refined, ethereal, delineated, well defined, diverse, harmonious, exciting, mind-blowing

Are unfiltered wines better?

Have you ever spotted the word "Unfiltered" on a wine label and wondered what *that* was all about?

Something of a contentious topic in FINE WINE production and scorned by many wine critics, FILTRATION is nonetheless a very common winemaking process. The issue with regards to quality is not so much whether or not to FILTER ever but *how much to FILTER* and *when* since nearly all wines produced for commercial sale will receive some degree of FILTRATION at some point during winemaking, if simply to perform a light FILTRATION to rid juice or wine of residual harvesting debris (leaves, STEMS, bugs, etc.) and/or lees for examples. The bone of contention largely has to do with the common and somewhat habitual practice of a final FILTRATION prior to bottling. Here there is a big difference between a "light" FILTRATION with particle catchers that are only wide enough to take out large particles such as those visible with the naked eye and "sterile" filters such as CROSS-FLOW FILTERS that routinely strip out microscopic microbials like YEASTS and bacteria plus inevitably a certain amount of wine FLAVOUR and textural compounds that can lend COMPLEXITY to wines, though to what degree this alteration is detectable is a moot point. Nowadays many FINE WINE and NATURAL WINE makers opt for very little (light) or no final FILTRATION prior to bottling, necessitating that hygiene conditions in the winery and especially on the bottling line must be impeccable to allow any degree of assurance that that wine will not be bottled with any ambient microbials (e.g. YEAST or bacteria), which could spoil the wine. Otherwise precautionary winemakers will sterile filter (with a CROSS-FLOW FILTER or several other means) prior to bottling, stripping any possible residual microbials from the wine but also, arguably, some of the delicate quality-enhancing nuances that contribute to COMPLEXITY. The alternative to FILTERING is careful SETTLING and RACKING.

Arguably another form of FILTRATION that is even more controversial is the use of REVERSE OSMOSIS – so controversial that it is indeed rare to find a winemaker that will admit to using this device, although they are in fact quite common in top wineries around the world (especially since these are the only wineries that can afford them). A REVERSE OSMOSIS machine essentially functions as a FILTRATION device though it works differently than a standard filter. It possesses the ability to separate out the smallest of microscopic compounds - even smaller than those that can be stripped out by a regular CROSS-FLOW FILTER - down to molecular dimensions. Based on the CROSS-FLOW FILTRATION principal, it works by passing the wine tangentially over a semipermeable membrane. Pressure is created on the "wine" side of the membrane to cause very small particles (determined by the pore size of the holes in the membrane) through to the side of less pressure, ultimately performing "osmotic" effect in reverse. In a greater context it is a method used to purify or desalinate water, though with regards to wine is mainly used for one of two purposes: 1) to concentrate MUST by removing water resulting for example from a dilute / rain-affected crop or 2) to dealcoholize wine by removing ETHANOL and water molecules after which this small amount of the concentrated, dealcoholized wine can be reconstituted with pure water and BLENDED back with a larger batch of wine to produce a wine of lower ALCOHOL. REVERSE OSMOSIS is also occasionally used to remove VOLATILE ACIDITY and more recently smoke TAINT or the major by-products of BRETTANOMYCES (4-ETHYLPHENOL and 4-ETHYLGUAIACOL). While REVERSE OSMOSIS is a very advanced not to mention expensive piece of equipment, it is not exact in what it removes from wine since the removal is based on particle size, so there is probably some loss of other desirable components besides targets such as water, ETHANOL, 4-EP, 4-EG and VA based on molecular dimensions. Although legal to use in most major wine regions for particular purposes and not uncommon in those at the pinnacle of wine quality production such as Bordeaux (mainly used for MUST concentration) and Napa Valley (mainly used for lowering ALCOHOL), the major criticisms against REVERSE OSMOSIS are the use of excessive manipulation, the possible stripping out of some AROMA compounds that contribute to COMPLEXITY and, in the case of MUST concentration, the concentration of any under-ripe and harsh components that may exist in the MUST such as PYRAZINES and unresolved TANNINS.

LENGTH & NATURE OF FINISH

....

"The art of love is largely the art of persistence."
Albert Ellis

....

REMEMBER AS A kid whenever you were given an ice cream cone or candy you wanted it to last forever, for the taste to never end? It's likely that you still feel this way about good things – the things you enjoy. You would love for that romantic beach vacation in Bali to last as long as possible. It would be amazing if your favourite television series could go on for another episode. How awesome would it be if you could test drive that Lamborghini for just ten more minutes? Or if you could hear just a few more chords of your favourite song / musical piece? And even though you may have graduated from ice cream cones, even now wouldn't it be great if they could make a bottomless Haagen Dazs tub?

It's just human nature that we all have an innate desire for our best experiences to be made better by lasting longer. And it only stands to reason that those who have truly embraced wine - have taken their level of involvement that one step further - would feel the same about a sip that they're particularly enjoying.

One of the keys to assessing a wine's quality for wine drinkers who are, for want of a better term, 'all in' (at the top of the WINE PURPOSES PYRAMID), is the measure of the taste or FLAVOURS that linger in the mouth after the wine has been spat or swallowed. Great wines have long, pleasant, and often COMPLEX FINISHES.

Why would high involvement drinkers at the top of the WINE PURPOSES PYRAMID care more about how long the FLAVOURS of a wine last in their mouths? Well, let's go back to our image of a childhood chocolate ice cream with multi-coloured sprinkles in a sugar cone or nowadays a walk with a lover on a white sand beach in Bali. The more intensely you feel about something, the more you want it and the more you want it to last.

Like most experiences, apart from the length of the experience contributing to the quality, there must also be a certain quality to the length of the FINISH. Imagine for example if the last bite of a dish that you are savouring is a flavourless piece of wilted garnish or your last sip of tea is a mouth full of bitter tea leaves. You want all the quality of the first exciting experience to last throughout the long FINISH and perhaps add something more. Furthermore an overly abrupt FINISH to the "flesh" components of the wine (i.e. GRAPE DERIVED FLAVOURS other than ACID and TANNINS) as opposed to structural elements usually confirms a fundamental short-coming in the wine: that the wine is mainly "skeletal", generally lacking CONCENTRATION and INTENSITY of the grape FLAVOURS.

The Nature of a Great Finish

What's in the FINISH of a great wine? Well to begin with simpler FINISHES - some grape varieties, wine STYLES and young wines destined for long ageing will yield long FINISHES

Australian "Port" was historically the tipple of choice for Australians. Century old or more barrels of these Port-styled, FORTIFIED WINES still exist and are now amongst the world's most highly CONCENTRATED (through many years of slow evaporation), thick, syrupy, unctuous wines that yield epically long finishes. Pictured here is a veritable museum full of such nectar at the Seppeltsfield winery in the Barossa Valley, Australia.

that are primarily composed of ACIDITY, SWEETNESS and/or TANNINS in their flush of youth. While such a FINISH may seem disappointing in the wine's formative stages, it is up to the critic to make a judgement call as to whether this straightforward / simple and predominately unbalanced AFTERTASTE situation may eventually be redressed with bottle ageing. In **Chapter 4**, in the section, "**How do some wines become better** BALANCED **after ageing?**" it was demonstrated how in some wines the SWEETNESS, TANNINS and/or ACIDS can become diminished and/or less prominent with bottle age. Ideally this "softening" of STRUCTURE will allow the grape, TERROIR and TERTIARY elements to come forward, manifesting themselves over time and eventually taking centre stage in the FINISH when the wine is at the peak of its DRINKING WINDOW. But as all good things must come to an end so does the greatness of FINISH. At a certain point in bottle ageing as the wine passes its drinking "peak", the fruit begins to dry out and fade, until once again all that remains in the FINISH is tart ACIDITY and powdery TANNINS.

It's also worth noting that sweet and especially very sweet wines can offer epically long FINISHES thanks largely to the viscous stickiness caused by their high SUGAR contents. Extreme examples include Sweet PX Sherries, Tokaji Aszu Essencia and Rutherglen FORTIFIED Muscat. The critical aspect of the FINISH for tasters of sweet wines to look out for is that the FINISH is not simply SUGAR laced. Ideally the COMPLEX FLAVOUR characters should linger right along with the SUGAR...are carried with it if you will. The exact same principal is true of a DRY wine that is naturally high in ACIDITY such as a Riesling. You don't want to taste just ACID in the FINISH but the FLAVOUR elements derived from the fruit that are, in an ideal situation, carried along with the ACID.

As a cautionary note, tasters looking for that extended experience should be wary if, like many things in life, a FINISH seems too good to be true. A classic winemaker trick to give the illusion of CONCENTRATION, TEXTURE and length is to retain some RESIDUAL SUGAR in the wine, not enough so that it appears overtly sweet but just enough to fool the palate. This is part and parcel of the production of many large-volume, cheaper, BRANDED WINES (whites, reds and roses) to make the wine appear as though there is more "fruit" and real grape substance than there actually is. Another cheat is over-oaking (usually with OAK chips or staves) a wine such that this oaky taste is all that comes through in its final throws. While cheats like these will certainly boost the length of FINISH, ultimately they are not considered by critics as quality enhancements but cover-ups for inadequacies and distractions from the fruit expression.

Finally, at the pinnacles of greatness it is not enough for a wine to possess a long FINISH, even if this is composed primarily of fruit as opposed to SWEETNESS or STRUCTURE (ACIDS and/or TANNINS). A long FINISH can be simple or COMPLEX, depending to some degree on the grape and/or STYLE as much as the CONCENTRATION. Many good to very good wines (but not outstanding or exceptional) have long FINISHES that can be relatively simple, imparting just a handful of lingering FLAVOURS. A good example might be a well-made, typical Sauvignon Blanc from Marlborough, New Zealand. The wine may have great CONCENTRATION and length, but generally lacks COMPLEXITY in its FINISH of just green/bell peppers and apples, for example. So apart from the length of the FINISH, critics may also look for further COMPLEXITY in the FINISH of a truly great wine, adding to that which came through in the initial impressions and MID-PALATE. These will often come through as a multi-layered affect to a wine's FINISH with new FLAVOURS manifesting themselves moments after the wine has been swallowed or spat.

How long is long?

How do you measure the "length" of a FINISH? Believe it or not, empiricists might take out a stop-watch or surreptitiously gaze at the second hand of a watch while the Zen wine masters amongst us (see **Chapter 8)** will simply "get" that a FINISH is long and layered or short and simple. And if we had to name a figure, exactly how long is a "long" FINISH? Well, there is no generally agreed period of time but there are some critics who are willing to put a number to it. For example, Robert M. Parker Jr. often refers to FINISHES that are 45 seconds to a minute long or longer as being extraordinary and I would generally agree that any wine that lingers around this long on your palate qualifies as a superlative marathon runner!

Communicating Finish Assessments

A FINISH can be said to be Short, Medium, Long or shades in between these assessments (e.g. Medium to Long). To qualify beyond this the taster can note that a FINISH is simple or COMPLEX. Other commonly used expressions in reference to the actual length, quality and nature of the FINISH are "clipped", "abrupt", "epic", "clean", "attenuated", "pure, "refreshing", "sustained", "straightforward", "uncomplicated", "persistent", "**layered**" or "multi-layered" and "lingering".

SUPPORTING QUALITY FACTORS

....

*"The moment we want to believe something,
we suddenly see all the arguments for it, and
become blind to the arguments against it."*

George Bernard Shaw

....

SO FAR WE'VE covered the FUNDAMENTAL QUALITY FACTORS of wine; factors that most wine critics will agree are all essential to determining wine quality. It needs stressing however that wine quality assessment is far from an exact science. For as many critics that may be assessing the quality of a particular wine, the results of its quality evaluation could well be that many differing assessments...and some could vary enormously. This is partly due to the cold hard fact that not everyone is on the same smell page, as detailed in the **Prologue, Part 2** of this book. And, truth be told, there are many pretenders to the throne since *anyone* can self-proclaim him or herself as a wine critic...generally no dedicated exam, degree or set level of experience let alone natural ability is required. This is more common than ever in our modern era of blogging. But even the greatest, most indisputably experienced, knowledgeable and talented critics in the world will differ wildly sometimes in their assessments because often their conclusions are not based on the FUNDAMENTAL QUALITY FACTORS alone. With many critics there are one or more SUPPORTING QUALITY FACTORS that also come into play.

SUPPORTING QUALITY FACTORS are less universally agreed quality factors. The major ones that are most frequently taken into account include:

- The wine's Ability / Potential to Age
- Regional Typicality
- Value for money
- Drinkability
- Compatibility with Food
- And Uniqueness of grape variety, STYLE and/or region

Before we go any further I should point out that these quality factors push the boundaries of objectivity far further than those discussed in the previous chapters. So much so that not all critics agree that all or even some of these should be taken into account when evaluating a wine's quality. Moreover, these contentious issues have wider-ranging definitions and interpretations than the FUNDAMENTAL QUALITY FACTORS. But they are important to be aware of not only because they are often valid points that should be noted in a comprehensive review of a particular wine but some critics will take to fiercely defending such aspects to back-up their assessments. My word to the wise when it comes to applying these factors to your assessments is to try not to get too dogmatic about them as you may run into trouble if you try to apply them to all wines and STYLES simply because each factor tends to work best when applied to isolated cases. This is precisely what makes them subjective to the critic's extrinsic views rather than related to the intrinsic FUNDAMENTAL QUALITY FACTORS of previous chapters, which can be assessed with far greater objectivity.

Ability / Potential to Age

A good many critics agree that a wine's ability to age is a key factor when assessing the quality of a wine that approaches the pinnacles of wine greatness. This is largely an issue of complexity. As suggested in **Chapter 5** addressing the question "**How do some wines become more complex with age?**" a very small proportion of wines produced in the world have the ability to develop into something more complex and sometimes far more complex over a period of time in bottle when stored under ideal conditions. That wine has this somewhat unique ability to develop TERTIARY CHARACTERS while cellared over a period, which can in rare cases extend to over a century, is one of its many extraordinary features. However, having the ability to age and yield something more COMPLEX over time depends heavily on maintaining conducive shipping, storage and cellaring conditions throughout the aging period.

A few extraordinary wines have the ability to age and gain COMPLEXITY over decades and in rare cases over a century! Pictured here is an amazing pair of well-preserved Chateau Cos d'Estournel bottles, 1906 and 1918, both fully mature, complex and still well within their DRINKING WINDOWS.

The counter argument here is that not all great wines have the ability to age significantly. This is usually a consequence of a grape variety that offers an awful lot in its flush of youth but deteriorates rather than gains as it ages. A prime example is Viognier. If we consider a splendid Condrieu (100% Viognier produced in the tiny Condrieu AC in Northern Rhone, France) that ticks all the FUNDAMENTAL QUALITY FACTOR boxes, offering wonderful COMPLEXITY when young but disappoints after 4-5 years as its PRIMARY AROMA perfume fades, we can see that this simply does not apply in this case. Although admittedly great Viognier is one of a few rare exceptions!

What are the ideal shipping and storage conditions for aging wine to preserve wine and/or promote the development of COMPLEX, TERTIARY CHARACTERS?

SHIPPING WINE

The search for ideal shipping and storage methods for wine has long been a problem for wine merchants and consumers. Indeed the STYLE of Madeira as we know it was discovered by fluke following wine shipping conditions during the long, hot sea voyages from the island of Madeira off the coast of Portugal to places in the New World and the East Indies. Unfortunately, not all wines benefit so fortuitously from sustained periods of heat. Bottled wine is heavy and delicate, sensitive to temperature extremes and breakage.

METHODS OF TRANSPORTING WINE

The three major issues when considering the method of transporting wine are time (from point of purchase to destination), temperature (that the wine will be maintained at throughout the journey) and cost.

The biggest cost issue is the time factor although temperature control will also increase the expense of transporting wines. But if the wine is required in a rush expect it to cost considerably more than if there is a long lead-time. The only means of transporting wine over a long distance quickly (e.g. within a week) is to air freight it via a logistics or specialized courier company – typically costing as much as ten times more than sea shipping when broken down to a per bottle basis.

The ideal temperature for transporting wine should be no higher or lower than optimum cellaring conditions. Thus it is important to ensure that wines are kept within a constant temperature range of 10-15 degrees Celcius. Wine must not be exposed to temperature extremes during transportation. When exposed to temperatures much above 30 degrees Celcius, particularly when the wine has come from a cool environment, the liquid in the bottle may expand, commonly resulting in leakage or, in the worst cases, CORKS that are partially or completely forced from bottles. Conversely, if bottles are exposed to excessively cool temperatures much below -5 degrees Celcius, the wine could turn to ice also resulting in expansion but in this case there is a further danger of the wine bottle actually bursting from the pressure. Even if the wine doesn't actually freeze, the exposure to excessively cool temperatures below 0 degrees Celcius could begin the premature precipitation of TARTRATE CRYSTALS out of solution, rendering aesthetically annoying though harmless crystal sedimentation in the bottle. Finally, temperature extreme scenarios must be avoided since even if the bottles and CORKS remain intact, the wine itself will almost certainly have been irrevocably altered.

LORRIES / TRUCKS

The use of Lorries / Trucks is an inevitable link in the wine delivery chain. Movement of wine from cellar to a vehicle of overseas transport (ship or plane) and then to the final destination cellar or storage facility requires a specialized temperature controlled transport vehicle, in all but a few exceptional climates and/or temperate months. A refrigerated lorry for wine collection and delivery seems an obvious no-brainer, yet many of the large shippers do not always use them because of the vehicle expense and cost to run. Particularly if wines are being collected during summer months, it is best to insist that the shipper uses a refrigerated lorry from cellar to cargo vessel.

The optimum situation (though not always available) is for the wine to be loaded from the cellar directly into a refrigerated (reefer) sea container with the container's refrigeration unit plugged into the lorry. The container is then transferred onto the boat, ideally unplugged only for the short period of time between leaving the lorry and being placed in the cargo hold.

SEA FREIGHTING

Sea freighting is still by far the most common method of transporting wines over long distances, primarily because it is considerably cheaper than air freighting. But sea journeys are relatively slow with a trip from Europe to Asia for example taking anywhere from 3-6 weeks, depending on the distance of the final destination, condition of the seas and number of ports of call involved.

Cargo vessels are managed by large multi-national firms that transport a broad range of food products and manufactured goods. Unlike wine, most of these goods are neither fragile and nor particularly sensitive to temperature, so it is best to go with a logistics company that has had some if not considerable experience with shipping wines.

CONTAINER OPTIONS

Steel ISO shipping containers are the standard means of securing wine over long journeys. They can be carried by truck, rail, ship or airplane. When loaded on a container ship they are normally stacked to around seven units high. For wine containers it is beneficial to find a logistics company that will try and negotiate container placement below the ship's deck where it is generally kept cooler and less exposed to climatic elements.

ISO regulations ensure that shipping containers come in standardized sizes. They are therefore eight feet high by eight feet wide with a range of optional lengths. Most wine logistics companies offer two lengths of shipping container, the twenty foot or forty foot options. A twenty foot container can hold about 600-800 twelve bottle, 750 ml cases while a 40 foot container can take up to around 1200 such cases. It should be noted that generally Bordeaux shaped bottles are less bulky than Burgundy shaped bottles and therefore more can be squeezed into a container.

While is seems obvious, it is worth stating that it is important to ensure that bottles are all packed in cases (either cardboard or wooden) and not left loose to shift about in the container during the long sea journey. Further to this point, the cases should ideally be palletized and shrink-wrapped. Palletization means that the cases can be easily moved and stacked with a fork lift, further reducing labour costs. Shrink-wrapping the pallet not only secures the cases to the pallet but it is a great security precaution since it is immediately apparent if a pallet has been tampered with and therefore if any missing bottles are a result of the transportation.

The smallest container size required should always be used and the container should preferably be filled to capacity or near capacity. This helps ensure that the boxes / pallets of wine don't shift too much during the journey, which can cause damage to the bottles.

DRY VS REEFER

The most important container decision to make is whether to ship via a dry (non-refrigerated) or reefer (refrigerated) container. A reefer container can maintain a constant temperature of around 14/15 degrees Celcius. The big deal here is cost vs quality. The use of a reefer container can cost up to three times the amount of a dry container. In my opinion reefer containers are essential for transporting wines during summer months, long journeys and particularly if the cargo vessel will be crossing the equator or passing through / stopping in tropical climates. Consider for example that an ambient temperature of 40 degrees Celcius in a cargo ship, certainly not uncommon for those travelling to Asia in the summer months or to SE Asia anytime of the year, could raise the temperature within the container to 60 degrees Celcius. Great if you are looking to make your own Madeira!

Another cheaper option is to use an insulated liner in the container made of energy reflecting material (liner foil or VinLiner) or Styrofoam. These are much more cost effective but not nearly as efficient or reliable as a reefer container.

In Japan many large importers that guarantee to only ship wines with reefer containers have started advertising this on the bottle. I would like to see this labeling information occurring throughout the world and believe me, given the option I would always choose to pay a bit more for the bottle of wine guaranteed to have been shipped via reefer container.

LCL CONTAINERS

Can you still sea ship your own wine even if you haven't got enough cases to fill a container? In most cases, yes. LCL (Less than Container Load) options are designed specifically for this purpose and can be arranged by most logistics companies. They involve the logistics company grouping together the consignments of several clients (known as groupage) so that the space and costs are shared by all parties. A problem with LCL shipments is that it often equates to extra waiting time as it may take a while for the logistics company to find enough clients to fill the container. Also logistics companies don't offer LCL *reefer* containers for all routes, so you'll need to check before you plan a shipment, if reefer shipment is important to your needs.

AIR FREIGHTING

A shipment of wine that can otherwise take a month or more to arrive can be turned around in a few days via air freighting. Plus if you are planning to transport only a few bottles and the increased expense is acceptable, then this is most certainly the way to go. However, the carrier must be able to cope with the fragile nature of wine and be made well aware of its temperature requirements and thus liable be made for any damage. Be warned - unless provided with detailed instructions a carrier may well leave a consignment of FINE WINES sitting in the baking sun on the hot tarmac while it awaits transfer to a bonded area for customs clearance!

PROTECTING YOUR ASSETS

TRACKING TEMPERATURES

For peace of mind, a range of temperature tracking devices is available to accompany wine shipments.

Data Loggers

Data loggers are devices offered by some logistics companies to use with reefer containers. They record container temperature and humidity throughout the voyage, creating data that can be downloaded into Excel format.

PakSense Labels

These are small, newly developed temperature-sensitive labels that can be adhered to cases or bottles. Essentially, if the label stays within the desired temperature range, it flashes green. If it is exposed to temperatures outside the range, it flashes yellow. Information from the label can then be downloaded into a computer to show exactly how high or low the temperature ran and when the mishap occurred, for liability purposes. Originally developed for the food industry, these labels are currently being distributed in Napa California for around US$20 per pack.

The labels are manufactured and distributed by **PakSense**

RADIO FREQUENCY ID (RFID)

These are microchips that can track shipments and temperatures of wines throughout a journey. They can be placed within a case to record temperatures. Another type can be placed at the base of the bottle to provide security and aid inventory management. Or a proprietary, tamper-proof neck seal with a covert code applied at the base of the capsule can be applied to authenticate the wine inside the bottle and thwart counterfeiters. These types of tags are already being using by some top Bordeaux Chateaux.

RFID devices for wine are manufactured and distributed by **eProvenance**

INSURANCE

Marine and Air insurance for wine can be very expensive and is probably justifiable only for FINE WINES. However it is certainly recommended for high value consignments since it means that the shipper is liable for compensation if the wine is damaged during transit.

LOGISTICS COMPANIES

To follow is a list of logistics companies have experience with shipping wines and can provide one stop shops for road, sea and air transport needs. This list is by no means exhaustive – there are many logistics companies – and these companies are not necessarily recommended.

JF HILLEBRAND

ZIEGLER LOGISTICS

DANZAS (DHL)

ORIENTAL LOGISTICS

CROWN WORLDWIDE GROUP / CROWN CELLARS

SPECIALISED AIR FREIGHTING COMPANIES

It can sometimes be cheaper to air freight wines via a specialized air freighting company so it is always worth getting a second quote. Some examples of such companies:

INTERNATIONAL LOGISTIC SERVICES

TNT

DHL

STORING WINE

Living in the tropics of SE Asia truly opened my eyes to how quickly wines can deteriorate due to improper storage. A bottle left malingering in a non-air-conditioned environment in Singapore for just a few days can be rendered undrinkable. Yet I've seen liquor stores here selling bottles of wine displayed in sun-drenched windows, merely with doors propped open to allow for a breeze to freshen the otherwise unbearably hot 30-odd-degree Celcius retail environment. Ok, this is an extreme scenario and there are many serious players in the wine trade here are doing an excellent job at shipping and storing wines in optimum condition, but what happens when that carefully nurtured bottle walks out the door? Understanding proper wine storage conditions is as critical to enjoying the true taste of wine as not glugging it from a dirty coffee mug or mixing it with Coke.

One of the fundamental problems with wine storage is the lack of area to devote to cellar space. Urban real estate prices have had a shrinking effect on retail units and modern housing in the large cities where wine tends to be most popular. With space at a premium, it is very difficult for a lot of wine retailers and consumers to dedicate space to the conditions necessary for keeping wine. So how can people with a growing passion for wine ensure that they are buying a bottle in pristine condition and then, that when they eventually come to drink it, it will still be in that condition? To begin, it's worth reviewing the necessary parameters for maintaining the condition of wines during storage.

TEMPERATURE

The temperature of wine storage is by far the most important factor to control since it can have the most immediate and dramatic impact on the condition of wine. The optimal temperature range for long term storage is 10-15 degrees Celcius with 11-12 degrees Celcius being ideal. The choice of temperature within this range depends upon the desired wine development rate and of course the significant cost of maintaining a space at that temperature.

Higher temperatures speed up chemical reactions in wine leading to premature aging. The higher the tempera-ture the more rapidly aging oc-curs. Exposure to heat above 30 degrees Celcius is to be particularly avoided as this can very quickly lead to OXIDATION and/or imparting a cooked or MADERIZED character. Likewise, prolonged storage at "room"

The temperature of wine storage is by far the most important factor to control since it can have the most immediate and dramatic impact on the condition of wine.

temperatures much above 22 degrees Celcius can also lead to premature aging. Though for short term storage (a period of up to a few months), most wines should come to no harm when kept at 16-22 degrees Celcius.

Another danger is extremely low temperatures, below 0 degrees Celcius. At temps below around -4 to -8 degrees Celcius, wine will begin to freeze forcing the CORK from the bottle or even the bottle to burst. Very low temperatures will also encourage the precipitation of TARTRATE CRYSTALS from wines that have not been STABILISED (including many FINE WINES), although this impacts mainly the aesthetics of the wine with a very minor effect on the FLAVOUR.

Exposing a wine bottle to rapid temperature fluctuations is to be particularly avoided. These are apt to cause the bottle to "breathe", expanding or contracting the wine and gas in the bottle and forcing small to significant cork movement. Once the integrity of the cork seal has been compromised, the wine is at risk of oxidation. Damage can be compounded by the fact that acetic bacteria (acetobacter), responsible for turning wine into vinegar, love warmer temperatures and thrive in aerobic (oxygen present) conditions. In worse cases, the bottle will leak wine or the CORK can actually be pushed out of the bottle. Because of the seriousness of the rapid temperature fluctuation risk, some professional wine storage facilities offer a temperature controlled "transition zone" prior to receiving and dispatching wines. For example, a storage facility in Singapore offers a transition zone area where incoming/outgoing wines are held at 18 degrees C for at least 24 hours.

UV LIGHT

Lighting is a very important factor that I fear many shop owners still tend to overlook. I see a lot of FINE WINE shops with sun exposed window displays filled with bottles to be purchased or florescent lit shop floors featuring whole exposed cases of older FINE WINEs. UV light is detrimental to wine quality degrading otherwise stable organic compounds and altering the character of wines. The sun emits a significant amount of UV light, though fluorescent shop lighting can also emit damaging UV rays and prolonged exposure to unfiltered fluorescents can affect the quality of wines.

UV protection is one of the key reasons why most wine bottles are green or amber. Amber glass is actually much better at filtering out harmful UV rays than green glass, yet the general marketing trend for wines has moved away from amber, presumably because of its connotations with cheap hock and beer. Therefore most wine bottles provide only a certain amount of protection and for medium to long term storage it is essential that bottles are protected from UV rays.

Be very wary of buying FINE WINEs that you suspect may have displayed near a sunlit window for any length of time or have been exposed to unfiltered florescent light for a prolonged period of time. Note that a good wine storage facility should have UV filters to encase their lighting and protect wines from harmful rays when it is necessary to light the warehouse. If at all possible, ensure that wines are stored and transferred in cases (cardboard or wooden) to keep them protected from light.

HUMIDITY

Humidity affects wine CORKS and labels. CORKS need a certain amount of ambient humidity in order to remain moist and retain their elasticity. For long term storage, a humidity range of 50-80% is recommended with around 70-75% being ideal. Humidity at the higher end of the range or above 80% can deteriorate labels and cardboard boxes though the wine itself will not be harmed.

Many FINE WINEs for long term aging are now being bottled under SCREW CAP, which has the benefit of taking the need for high humidity out of the storage equation.

When buying wine, be aware that a lot of wine shops may have air conditioning but have no means of humidity control. Without a specially contained fine wine area to control the storage temperature and humidity for FINE WINEs, shop floors can have a damaging effect on CORKS. If a bottle has been stored under such conditions for years (and especially if it is stored upright), the cork could well be drying and allowing oxygen ingress resulting in premature oxidation. Note that you will not necessarily notice any leakage if this is occurring, rather when you open the bottle the cork will be very brittle and break easily, or worse, it may be so loose that it slips out too easily or gets pushed into the bottle by the corkscrew. This is a sign of a storage fault and should be avoided at all costs!

VIBRATIONS

Vibrations over a prolonged period of time are said to be detrimental to wine quality. It is believed that the agitation of wine particularly if there is sediment present can alter its character. Logically, it makes sense that agitation could alter development, since whenever compounds are shaken or stirred chemical reaction rates are increased.

BOTTLE POSITION

Wines under CORK should be stored on their sides or upside down to help keep them moist and maintain the seal. If a SCREW CAP or SYNTHETIC CORK (PLASTIC CORK) has been used to seal the bottle, the position makes little difference. As an aside however, wines under SYNTHETIC CORKS are not intended for aging beyond a few years at most as these closures are not designed protect wines over extended periods of time.

ODOUR-FREE

Since there is a certain amount of gas exchange through most closures, storage areas for wines should be free of powerful, persistent smells that can sometimes TAINT wines. Smells from paints, wood treatments and sealants used in newer storage rooms and warehouses should be eradicated prior to use. Some wine storage facilities provide extra odour protection by installing charcoal filter systems to maintain a constant odour-free environment.

STORAGE OPTIONS

WINE CABINETS / REFRIGERATORS / CAVES

Specially designed wine cabinets are ideal for storing small amounts of FINE WINES for an indefinite period. The advantages are that they offer the desired storage conditions for small to medium sized collections of wines and provide quick, easy access. There are a wide variety of brands and designs to choose from with most providing the basic need of in-built temperature and humidity controls.

Other factors to consider when choosing a wine cabinet include:

Temperature / humidity range
Size and shape of the bottles that you're likely to store and what the unit can fit
Capacity
Level of insulation and energy efficiency
Noise
Ease of accessing bottles (e.g. sliding shelves)
Lock on the door for security
Carbon filter for odours
Anti-vibration
UV Filtered glass (if glass doors are desired)
Design aesthetics

WAREHOUSES

If you don't have a large area or room at your home to devote to wine storage and you have ten cases or more that need cellaring, it is probably worth seeking the assistance of a specially designed commercial wine storage facility or warehouse. The choice of warehouse is an important one since it can be costly and detrimental to wine quality to be constantly moving parcels of FINE WINES. Apart from meeting all of the desired storage conditions already outlined above, there are a number other major considerations when choosing a warehouse.

BONDED VS DUTY PAID STORAGE

In most countries with the notable exception of Hong Kong and Macau, wine is susceptible to duties and taxes. When purchasing and storing wines there are circumstances when the deferment of duty payment is preferred, particularly if there is a likelihood that the wine might be re-exported. Many but not all commercial warehouses therefore offer bonded and duty paid storage areas. If held in bond, the duty is payable only if and when local delivery is taken or if it is moved for any reason out of bonded conditions. Bonded warehouses and deliveries are strictly monitored by local governments and the warehouse's terms, conditions and capabilities should be investigated prior to making any storage commitments.

SECURITY

It is recommended that the security systems and liability insurance conditions of a warehouse are thoroughly investigated. In some cases just basic industrial insurance is offered with optional insurance provided at an additional cost to cover incidences of fire, breakage, theft, water damage, etc.

Another vital security issue to consider is how the warehouse maintains the separation of your wines from wines held by other clients to ensure no mix-ups. There are several means of doing this from account individual code numbers to designated zones. Whichever way, it is important that you are confident that when you eventually go to take shipment of your case of Petrus 1990, that it will be *your* case (presumably of known provenance) that is delivered and not someone else's case.

LOCATION

The location of the warehouse is important to your specific need for access to your wines. For long term aging and the cellarage of investment wines, you may choose an overseas warehouse in Europe, for example, which might be closer to the point of purchase and offer better rates. Most wine collectors however like to have regular access to most if not all of their collection and therefore choose facilities closer to home.

UNIT CHARGES

Wine warehouse storage fees are expensive, period. They can be even more expensive if you choose to store your wine in a city centre. Therefore you need to ensure the wine that you're storing is worth the expense and is going to improve / appreciate enough to justify the storage cost. Storage can be especially expensive if a warehouse charges uniformly for every wine unit, whether is a single magnum in a wooden box or a six bottle case, as though it were a twelve bottle case. A more cost efficient means is to find a warehouse that offers the flexibility of charging by the 750 ml bottle equivalent. It is also prudent to check if the warehouse charges for a full year only or if there is a by-the-month option.

ADDITIONAL SERVICE CHARGES

Service charges at warehouses can really mount up. It is worth noting the collection / delivery fees offered by warehouses as well as costs for landing / dispatching stock and any charges of overseas shipment and customs clearance, if required.

ON-LINE ACCESS

Some warehouses nowadays are offering on-line access to your inventory or virtual tours of your cellar so that you can take assessment of your collection in cyber-space anytime.

Regional Typicality

I've said it before and I'll say it again, that a wine can express the sense of a place – whether it be a country, a legally delineated region, a vineyard or a single block of vines – is one of the attributes that makes it truly unique in the beverage world. But, as I've also pointed out before, not all wines do express the place from which they come from, nor are they designed to do so. Many large volume BRANDED WINES are BLENDED across several regions in the effort to target a specific taste that consumers can enjoy again and again and therefore aim to achieve a consistency of this taste vintage after vintage. And some of these wines are *fundamentally* great – take Penfolds Grange, a blend of regions from South Australia, for example. This is an extreme example of muting regionally typical expression but there are many more subtle winemaking means of producing a consistently good, arguably better BALANCED wine that in doing so minimises the wine's expression of place. And yet such a wine may be (and often is) labelled as the product of a delineated region and therefore representative of its TERROIR. So it's really up to the critic to see through the winemaking and judge the TERROIR expression to the extent that it's an important quality factor in the view of the critic, which implies a good dollop of subjectivity.

Common examples of techniques whereby winemaking can overpower TERROIR expression include permitted FLAVOUR additions such as OAK (especially staves, chips or OAK essence, which do not involve barrel MATURATION and therefore do not integrate so well with the fruit), use of too much "new OAK" during barrel MATURATION, added TANNINS and imparting SWEETNESS in a "DRY" table wine STYLE. Some critics argue that the use of excessively overripe or under-ripe fruit by purposely practicing delayed or early harvesting can minimise TERROIR expression...but as discussed in **Chapter 2** the concept of RIPENESS is largely subjective. CHAPTALIZATION, ACIDIFICATION and MUST concentration (e.g. REVERSE OSMOSIS) all alter the expression of the true products of climate and/or vintage. The use of CULTURED YEASTS to create AROMA instilling THIOLS from otherwise unexpressed AROMA PRECURSORS arguably manipulates terroir expression. The over-use of STEMS, particularly in the making of Pinot Noirs and some Syrahs, sometimes overpowers fruit / TERROIR expression in a wine, imparting a green wood character and harsh TANNINS. However, there is a notable grey-area that exists with all this. Winemaking techniques like carbonic MACERATION (e.g Beaujolais), OXIDATIVE WINEMAKING (e.g. Vin Jaune and Tawny Port) and sparkling winemaking (e.g. Champagne) that create distinctive aromatic compounds, ESTERS, characters and STYLES are largely accepted as part and parcel of regional expression even if their very employment minimises fruit expression and therefore that sense of TERROIR. And so here's where regional tradition and culture tend to overrule even the staunchest of terroiriste's insistence on the importance of tasting the place over the winemaking.

Value for Money

Everyone loves a bargain, right? Most critics agree that given the right piece of land, vines / vineyard management and a competent winemaker with all the latest winemaking tools, it's not particularly challenging to create a great wine at great expense…and with a great big price tag! High quality factors such as prime location, hand tended vines, low YIELDS, rigorous fruit selection, state of the art winery equipment and the best quality **oak** barrels all come at enormous costs. In truth it is far more difficult to produce a superlative, knock-out wine cheaply. For some critics the ability to do so is a true testament to the winemaker's skill. In fact many reviewers will occasionally if not always make a comment on the wine's "value for money", sometimes referred more scientifically to its QUALITY / PRICE RATIO or "QPR". For a few critics the price of the wine relative to its quality is a major factor in their final quality assessment. So for example, a wine of average quality with a luxury price tag may be judged qualitatively against other high priced wines and ultimately deemed of relatively poor quality. And vice versa for a low cost wine that punches far above its weight. Other critics completely disregard price when making quality assessments or at least in the assessment as expressed by a RATING so as to "fix" the RATING scale and show the wine's quality level relative to all wines within its peer group (if thus tasted). For more information about WINE RATING systems and methodologies, see **Chapter 9**.

What is wine QUALITY / PRICE RATIO (QPR) and how can I work it out?

QUALITY / PRICE RATIO (QPR) is a somewhat scientific way of calculating value for money. It specifically relates the quality of a wine to the price that's being charged for it and rates it according to value. Our modern practice of allocating wine quality SCORES (see WINE RATINGS in **Chapter 9**) has made this RATING a little easier to calculate, though it's far from an exact science because ultimately something is only worth what you're willing to pay for it. Plus given the finite nature of any given wine from a particular vintage and that the highest quality wines are often by nature made in smaller quantities, supply and demand is a major force that skews the highest quality wines (or higher scoring wines) away from a straightforward calculation of value. In other words, most serious (highly involved) wine consumers would agree that if you simply divided the score by the price the ensuing calculation doesn't actually reflect the "good" value of many higher quality and/or rarer wines compared the mass produced, lower quality, lower priced wines, which let's face it most highly involved consumers are less inclined to buy anyway.

An Example of a QPR Calculation

Want to put the theory into practice? Bearing the points made above in mind and using the 100 point wine scoring system (the most widely used today in the wine world), it therefore stands to reason that most consumers that are looking for value amongst the higher quality wines – say those rated 87 points or above. Thus it makes sense to use 87 points as the lowest quality consideration – the "root score" – and accept that the calculation will only be useful from this score up. In order to render this QPR calculation relevant I further suggest that bonus points are added to wines scoring 90-95 points and higher bonuses to those that score 96-100.

Thus my formula looks like this:

Wine Score ÷ Retail Price (in $USD) + Bonus Points = QPR RATING

For my own QPR calculation I add 0.5 bonus points to a score of 90 and then add an extra 0.5 to each score above 90 until 96 points. At 96 and above SCORES receive an incremental 1 point bonus. So the scoring bonus looks like this:

Score	Score
87-89: No Bonus	95: add 3
90: add 0.5	96: add 4
91: add 1	97: add 5
92: add 1.5	98: add 6
93: add 2	99: add 7
94: add 2.5	100: add 8

Relative value for money can then be measured against a 1-10 scale QPR RATING Chart:

QPR 10+ = Extraordinary value - BUY!
QPR 9 = Outstanding value
QPR 8 = Excellent value
QPR 7 = Very good value
QPR 6 = Good value
QPR 5 = Above average value
QPR 4 = Average value / fair market price
QPR 3 = The price is a little steep
QPR 2 = Expensive for what it is
QPR 1 or less = You're being ripped-off!

Straight away you'll note that my bonus allocation assumes that 100 point wines start out at "Excellent value" regardless of price…and not to be flippant but this assessment assumes that anyone considering buying a "perfect" wine will – like it or not - need to adopt this premise.

Drinkability

Revved-up, monolithic fruit-bombs can shine like a beacon within tastings of many wines of a similar, less overt STYLE…but are they easy to drink? When you slow down to consider such a wine, really *drink* it, does each swallow leave you thirsty for more? Or is it more of a taster's wine that is so big and CONCENTRATED (e.g. over-ripe Cabernet Sauvignon, Syrah or Grenache) or even ultra-lean, ASTRINGENT, TANNIC, ACIDIC and/or plain angular (e.g. some Pinot Noirs, Nebbiolos or Rieslings) that it ticks all the FUNDAMENTAL QUALITY FACTORS boxes but just isn't very "drinkable". To a certain extent this consideration basically necessitates that a wine be BALANCED. But it also might take into account certain circumstances such as when and how it will be consumed. For example, is it "drinkable" with food? Or as a stand-alone aperitif? Is it too super-charged and alcoholic for simple, everyday sipping? Too innocuous for a special occasion? Or too TANNIC or acidic for a quaffing wine by the glass in a bar? And herein you can appreciate where the subjectivity of this factor lies.

Compatibility with Food

This SUPPORTING QUALITY FACTOR often goes hand-in-hand with Drinkability. It specifically demands of the taster, "Can you enjoy this wine with food?" I find this one of the most subjective of supporting quality assessment factors, first and foremost begging the counter question, "What food?" For any given wine there is almost certainly a food item somewhere on this planet that will marry well with it. Secondly, food and wine pairing is far from a formulaic endeavour and is highly individual. But once we get beyond the first two hurdles of this moot argument, the inherent grain of truth here is that generally wine almost by design pairs well with food.

Compared to other beverages such as coffee, tea, cola and fruit juice, most table wines possess a combination of higher ACIDITY and relative DRYNESS (lack of SWEETNESS) that allow them to complement and "lift" most cuisines without lending cloying SWEETNESS that could detract or overpower the dish. If we compare wine to other alcoholic beverages such as spirits, liqueurs or beer, the relatively higher ACIDITY and moderate ALCOHOL of most table wines more adeptly cut through the richness of foods without overpowering. And the FLAVOURS of wines simply complement many foods. Therefore the argument against wines that are deemed incompatible with "food" usually relates to wines that fall outside of the table wines I've described above, namely those that are overly sweet, alcoholic and/or relatively low in ACIDITY. But when it comes to wine - for every rule there is almost certainly an exception and this is definitely the case with wine and food pairings!

A Simple Guide to Wine & Food Pairing

Wine & Food Pairing – First Rule
- First Rule - There are <u>no</u> rules when it comes to wine & food pairing!
- Whatever combination you want to eat and drink is just perfect.
- But there are some *guidelines* that can make your experience of both food & wine better…

Wine & Food Pairing – 3 Basic Elements of a Good Pairing
- Aim to find FLAVOUR Complements
- Match the INTENSITY & Weight of the wine with the dish
- Match food and wine TEXTURES

Flavour Complements
- When considering wine and food matching one of the main aims is to isolate FLAVOUR complements.
- This is not the same thing as trying to pair identical FLAVOURS.
- It is about finding FLAVOURS that magically combine into a better flavour experience in your mouth.
- An appropriate food example is a sweet and sour combination such as sweet and sour pork.
- Moderate salt in the food will soften the appearance of ACID in the wine and make it seem fruitier. This works well with high ACID wines such as Riesling or Champagne.
- Gamey or strong FLAVOURED bird meats such as duck, pheasant or quail are complemented by "fruity" reds with notable berry FLAVOURS such as Pinot Noir, Grenache or Beaujolais.
- UMAMI taste (mushrooms, MSG, fish, ripe tomatoes / tomato sauce, etc.) in food can accentuate TANNINS so pair with a white wine or soft / low TANNINS red wine.

Intensity & Weight
- To get the most out of the food and the wine, it is important to find foods and wines with

similar intensities and weights.

- The food should not overwhelm the wine so that you can't taste it. Example: A strong chilli component in a dish would completely negate the FLAVOUR of delicate Chablis.
- The wine should likewise not overpower the food so that you can't enjoy the special FLAVOURS of your dish. For example, you wouldn't pair a big, robust Barossa Shiraz with a dish of steamed prawns or poached fish.
- Examples of good INTENSITY / weight combos: Oysters with Champagne. Lamb with Cabernet Sauvignon.

Textures

- Try to match or complement the TEXTURES of food & wine
- Delicate textured foods such as scallops need a light bodied, less TEXTURED wine such as DRY Riesling or Champagne
- Light textured fish such as snapper or cod also needs a delicate wine such as a Sauvignon Blanc
- Chicken has more texture and needs a white with more texture and "richness" such as Chardonnay or Pinot Gris.
- Proteins in red meats will combine with the TANNINS in the wine and make them appear softer. Therefore beef can work well with more TANNIC reds: Barolo, Chianti, Cabernet and Syrah.
- The rich, oily texture of foods such as Foie Gras need a good amount of ACIDITY in a wine to cut through it and lend freshness. The oily SWEETNESS of Sauternes can work well here as can the bubbles of a sparkling wine.

Wine & Food Pairing: Cheeses

- Sweet & Salty: SWEETNESS and Salt can be a great FLAVOUR combination. Salty blue cheeses pair very well with sweet wines such as Sauternes or Port.
- Goat's Cheese pairs well with Sauvignon Blanc.
- Creamy (e.g. Brie) / and Semi-Hard to Hard Cheeses (e.g. Gruyère and Comté) are better with full bodied whites such as Chardonnay or soft (low TANNIN), fruity reds like Beaujolais and Pinot Noir.
- TANNIC red wines and especially fine red wines can be a difficult match with cheeses, though strongly FLAVOURED hard cheeses such as Cheddar can work well so long as they do not overpower the nuances of the wine.

Wine & Food Pairing: Sweet Dishes

- A sweet dish will call for a wine with good ACIDITY, but you will also need to find a wine with a similar SWEETNESS level to the dish.
- If the dish is much sweeter than the wine, it will make the wine seem overly tart or sour.
- Fresh fruits such as strawberries are great with sparkling wine.

- Fruit tarts are better with sweeter, fruitier STYLES ranging in SWEETNESS levels from Moscato to Sauternes, depending on the SWEETNESS of the tart.
- Chocolate is difficult but pairs well with Tawny Port and other similar FORTIFIED sweet red wines.

Uniqueness

As the world globalises seemingly closer each day to one great homogenous mass of BRANDED blandness, the backlash has been an outcry for maintaining biodiversity and cultural identities. This has been one of the major factors in a renewed appreciation amongst wine authorities for indigenous varieties and regionally traditional STYLES, resulting in uniqueness of grape variety, STYLE and/or region qualifying as a popular SUPPORTING QUALITY FACTOR nowadays. In all sincerity I feel this is a noble cause and can empathise with the arguments and rational behind resultant emerging dogmas in the wine world. But while I'm all for preserving and indeed celebrating uniqueness I'll come right out an declare that I don't think it should be taken out of the context of the FUNDAMENTAL QUALITY FACTORS and used as a stand-alone justification for heralding wine greatness.

Making wine in amphorae like those pictured above hearkens back to ancient traditions and certainly is unique...but are the wines ultimately better?

In Summary...

...some or all of these SUPPORTING QUALITY FACTORS may come into play when making a final assessment about a wine's quality, but the crux of your judgement should largely depend upon the major factors that we've just discussed throughout **Chapters 1-6:** FAULTS, RIPENESS, CONCENTRATION / INTENSITY, BALANCE, COMPLEXITY and length /nature of FINISH. Why? By nature of their very vagueness these SUPPORTING QUALITY FACTORS are far more subjective than the major factors that have been clearly discussed and defined in the previous chapters. And since being a professional wine critic involves (or should involve!) being as objective as humanly possible, while an opinion on these supporting factors adds to the interest of tasting notes and goes towards making them more poetic / less prosaic, these supporting factors should not be taken into account in a definitive quality assessment that purports to relate to intrinsic quality.

WINE ZEN

....

*"The truth knocks on the door and you say,
'Go away, I›m looking for the truth,'
and so it goes away. Puzzling."*

Robert M. Pirsig, Zen and the Art of Motorcycle Maintenance

....

SO THERE YOU have it - the mechanics of wine quality - fully dismantled and laid bare. But before you go stampeding out into the wine world clutching at a Riedel glass full of very special old plonk in one hand and a notebook overflowing with empiricist wine quality revelations in the other, let's step back and get a little Zen for a moment. Does the knowledge of wine quality mechanics offer you a complete understanding of the quality of wine?

Zen is a branch of Buddhism that somewhat defies being labelled as a religion or philosophy mainly because it largely rejects labels and even words. For the purposes of this book I'd like to stress that it is extremely difficult not to oversimplify what is a vastly complex concept here. Furthermore I'll come right out and confess that this consideration of the "Wine Zen" is not formally taught in any wine schools. Professionals and wine academia would likely dismiss the concept as nonessential to assessing wine quality, though often it sits in the background of nearly all the quality considerations of true wine lovers and very experienced tasters. And it should. Taking a thoughtful moment to reflect upon an extraordinary wine just as it is, its 'suchness' beyond words and numbers, will certainly enhance your experience and perhaps offer a truer understanding of wine. Nowadays it is sometimes hard for consumers and especially for us critics to remember that recognizing and appreciating a wine's quality needn't involve technical evaluations, critical pronouncements, descriptive words and scores. Put aside your wine tasting notebook once in a while. There is a reality of intrinsic greatness of wine that cannot be expressed with scribblings and sums.

To help demonstrate what I mean by Wine Zen, here's a short retelling of a classic Zen Buddhism story known as, "Pointing at the Moon".

Pointing at the Wine

Imagine that a wine expert, maybe a MASTER OF WINE, me perhaps, is driving through Burgundy, in an imaginary township somewhere north of Nuits St Georges and south of Gevrey Chambertin. I'm driving down a desolate country road off the Route Nationale 74 and I stumble across a beautiful, well-tended vineyard poised mid-slope on a limestone outcropping, facing South-East and planted to Pinot Noir. As I drive a little further I see a little farmhouse and winery, the name of which I don't recognize. But the beauty and potential of this unknown's vineyard has so inspired me, I must stop to taste the wine. A little old vigneron / winemaker woman receives me and takes me down to her cellar. I taste barrel after barrel of extraordinary wine, each one more exquisite than the other. The final barrel is the most mind-blowingly awesome Pinot Noir I've ever had the pleasure to sip. I start asking the woman technical details about her clones and pruning techniques in the vineyard, her use of BIODYNAMIC methods, how she controls BRETTANOMYCES and OXIDATION, her ideal temperature for FERMENTATION, her types of YEAST and about her RACKING regimes and SO_2 additions. The woman looks at me blankly and I therefore assume that she, like many great winemakers of the world, is self or family-taught and has no institutionally imparted technical knowledge.

I smile, just a little patronizingly, as learned words of praise from my formal wine education trip effortlessly off my tongue: "But it is so wonderfully pure, clean, ripe, INTENSE, CONCENTRATED, BALANCED, COMPLEX and with a multi-layered FINISH that goes on forever…," I proclaim, trying not to omit any of my learned quality factors. Then, pointing to the final barrel I tasted containing that spectacular nectar I say, "This is without doubt wine of the highest quality!"

The old woman shakes her head slowly, ever so regrettably. I think that she does not understand me; perhaps she does not even know the quality of the wine she has made. So I ask if I may buy the wine.

"No," she replies, "you may not buy it because you do not comprehend it."

I'm aghast. I explain that I am an MW –a qualification at the utmost pinnacle of wine education.

"But you still do not comprehend this wine," she insists, pausing with sage-like patience. "If you did you would not have asked me such questions nor have been so trite with your description."

"Trite?" I query, bristling.

"See how your finger points at the wine?" She asks. "Imagine that your finger represents your technical knowledge and all those words that you use to describe the quality of this wine. And although your finger points to a wine of quality, your finger is not the quality nor is it the wine. Your finger could be used to show me the wine of quality, but ultimately I can see, embrace and truly comprehend the wine with or without your finger. You, I'm afraid, cannot." And with this she lowers my finger, takes the tasting cup from my other hand and shows me out of her cellar door.

"Getting" Wine

To get the utmost out of a glass of wine – to truly "get" it - it is extremely important to always bear in mind that the knowledge you possess about wine quality mechanics (technical knowledge if you will), your MENTAL WINE LIBRARY, even words you use to describe wine quality and whatever RATING you may give a wine are not quality themselves. True quality is in the wine and the feeling(s) of suchness or existence that it imparts within you.

That all said, humans are highly social creatures and practically speaking you are likely to want to convey those wine feelings as well as what you contextually know about the wine and can sense with your eyes, nose and mouth in professionally recognized words and phrases to someone or a lot of some-ones. Wine is after all a highly convivial thing and especially given the popularity of social media / blogs, wine drinkers are more inclined than ever before to want to share quality experiences. To do so you will therefore need to adopt the common language of wine (WINE-SPEAK) to produce tasting notes and, if you so choose, a RATING system with which to communicate your experiences and discoveries.

WINE SPEAK, TASTING NOTES & RATINGS

....

"Don't criticise what you can't understand."

Bob Dylan

....

THUS FAR YOU'VE been armed with an understanding of what wine quality means and how to see, feel (texturally within your mouth), smell and taste it in your glass of wine. Now you may well want to tell people about your discoveries and quality opinions. If you are intending to communicate with other wine-minded people around the world, you will need to learn at least a little WINE-SPEAK - the language of wine - in order to make yourself clearly understood. And you'll probably also want to adopt or adapt either or both of the universal formats for communicating wine quality conclusions about wines: tastings notes, possibly incorporating those WINE-SPEAK words and terms commonly used in the wine world and WINE RATINGS, which can be of your own devising or borrowed from a number of systems that are commonly in use.

Wine-Speak

Love it or loath it, the ever-growing community of winos appreciating and communicating about wine has evolved what could / would have been an onerously exhaustive list of wine related gobbly-goo down to a relatively manageable lexicon of DESCRIPTORS, old-school carry-overs, technical and industry words and terms specific to our world. This includes a lot of fragrant to stinky food, spice, flora and fauna items (ubiquitous and regionally obscure) and earth / turf related smells that share AROMAS and FLAVOURS with wine along with everything from scientific naming to doggedly employed OUTDATED WINE JARGON. Our language of wine borrows from no less than seven different wine producing and drinking nations' languages and colloquialisms (especially France, the UK, Spain, Italy, Germany, Australia and the USA) and employs plenty of nick-names and acronyms. To an outsider, WINE-SPEAK must surely appear like the cryptic lingo of an elitist club. But there is really nothing subversive about it. Developed largely over the last century throughout a hodgepodge of admittedly mainly Western wine drinking nations, WINE-SPEAK is really just a language treaty amongst this myriad of idiosyncratic cultures to weed out many of the more obscure DESCRIPTORS and foreign names for things and describe wine using the same "tongue".

On a basic level, the DESCRIPTORS used in WINE-SPEAK are an attempt to verbalise specific smells, FLAVOURS and TEXTURES that are experienced during tasting and/or drinking. Nowadays there are a number of ready-made lists available to students of wine to help guide them towards generally accepted terminology. Much of my lexicon of DESCRIPTORS was initially adapted from Michael Broadbent's "Full Glossary of Tasting Terms" in his "Pocket Guide to Winetasting" (that used to be given out at WSET courses)... though this is admittedly a bit outdated now. Another very popular source (and one of the originals) is Ann Noble's Aroma Wheel, which can be readily accessed on the internet: www.wine aromawheel.com. This is still very relevant but is a bit limiting in the number / range of DESCRIPTORS it offers. One of the more modern tools for accessing DESCRIPTORS that I think is very well done is the handy fold-away, pocket sized "The Essential Wine Tasting Guide": www.essentialwinetastingguide.com. But of course new DESCRIPTORS are being added to WINE-SPEAK every year and, more to the point, with the more tasting experience you gain the more confident you should feel in coming up with your very own DESCRIPTORS. Though I would recommend caution against coming up with words or phrases that are too obscure like, "smells of grandmother's drawers" or "scented of even-toed ungulate gland excretions". These probably aren't going to offer-up very vivid aroma imaginings to anyone but you.

One of the drawbacks to the DESCRIPTORS commonly used, recommended and taught by wine professionals is that they are mainly Western in origin / nature and are to some extent meaningless in Eastern cultures and elsewhere. For example, just try asking someone in China what cassis smells like or a national of Vietnam what a blackberry is. Even seemingly commonplace DESCRIPTORS like brioche, butterscotch, gooseberry and oatmeal can fall on deaf ears in countries where these foods are not generally consumed or are readily available. During my time living and working in Asia, I developed an "**Asian Food Lexicon for Wine**", available in the Appendix of this guide to offer a brief list of local DESCRIPTOR examples for Asian cultures and certainly this sort of lexicon can be individually created to reflect local foods anywhere.

Technical WINE-SPEAK words are largely a late 20th Century (continuing into the 21st Century) interloper to our otherwise lifestyle oriented, sometimes artistic and often philosophical pursuit. They do seem to grate in a sterile, prosaic way on our otherwise poetic ears, but sometimes there's just no other way to accurately describe the plethora of detailed information that we now know about wine thanks to science. Then there are simply a good many common WINE-SPEAK words that appear to be just ordinary words but which take on entirely different meanings in the context of wine to those that may be found in a dictionary. Examples include terms like: CLOSED, FORWARD, DUMB, MUTE, HOLLOW, TIRED or past-it. But out of all the WINE-SPEAK sorts, industry specific WINE-SPEAK words are probably most guilty for making wine consumers feel left out of the club. Words like negociant, bonded warehouse, courtier, en primeur, futures, reefer, barrel tasting and ullage are daunting enough. But then there are the acronyms, such as FOB, IB, LCL, RFID, DP, AOC, DOC, MW, WSET, CIA, CIS, TCA, ISO, AWRI and MS, just to name a few. For your reference (and to help you crack the code) some of the more common wine quality relevant WINE-SPEAK words and technical terms have been compiled and defined at the end of this book in the **Glossary of Wine Quality Terms.**

Finally, hate to say it but there is a lot of half-baked, OUTDATED WINE JARGON hanging about our trade that has simply remained stuck to us like gum on a shoe. These largely include old-school words, comparisons or phrases that were spawned in more conservative and chauvinistic times and when we knew a lot less about wine and especially wine chemistry than we do now. One of my least favourite bad habits of the industry is to refer to a wine's STYLE as being masculine or feminine. In fact any comparisons between wine and a beautiful woman are enough to make me reach for the sick-bag…but they are still more common than you'd think. A pair of phrases that really ought to be phased-out is Old World vs New World (see the text box in this Chapter, **What is wrong with the term "New World"**?). Another common example of OUTDATED WINE JARGON that irks me is "BOUQUET". This is a common WINE-SPEAK term for a collection of winemaking, MATURE or EVOLVED (barrel and/or bottle aged) AROMAS. I'm probably being a little too nit-picky here; after all there is admittedly a certain logic to the metaphorical blossoming of fruity / PRIMARY AROMAS into a COMPLEX "BOUQUET" of MATURE / aged wine notes. But this somewhat imprecise, sentimental term is tritely trotted-out by wine snobs and too often misused by the very nature of the image it conjures, so I prefer more specific references that just say what they mean such as: "EVOLVED fruit characters", "MATURE notes" or simply "winemaking", "bottle aged" or "SECONDARY" and "TERTIARY CHARACTERS". Other throw-back terms that I hate because they are meaningless, misleading, euphemistic or just plain pretentious include: charming, foursquare, manly, mawkish, mellow, stringy, suave, supple, gout de TERROIR, honest, needs food and corky (as opposed to CORKED). Can we ban them please?

What is wrong with the term "New World"?

The term "New World" was first coined around the 15th Century when explorers from Europe began discovering new continents and countries that previously had not featured on their Eurocentric maps. We don't really hear this term used anymore except in the context of wine. Think about it, if a Londoner were to walk up to a New Yorker and refer to him as someone from the 'New World', the Brit would sound like a cringingly patronizing eccentric living in the past. But then we wine folks are kinda used to this description. We've embraced the term New World to generally refer to any non-European wine producing nation. It's a simple, neat and handy way of categorizing the wine world.

When I began my wine studies in my naivety there seemed to be a clear line between Old World vs New World and I even had a checklist with the respective attributes and philosophies. Going back to that check-list now only confirms that the distinctions that were so apparently clear-cut to me twenty-odd years ago are now with the benefit of hindsight merely outdated stereotypes. And that line dividing the differences in wines made in Old and New Worlds has not been just blurred, it's completely obscured. So I'd like to think that where the term New World was once an all-encompassing BRAND name for non-European countries that brandished bold labels in English touting the grape varieties and promising sunshine in a glass, this is now being replaced with well-defined regional characteristics in the minds of wine communicators if not consumers. And oversimplified categorizations of the wine world are increasingly considered misleading. Today we're also seeing countries with ancient cultures such as China and Japan producing internationally competitive wines from regions where grapes, albeit table grapes, have been grown for centuries. To call them 'New World' is completely inappropriate on multiple levels.

I question if the term New World should be used by wine communicators anymore except as an historical reference and example of OUTDATED WINE JARGON. I suggest that today's new approach to the wine world seeks to challenge such stereotypes, dispelling the idea that the many wonderfully diverse wine producing countries can be stylistically lumped together. Let's discuss the personalities and cultures of individual nations and try not to cram them into an antiquated catch-all phrase that just doesn't fit.

Tasting Notes

By the very fact that you've persevered this far into the depths of wine quality, I'm guessing you've probably heard about wine tasting notes. You may have already written a few... maybe books full of them. These observational jottings are simply written accounts to remind ourselves of that fleeting experience that is wine. On a basic level tasting notes are descriptions of the sensual experience of seeing, smelling and tasting – sort of scent-o-graphs of the moment. If you are not a professional in the wine trade or aspiring to be one, then how this aide-mémoire is composed is your own affair. A tasting note can go on for a page or more. Or, more often than not, it can be a simple one word exclamation:

Wow!

Terrible!

Yum!

Yuck!

Great!

Awesome!

Shocking!

Most wine education institutions dictate that tasting notes should be guided methodically by your senses: seeing, smelling and then tasting and feeling within the mouth. They go on to recommend that each sensory experience is detailed in turn within the note and some will go so far as to break practice tasting sheets into Sight, Nose and Palate categories, for the student to detail his / her comments in the expected methodical manner. And while all these senses are indeed necessary to describe and evaluate wine, tasting notes needn't be quite so mundanely structured with pedantic comprehensiveness. Furthermore such a straightforward, formulaic listing of sensory observations can somewhat miss the point, which is of course to put them in context. And often formal tasting classes place disproportionate importance on largely superficial aspects of tasting such as the relevance of tears / legs clinging to the sides of the glass or the colour of a wine. Still at a rudimentary level this methodical approach does get the ball rolling for newbie tasters and certainly gives boxes to tick when searching for something to say about a wine other than, "Wow!".

Professionals such as oenologists (wine-makers), wine buyers for retailers and wine critics need to adopt a more relevant if equally formal and standardised approach with their tasting notes. Professional tasting notes should additionally aim to accurately describe the STYLE and character of the wine so that someone that has not tasted it can understand what the wine is like. The tasting note should further include details of aspects of the wine that ultimately support a quality conclusion.

Quality conclusions based on wine tastings, apart from being the main purpose of this book, need to draw from the findings detailed in a professional tasting note and should be stated either within the tasting note or expressed as a RATING that accompanies the note or both. In fact for a professional critic it would be pointless to describe a wine without somehow, however subtly or blatantly, stating whether it is good, bad or somewhere in between. Apart from the use of DESCRIPTORS, to back-up quality conclusions professional critics will often single out and make reference to specific FUNDAMENTAL QUALITY FACTORS and their contribution or lack thereof within the wine. Not all the factors need to be addressed in every note – for brevity's sake (and to keep to the average attention span that most consumers are willing to commit to a note) most critics will just point out the major successes and failures of the wine. Examples might include:

This wine is dilute and lacks fruit expression. The unresolved, bitter TANNINS suggest under-ripe fruit along with the overpowering herbal streak. It FINISHES abruptly and tart.

Or...

It fills the mouth with rich, COMPLEX FLAVOURS that are well supported by a backbone of firm, ripe TANNINS and BALANCED acidity. The multi-layered FINISH goes on for at least a minute.

And how do you deliver the punchline, so to speak? Well some critics come right out and say at the end, "*It's awful.*" Or, "*This is a magnificent effort – kudos!*" Otherwise a critic might let readers come to that inevitable conclusion with the words he or she chooses to describe a wine: "*It smells of green beans and rotten eggs, imparting a bitter, unpleasant* AFTERTASTE." Other critics may pedantically describe the characters of the wine with noncommittal references to its shortcomings and dish the final verdict out in a damning score: "75/100". What's the best way? To a certain extent it is whatever works for you. If your notes are only ever going to be talking back to you, then you can even have your own secret quality-code. Tasting group members and bloggers can be fairly casual / free-form about how they express their wine views...they're amongst friends. Critics cannot be so casual and need to weigh every word, though like any writer I'd like to stress that each critic should seek to develop his or her own "voice", which will add valuable personality to the tasting notes. This said, critics and other wine professionals offering an opinion upon which money will ride have been under increasing pressure by consumers who value advice to conform – less with the format of tasting notes with which they have more poetic license and specifically so with the rising importance of WINE RATINGS.

WINE RATINGS

"Scoring wines is simply taking a professional's opinion and applying some sort of numerical system to it on a consistent basis." – Robert M. Parker Jr.

The very idea of evaluating wine by numbers is contentious to many romantic lovers of the vine. The practice is for sure the polar opposite of the school of WINE ZEN (**see Chapter 8**) and its ilk. The British, amongst the earliest pioneers of modern wine commerce and criticism and perhaps those that have been the most resistant to adopting the practice of RATING systems, would probably even pipe-in that *it's just not cricket.* RATINGS are however incredibly practical and, in our fuzzy wine world bereft of any formal wine criticism qualifications, lend credibility to our vocation...when the RATINGS are consistently applied with consistency. This is largely because standalone tasting notes are wide open to a broad range of quality conclusion interpretations and one often doesn't really know for certain where the critic stands. Nowadays most wine experts and critics around the world have embraced the usefulness of not just alluding nebulously to quality with the chosen DESCRIPTORS in tasting notes or stating it plainly with terms like, "average quality" or "excellent quality", but in assigning a RATING to it or a score. Plus a tasting note alone can never show precisely where a wine sits qualitatively in relation to another. Cue the RATINGS.

WINE RATINGS are a fairly recent phenomenon in the history of wine. Until the mid-Twentieth Century it would have been considered preposterous to hang a number on a bottle. Then in the 1950s The University of California at Davis developed a 20 Point Scale System and ORGANOLEPTIC Evaluation Scoring Guide for Wine. It was originally created by Dr. Maynard A. Amerine, then a Professor of Enology at UC DAVIS, and his staff in 1959 as a method of RATING the large number of experimental wines that were being made at the university. The basic purpose back then was to weed-out "spoiled" or FAULTY wines at the bottom of the scale and award "wines of outstanding characteristics having no flaws" at the top. But little did the professor know that with the introduction of the 20 Point Scale, Pandora's Box had been opened.

There are a number of wine critics and critical publications that still use a 20 Point Scale for RATING wines, including *Jancis Robinson, Decanter* and *La Revue du Vin de France*. Australian wine show judging similarly adopts a 20 point system, although a few shows have recently migrated over to the 100 Point Scale. And there are a few other idiosyncratic methods of RATING wines such as the dishing-out of 1-3 "bicchiere"(wine glasses) by the Italian *Gambero Rosso* publication. Some people simply choose to use ticks, stars or other symbols as RATINGS. It really depends on the level of RATING precision you are looking to achieve.

Having developed out of the long tradition of British agricultural shows, Australian Wine Show judging was initiated in order to improve the overall quality of Australian wines by aiming to eradicate incidences of FAULTS. Nowadays with less and less faulty wines being produced, the current and future goals of the show system are moving away from the former focus on FAULT-spotting and more towards rewarding other quality factors.

SCOREBOARD

Name _____

Name or no.					
Appearance	2				
Color	2				
Aroma & bouquet	4				
Acescent	2				
Total acid	2				
Sugar	1				
Body	1				
Flavor	2				
Astringency	2				
General quality	2				
Total					

The UC DAVIS **20 Point System** is based upon the above scorecard allowing for points to be given to each of ten categories, which are totalled to equal the final score. The final score reveals the quality prognosis.

17 - 20 points : Wines of outstanding characteristics having no flaws

13 - 16 points : Standard wines with neither outstanding characteristics nor defects

9 - 12 points : Wines that are of commercial acceptability although they have noticeable defect(s)

5 - 8 points : Wines that are below commercial acceptability

1 - 5 points : Wines that are completely spoiled

But today perhaps the most widely implemented and powerful amongst systems of WINE RATINGS is the 100 Point Scale. This was created and introduced by Robert Parker in 1978 in what was to become *Robert Parker's Wine Advocate* magazine. It was devised partly to challenge shortcomings of other RATING systems such as the 20 Point UC DAVIS scale since Parker believed that a 20 point RATING system did not provide enough flexibility and often resulted in compressed and inflated WINE RATINGS. The other major benefit of this 100 point system is that it offers a figure that is immediately recognized and understood as a grade since it was based on the American scholastic grading system. Technically it is not a 100 point scale though, as in practice employs 50-100 point RATINGS. So a wine gets 50 points just for being called a wine. Since its inception, Robert Parker's 100 Point Scale has become the wine industry's standard and is now used by other major wine publications such as the *Wine Spectator* and *Wine Enthusiast*.

Robert Parker's Wine Advocate 100 Point Scale *score ranges correlate to the following assessments:*

96-100
An **extraordinary** wine of profound and COMPLEX character displaying all the attributes expected of a classic wine of its variety. Wines of this caliber are worth a special effort to find, purchase, and consume.

90-95
An **outstanding** wine of exceptional COMPLEXITY and character. In short, these are terrific wines.

80-89
A **barely above average to very good** wine displaying various degrees of finesse and flavor as well as character with no noticeable flaws.

70-79
An **average** wine with little distinction except that it is soundly made. In essence, a straightforward, innocuous wine.

60-69
A **below average** wine containing noticeable deficiencies, such as excessive ACIDITY and/or TANNIN, an absence of flavor, or possibly dirty AROMAS or flavors.

50-59
A wine deemed to be unacceptable.

Fixing the Wine Purpose Scale

If you've never scored a wine before then you may not have considered that to do so requires a set of boundaries within which any given wine will need to be rated if you're intending to rate anything more than just one wine ever. And if you're anything like me when I was first presented with the score-giving challenge, you're probably wondering what the heck I'm talking about. Well, let's go back to the very beginning of this book where you'll recall I assigned a fit-for-purpose definition as a sliding scale against which to measure wine quality, recognizing that wines have many purposes. Until now we had been viewing and describing wine quality while largely taking into account wine's many roles. So for example, someone may be seeking no more than a wine that is clean, sound and easy to drink, well BALANCED but it isn't required to be particularly COMPLEX or long in the FINISH because it is just for everyday drinking purposes. Therefore they may be assessing a wine that can be deemed, descriptively or in plain qualitative language, of excellent quality for that specific role because it suits its purpose well. It would however probably wade in at an average or even below average quality level if its role were defined as that of a "FINE WINE", which is expected to offer much more. In other words our fit-for-purpose scale is a sliding scale with as many notches as there are wine purposes, which are a lot!

When a critic goes to give a RATING the sliding wine purpose scale by which quality can be measured must become a fixed wine purpose scale. This concept of fixing the scale somewhat belies our journey thus far. It takes our wonderfully flexible concept and makes it rigid and restrained. So why fix it? Consistency. Consistency – that ability to repeatedly score wines of a similar quality similarly across an extensive database of wine reviews - is, like it or not, the cornerstone of trust. So in order to offer consistency, a critic must fix their wine purpose scale and stick with it.

RATING wines makes a critic's ability (or lack thereof) to review wines absolutely transparent. That a critic can consistently review the same wine repeatedly with a similar or ideally the same score or indeed score wines of the same purpose and quality similarly is critical to building trust as a reliable critical source. It is incredibly difficult, arduous and time-consuming to rack up the level of experience necessary to review and score wines with consistency. This is perhaps why many lesser critics do not score wines or, sad but true, are inclined to alter their original SCORES to offer a semblance of consistency to their readers.

So when it comes to RATING wines the wine critic will need to choose just one purpose for the wine. Of course this means the purpose scale will need to be fixed for references to relative quality within the accompanying tasting note too (if employed). If we go back to the original scoring system – the UC DAVIS 20 Point System – the scoring was largely based on a "faultless" wine being at the pinnacle. In other words, the purpose of the highest quality wine was to be bereft of FAULTS. Some other 20 point systems today still fix the scale thus, for example the Australian wine show judging system does it for the most part. And this stands to reason, after all these systems were designed specifically to improve the quality of winemaking within an institution or country. But they can equate to something of FAULT-spotting clinics rather than systems for judging intrinsic greatness, which is not a bad thing so long as both judges and consumers buying the awarded wines understand that purpose. Here too is where Robert Parker diverged when he created his 100 Point Scale in 1978. His system was specifically designed to highlight greatness in wines and therefore fixes the purpose scale so that 100 Points represents a wine of absolute quality "perfection" regardless of considerations such as price and assuming that its purpose is to offer not just a sound / faultless wine but a superlative FINE WINE example of its kind incorporating a far broader range of quality factors than, for example, the UC DAVIS system. He went on to qualify this fixed scale in further detail by stating, "The score given for a specific wine reflects the quality of wine at its best." Furthermore the numeral RATING given in Parker's system is a guide to how the critic considers the wine to rate vis-à-vis its peer group (e.g. STYLE, region and/or grape variety). Other 100 Point systems have for the most part been pressured to adopt the guidelines of Parker's fixed scale for consistency's sake (not just their own but within the wine industry as a whole) if no other. Thus a 90 point wine means the same or roughly the same thing across many critics and publications with the only real difference being how expertly the reviewer assesses quality, how large the peer group is (e.g. in the context of a wine region, a country or the whole world) and how generous he or she is with his/her scoring.

Another point that requires consideration when RATING wines is context. Wines that are rated are of course judged in relationship to other wines, sometimes directly within a tasting flight of wines and often with reference to the critic's MENTAL WINE LIBRARY. Robert Parker and many other critics site tasting wines amongst their "peers". But what the critic needs to get absolutely clear in their head (and convey to his or her readers) is how large is the reference or peer group? For example is a Cabernet Sauvignon based wine from Bordeaux rated in the context of other Bordeaux red wines, other Cabernet Sauvignons fetching from anywhere in the world, other red wines coming from anywhere or in the grand context of ALL wines from throughout the world regardless of their colour, STYLE or varietal? Many local wine critics will simply review wines in the context of the area or country within which they write, e.g. Australia or Burgundy. There is no right or wrong answer; the critic simply must be as consistent with the scope of this peer group as they are scoring consistently to a single wine purpose.

A final cautionary note for you to consider on this subject of SCORES from the greatest and most famous proponent of wine SCORES, Robert Parker: "SCORES however do not reveal the important facts about a wine. The written commentary (tasting note) that accompanies the RATINGS is a better source of information regarding the wine's STYLE and personality, its relative quality vis-à-vis its peers, and its value and aging potential than any score could ever indicate.

How many wines can a professional wine critic taste in a day?

Unfortunately there is no neat, quantitative reply to the wine critic's ultimate question. Numerous variables are involved including the type of wine being tasted, the format of the tastings and what you are expected to produce in terms of tasting notes. For example, when judging for a wine show it is not uncommon for judges to be required to taste through 200 or more wines of similar STYLE in a day, but then they are merely expected to sort the wheat from the chaff and/or place the wine into STYLE / quality categories. To write full tasting notes and rate the wine is a whole other ballgame.

A few years ago I sent round a survey to wine professionals, including to some of the most famous and influential names in the wine world. Experts of all sorts were consulted - critics, journalists, wine buyers, merchants, winemakers, educators and sommeliers. There were a good number of experts with oenology degrees and/or MASTERS OF WINE amongst the group and they fetched from ten different countries. My question was simple, requiring a short response in the form of a number:

"If you had to put an exact figure on it, at most how many wines could you taste in a day?

I added the proviso: *"Assume for argument's sake that you're doing a tasting marathon involving a STYLE that is within your comfort zone. How many wines do you think you could taste in a day and produce good quality tasting notes that do justice to the wines?"*

Of the 50+ people that responded with a number, many came back with tips on how maximize performance during these wine marathons. Advice included taking a light lunch with regular snacks of warm, nourishing broth. The necessity of breaking the job up into a number of flights with frequent breaks was mentioned by quite a few, some adding that stretching or pacing between flights helped. Dictating notes into a Dictaphone was suggested by a couple of people. I tend to nibble on bread / crackers / water biscuits between so many red wines to help reduce the TANNIN build-up but others considered this of little use.

Rather than the oft discussed "palate fatigue", these experts pointed out that the mental fatigue of producing tasting notes and ratings is a bigger problem. It is the concentration of writing notes that really slows critics up. In wine show judging you can whip through a large number of wines with no issues as there are no notes required.

Without further ado, the magic number – the average of all the figures given by the experts polled – is **104**. If you're interested in reading the results, I've reproduced the chart below showing the country of residence and occupation of each expert and their figure given.

Results of "How Many Wines Can You Taste in a Day?" Poll

Occupation	Country of Residence	Number
winemaker	Australia	150
winemaker	NZ	100
educator, MW	USA	96
journalist	UK	150
journalist	UK	80
journalist	Singapore	50
journalist, MW	HK	300
wine buyer	Singapore	80
sommelier	Singapore	75
journalist	USA	200
wine buyer	Switzerland	100
journalist	USA	140
winery agent	Singapore	70
winery agent	France	115
negociant	France	60
journalist, MW	UK	100
sommelier	Japan	60
consultant, MW	UK	150
wine merchant, MW	UK	150
journalist	France	80
journalist	UK	180
winemaker, MW	Australia	120
winemaker	NZ	90
sommelier	UK	80
wine buyer	Singapore	30
journalist	Singapore	75
auctioneer, MW	Australia	60
viticulturalist, educator	NZ	50

winemaker, MW	Australia	180
sommelier	USA	100
educator	Singapore	150
consultant, MW	Australia	80
wine merchant	USA	130
wine buyer	Singapore	160
wine buyer	Japan	36
wine merchant	UK	100
journalist	Singapore	50
consultant	UK	220
journalist, MW	HK	140
wine merchant	HK	80
journalist	France	30
consultant	HK	120
educator	Japan	60
wine merchant	Japan	100
winemaker	France	50
journalist	UK	96
winemaker	Italy	70
educator	NZ	80
consultant, MW	UK	120
wine buyer	USA	100

The 100 Pointer Debate

Many critics, including those that have adopted the 100 Point Scale, debate if there can be such a thing as a 100 point – "perfect" – wine. Does it / should it exist? Of course Robert Parker and his team of reviewers (myself included) for Robert Parker's Wine Advocate whole-heartedly maintain that if you apply a 100 point scale there must be such a beast. Other users of the 100 Point Scale claim that they will not give 100 points to any wine, presumably because they believe that wine "perfection" cannot exist. To a certain extent this is a rather childish philosophical stand-off amongst reviewers. It doesn't really matter if you use 100 points or 99 points as your pinnacle, because either way there will be those wines of the highest quality that sit at the pinnacle of your actual scale. But surely it is pointless for anyone that sets a grading system to make the top score unobtainable with a glass ceiling at an arbitrary figure somewhere below? I'd like to suggest that those who refuse to give out 100 points on principal rename their RATING system as the "99 Point Scale", which automatically excludes the possibility of a 100 point / "perfect" wine; otherwise they are misleading their readers.

DRINKING WINDOW

As a part of the service offered by some wine reviewers, suggested DRINKING WINDOWS for wines are given to accompany the tasting note. DRINKING WINDOW is a common wine-speak term for a period of time when a bottled wine is drinking at its best. More often than not this period begins soon after the wine is bottled. Many FINE WINES are however designed to develop and improve with bottle age, becoming better BALANCED and more COMPLEX. (See **Chapter 4** in the section **"How do some wines become better** BALANCED **after ageing?"** and **Chapter 5** in the section **"How do some wines become more** COMPLEX **after ageing?"**) Furthermore different grape varieties, regions, colours and STYLES may vary subtly to enormously in the way and pace at which they develop. And it needs to be said that every wine has its day when it is at the peak of its DRINKING WINDOW (although this "peak" is largely subjective) after which it faces a period of plateau and eventually decline, whereby the GRAPE DERIVED AROMAS are all but unrecognizable and all that is left are OXIDISED and ALDEHYDIC notes. In the declining stages of maturity the nose may progressively be referred to as "TIRED", "drying / dried out" and finally "past-it".

To be clear though, any DRINKING WINDOW proffered is at best a guesstimate relying heavily on two major factors: 1) the experience level of the critic and 2) the personal preferences of the consumer (e.g. at which stage of evolution does the drinker prefer his or her wine).

Anticipating the DRINKING WINDOW of a wine is perhaps one of the most difficult jobs of a wine critic or consumer. Essentially the taster must at the moment of tasting make a judgement call as if the wine is too young, ready to drink, will hold for a period of time, will improve with age or has gone past its prime. Whether this is done by a consumer or a professional, the accuracy of this task will depend first and foremost on an understanding the maturity level at which the taster or the critic's group of readers like to drink wines – and bear in mind once again that this may include a wide range of grape varieties, regions, colours and wine STYLES. Even with this personal preference variable clearly established, the taster must also have an extensive MENTAL WINE LIBRARY in order to understand how the wine that is being tasted may or may not develop over time.

The Critic's Check Sheet to Tasting Wine Quality:
At L.A.S.T., let's Taste!

What are the four stages of assessing wine quality?

- **Look:** At the wine's Clarity, Colour & INTENSITY
- **Air:** Swirl the wine gently within the glass to aerate it
- **Smell:** The wine's INTENSITY & AROMAS
- **Taste & Feel:** SWEETNESS, ACIDITY, FLAVOURS, CONCENTRATION, BODY, TEXTURE, BALANCE & FINISH

Preparation: Pour from a freshly opened bottle no more or less than 2.5 - 4 cm of wine into a tulip shaped, standard sized wine glass (i.e. roughly 8 cm wide x 12 cm tall without the stem).

Look: To Determine the Wine's Clarity, Colour & INTENSITY
- Tilt the glass of wine against a pure white background
- Check that the wine is clear (not hazy) and make note of any obvious spritz / bubbles
- Lack of clarity and the presence of bubbles in a still wine can suggest real FAULTS such as post-bottling microbial spoilage or more commonly it may simply be cloudy due to harmless suspended sediment (especially if it has some bottle age), PROTEIN HAZE (a SUPERFICIAL FAULT that doesn't affect smell / taste) or some largely innocent residual CO_2 from protective bottling. TARTRATE CRYSTALS or "wine diamonds" at the bottom of the bottle are also SUPERFICIAL FAULTS that may detract from the look but not the palate.
- Determine the colour and its INTENSITY (pale to deep)
- Clarity, colour & INTENSITY can give clues about a wine's age and possible FAULTS
- Colour & INTENSITY can give clues about the grape variety and winemaking
- But clarity, colour & INTENSITY DO NOT automatically indicate quality

Air: Swirl to Aerate the Wine
- Take the wine glass by the stem (or base if using a stem-less wine glass).
- Gently rotate the glass in a small circle
- The wine should swirl around the sides of the glass folding air into the liquid
- Aerating the wine encourages the release of (volatizes) aroma and FLAVOUR compounds

Smell: To Determine the Wine's INTENSITY of Smell & Specific AROMAS
- After swirling the wine, take a good sniff well into the glass
- Look for off-odours / wine FAULTS and under-ripe (e.g. herbal / vegetal) characters
- Consider the INTENSITY of AROMAS, e.g. Weak vs Pronounced
- Try to isolate individual AROMAS and consider how representative these are of the variety, vintage and region
- Consider WINEMAKING DERIVED AROMAS (SECONDARY AROMAS) in relation to GRAPE DERIVED AROMAS (PRIMARY AROMAS)

- Consider how COMPLEX the wine's nose is
- Consider how youthful or EVOLVED the wine's nose is

Taste & Feel: **Wine's** SWEETNESS, ACIDITY, FLAVOURS, CONCENTRATION, BODY, TEXTURE, BALANCE
& FINISH
- Take a good mouthful of wine and swish it around your palate
- Ensure that wine comes in contact with all parts of your tongue and including
  your inner-cheeks
- Hold it in your mouth while repeatedly sucking in air (it's GOOD to 'slurp'!)
- Continue to slurp for 5-10+ seconds to maximise RETRONASAL OLFACTION, then spit or swallow
- Consider FUNDAMENTAL QUALITY FACTORS: FAULTS / GREY-AREA FAULTS, RIPENESS (especially FLAVOURS
  and TANNINS), CONCENTRATION, BALANCE and COMPLEXITY
- Consider first impressions and MID-PALATE FLAVOURS
- Consider how youthful or MATURE the wine's palate is
- Consider the persistence and nature of the wine's FINISH after the wine has been spat or
  swallowed

CRITICAL BIAS

IMAGINE YOU'VE READ a glowing restaurant review and decide to treat your partner to a meal there for a special occasion. On that important night you discover the hard way that the food is lousy, the service is terrible and the ambiance atrocious. You can't believe the restaurant critic even visited the same restaurant! When you go back to the restaurant review to check the details, you discover an advertisement for that very same restaurant on the next page. Regardless of whether the critic that wrote the review was actually compromised by the financial agendas of the newspaper (in its acceptance of sponsorship / payment from the restaurant) this ad would no doubt place an element of doubt in your head. You can no longer trust the critic.

Factors that can compromise integrity, constitute conflict of interest and create bias should be important considerations for any conscientious, truly transparent critic and his or her followers. In the early 1970s when Robert Parker was conceiving of writing his own wine guide he was taken with the work of Ralph Nader, an American political activist who sought to 'out' corporate and political corruption by challenging compromised propaganda. Parker recognized that much of what was then being written about wine was compromised by the financial agendas of many of the famous wine writers of the day. He dreamt of a publication that could be free of financial ties to wineries and merchants, a guide that would produce wholly unbiased views on wines and that served only the interests of wine consumers. This would be a magazine that would be funded purely by subscribers – the people that buy, read and use it. And so *The Wine Advocate* started and remains true to this day. This was one of the key attributes of this publication that made me want to review for Robert Parker as one of his wine critics.

Today as the Editor in Chief of *Robert Parker's Wine Advocate* and its website RobertParker.com, critical bias and journalistic integrity are issues that I consider every single day. Maintaining the trust of our readers is paramount to every report we produce and every decision we make. But truth be told, the consideration of critical bias and preserving the lack thereof is still too rare in our profession. *Robert Parker's Wine Advocate* is still the only major wine publication that does not accept sponsorship from any wine related businesses. Apart from this stance, most other wine magazines and publications that carry wine reviews allow their critics to accept gifted flights, accommodation, meals, wine and/or other gifts in kind from wineries, wine retailers and/or wine marketing bodies...which many critics do accept without declaring them to their readers. *Robert Parker's Wine Advocate* employs Reviewers as full employees with binding contractual obligations that do not allow them to accept any such freebies from wine related entities.

And then there are the parties. Being a wine critic is as much a lifestyle choice as it is a profession. Ask any wine writer and they will certainly tell you they don't do it for the

Robert M. Parker, Jr. at his desk at The Wine Advocate office in Monkton, Maryland, where the now globally famous wine publication began

money alone! There is often a fine line between a winery providing a tasting of wines for critical review and putting on a party to secure the good will and sentiments of a critic. And sometimes there is not such a fine line. For anyone who is in the business of wine and has attended Vinexpo (the Bordeaux centric wine trade fair) and/or Primeurs Week (the week in April during which the major Chateaux / wineries offer barrel tastings of their pre-release wines of the previous year), the scale of the parties thrown by individual wineries for wine journalists would come as no great shock...but I'll bet it would for the readers of those reviews and buyers of those wines on the basis of the reviews. Beyond this (and sometimes as part and parcel of the parties), there are the "friendships" that evolve between the winemakers / winery owners and critics. Imagine giving a damning review, which you know could financially damage, to your best pal.

Apart from financial, gift, party invite and friendship agendas another major issue in the field of wine criticism today is the pressure on critics to be frequently quoted by wineries and merchants on websites and in advertising around the world to increase their popularity. This has resulted in what could be construed as a false inflation of wine scores from wine publications looking to grab readers' eyeballs and obtain free third party endorsement. Beneath all this is the harsh reality that eyeball-traffic (number of clicks on web links) to wine review websites, whether they require subscriptions or not, increases the fee that can be demanded of potential advertisers. If this all sounds too insidious to be true, well it isn't.

So the next time you read a review by a professional critic – be it a film, restaurant, book, art or wine critic – before you accept the validity of the review ask yourself this: Do you know how that critic is being funded? Do you know his or her policy on accepting gifts, trips or invitations to parties staged by the business that they are reviewing? Do you know all his or her prejudices and chauvinistic tendencies? Do you know this critic's friends, family and enemies that are associated with the industry for which they review? Do you know if this critic is under pressure from their publication to be frequently quoted and encourage more website clicks? If you don't know the answers to some or all of these questions, before you part with your money based on this critic's endorsement, perhaps you should.

GLOSSARY OF WINE QUALITY TERMS

A

ACETIC ACID / ACETIC Acetic acid is the most abundant of the volatile acids in wine, existing in very small concentrations as a by-product of fermentation. It is also a major component in vinegar, lending its distinctive aroma and taste. Wine doesn't ordinarily smell or taste of vinegar and indeed it shouldn't if its level of acetic acid is within the range that is naturally generated even with careful handling and production methods and is in balance with the other components in the wine. Exposure to oxygen and omnipresent acetic acid generating bacteria – acetobacter – can however generate unpleasantly high, vinegar-imparting levels of acetic acid in wine, constituting a fault. If a wine is said to be "acetic" this usually means that the level of acetic acid is notable and high enough to be considered a fault. Volatile (short for volatile acidity or VA) is another way of saying, "acetic".

ACETALDEHYDE (AKA ETHANAL) This is the most common aldehyde in wine, formed by the oxidation of the primary alcohol in wine, ethanol, which can further be oxidised into acetic acid. It has a somewhat bruised / old apple and nutty smell, which in proportion can lend complexity to the nose of an evolving / maturing wine or in the case of fino sherry defines the style. More commonly acetaldehyde can contribute to the faultiness of an oxidised wine, overpowering or detracting from the grape derived characters that may also be fading as a consequence of the oxidation.

ACETOBACTER This is an omnipresent acetic acid generating genus of bacteria. In the presence of oxygen (air) and usually as a consequence of oxidation acetobacter can convert the ethanol (alcohol) in wine into unpleasantly high concentrations of acetic acid (vinegar), constituting a wine fault. This fault is commonly referred to as "acetic", "volatile" or VA (short for volatile acidity). See "acetic acid" and "volatile acidity" for more information.

ACIDIC This is a common wine-speak word for a wine that appears too tart because the acidity is excessive relative to the other components in the

wine and it is therefore poorly balanced.

ACIDIFICATION Acidification is a winemaking amelioration that involves adding fruit sourced acids to juice or wine during winemaking in order to increase the total / titratable acidity and lower the pH. Usually involving the addition of tartaric acid (and less often malic or citric acids), it is commonly practised in warmer climates and vintages where legally permitted and where sugar levels can be sufficiently high but acidity may be lacking and/ or the pH is too high to the extent of producing a potentially unbalanced (e.g. flat, flabby, cloying or dull) and unstable wine. Tartaric acid additions are usually made to grape juice before or during fermentation to create a more seamless effect in the finished wine. Citric acid can be added after fermentation (never before as yeast can convert it into acetic acid), although the effects are often more clumsy. Malic acid is sharper / tarter than tartaric acid so needs to be used sparingly and with care if malolactic fermentation is to follow the addition. Judicious use of acidification with tartaric acid prior to or during fermentation can achieve imperceptible or almost imperceptible results. But over-acidification can result in a disjointed acid appearance on the palate occasionally to the point of being unpleasant. And over-acidification can stand out like a sore thumb on a big, rich, jammy or raisiny wine with a sour acid backbone that just doesn't belong (and is highly unlikely to occur naturally).

ACIDS / ACIDITY Along with sweetness, salty, bitterness and umami, acidity is one of the five major tastes relating specifically to the perception of acids on the tongue. Wine has a relatively high level of acidity compared to many other alcoholic beverages, which can be considered one of its defining features. Acids are major components in both grapes and wines, occurring naturally and they are sometimes artificially added to wines (acidification). The two most important acids found in grapes are tartaric acid and malic acid. In many wines (as opposed to grapes), there is a third acid that features prominently: lactic acid, which sometimes replaces malic acid either partially or wholly. Wines also contain trace amounts of volatile acids the most prevalent being acetic acid. Other minor acids in wines worth noting are citric, succinic, butyric, sulphuric and perhaps ascorbic acid (if added). The acids in wine are measured using "titratable acidity" or "total acidity", which are approximately but not exactly the same thing (total acidity is slightly higher) and both are (confusingly) abbreviated as "TA". The test for titratable acidity is generally easier and therefore the norm. The TA (titratable acidity) of wines can be expressed in terms of any of the acids present in wine (curiously the French like to use sulphuric acid), most often expressed in terms of the most abundant acid in wines: tartaric acid. It is common for wines to have a TA (titratable acidity) range of 5 – 8 grams per litre expressed as tartaric acid. Otherwise TA (titratable acidity) is often expressed as a straightforward percentage (grams of tartaric acid per 100 millilitres) with a normal range of 0.5 to 0.8% expressed as tartaric acid. There is usually a relationship between acidity and pH – e.g. wines with high acidity have a relatively low pH – although this is not a direct correlation and there are exceptions. Acidity in wine is an important structural and quality feature that contributes to its taste profile, perceived balance, stability and ageability. Wines with higher acidity and lower pH offer increased wine stability in terms of protection from microbial and oxidation spoilage. Plus the effectiveness of SO_2 increases at higher acid concentrations / lower pH levels meaning less SO_2 additions are necessary. For more information see "acetic acid", "acidification", "lactic acid", "malic acid", "pH", "SO_2", "stability", "structure", "TA", "tartaric acid" and "volatile acidity".

ADDED TANNINS (AKA OENOLOGICAL TANNINS)
Adding store-bought tannins to create or boost existing tannic texture and structure levels probably sounds like a bit of a swizz but it is actually very common practice and many of the greatest wines of the world contain "added" tannins, including some fine red wines from Australia, California, Bordeaux and Burgundy. Added or oenological tannins are commercially produced from a variety of sources, though winemakers can purchase types that only contain grape skin tannins or skin, seed and oak tannin cocktails. Some tannin additions contain tannins from more exotic sources such as other types of woods and nuts. I tend to find the uniformity of added tannins a little boring in younger wines but what these concoctions rob of wine in terms of individuality and sense of place, they make up for in control and consistency. They are sometimes apparent in their overly powdery texture. If the main reason that they're added is to increase the wine's ageing potential, then as the wine ages and tannins polymerise and eventually precipitate out of solution their contribution becomes less relevant anyway. How can you detect commercially produced tannins simply by tasting? Well, it is hard to point a finger at any particular characteristic, but if the tannins in a wine just appear too uniformly similar, soft and cuddly to be true, they're probably added! For more information see "tannins".

AFTERTASTE See "finish".

AGGLOMERATED CORK (AKA AGGLO CORK) An agglo cork is a wine bottle closure made of tiny cork pieces, usually treated to get rid of TCA and glued back together into a cork shape. In the early days of agglo corks there were lots of criticisms with some of these closures still exhibiting signs of TCA in wines. Another purported taint detectable with the use of the early agglos was a faint stink known as "glue poo", presumably coming from the glue that held the cork pieces together. Today agglo corks are for the most part far more advanced and offer a good if relatively short-term closure option. One of the best so far appears to be the Diam brand agglo cork, attracting very few if any complaints to date.

ALCOHOL A major wine component, in wine-speak the word alcohol is largely synonymous with the major alcohol type found in wine: ethanol (sometimes called ethyl alcohol). Wine however does also contain very minor traces of "higher alcohols", which are thought to contribute to the aromatic profiles of wines and add complexity. For more information see "ethanol".

ALDEHYDE / ALDEHYDIC Aldehydes are aromatic compounds generally formed by the oxidation of alcohol. The most common aldehyde in wine is acetaldehyde, formed by the oxidation of the primary alcohol in wine, ethanol, which can further be oxidised into acetic acid. When a wine is referred to as aldehydic, this is usually an uncomplimentary reference to unpleasantly high levels of acetaldehyde constituting a fault that is generally in conjunction with oxidation.

AMELIORATE / AMELIORATION Meaning "to make better", in the USA the winemaking wine-speak term amelioration usually refers to the practice of adding water to must or burgeoning wine. For the record, it's only under very rare circumstances that water may lawfully be applied to must or fermenting grape juice in some regions and countries (e.g. California, USA) if there is an immediate risk of a stuck fermentation due to sugar content so excessive that the yeast can't continue to function (i.e. potential alcohols of around 15.5% and above). The addition of water to wine is generally banned with regards to the production of wines from legally protected regions in wine producing nations around the world, which is not to say the euphemistically called "black snake" (water hose) of amelioration never finds its way into the tanks of warm areas / vintages! Further afield the definition of amelioration could include a larger range of permitted must adjustment practices such as chaptalisation, acid additions (acidification), tannin additions (added tannins) and added sweetness (e.g. sussreserve or dosage).

ANTIOXIDANT An antioxidant does what it says on the tin – inhibits oxidation reactions. In most cases antioxidants work by becoming oxidised themselves. As a simplified example, the antioxidant sulphur-dioxide (SO_2) protects wine from oxygen and therefore oxidation by binding with it - kind of like a policeman cuffing him/herself to a prisoner – and therefore the oxygen can no longer do its damage. Wine contains natural antioxidants and almost all wines contain some added antioxidants. The naturally occurring antioxidants found in wine include trace amounts of SO_2 and red wines also have tannins, which have antioxidant properties. Winemakers commonly add SO_2 to boost wine's limited natural protection from oxidation. Added or oenological tannins may also be used in part at least to increase protection from oxidation. Ascorbic acid (vitamin C) is sometimes used as an antioxidant additive. Usually used exclusively in white winemaking, ascorbic acid needs to be used in conjunction with SO_2 although its use does generally mean that less SO_2 needs to be used to achieve the same effect. Natural wine proponents often shun the use of added antioxidants including basic SO_2 additions.

AROMA An aroma is quite simply a smell, any smell, though it usually implies a pleasant one. In common wine-speak the word often specifically refers to grape derived (primary) smells as opposed to winemaking (secondary) or maturation / mature (tertiary) notes, though the general meaning and wine-speak usage are both acceptable in wine criticism. In the context of wine, the terms aroma and flavour are often used interchangeably since the flavours of wines predominately consist of aroma compounds.

AROMA PRECURSOR (AKA FLAVOUR PRECURSOR) An aroma precursor is an odourless, flavourless, non-volatile grape aroma that is transformed through the fermentation process into a volatile (detectable) aroma. Aroma precursors in fact make up the majority of grape derived aromas in wine since most Vitis vinifera grape varieties have no characteristic aroma, a couple of well-known exceptions being terpenes found in aromatic varieties such as Muscat and Riesling and methoxypyrazines found in Sauvignon Blanc.

AROMATIC VOLATILE THIOLS Aromatic volatile thiols are a set of reduction compounds that are sometimes actively sought-after by winemakers who may even choose specialised cultured yeast that are targeted specifically to generate aromatic thiols from previously odourless aroma precursors in grapes. For example, 3-mercaptohexanol is the reduction thiol of a grape-derived aroma precursor in Sauvignon Blanc that lends an appealing grapefruit or passion fruit like smell to the finished wine. 2-Furanmethanethiol is another aromatic volatile thiol thought to be generated from aroma precursors found in Petit Manseng, Cabernet Sauvignon, Cabernet Franc and Merlot lending the aroma of roast coffee to some wines produced from these grapes. For more information see "reduction" and "mercaptans".

ASCORBIC ACID (VITAMIN C) is sometimes used as antioxidant additive. Usually employed exclusively in white winemaking, ascorbic acid needs to be used in conjunction with SO_2 although its use does generally mean that less SO_2 needs to be used to achieve the same effect. Care needs to be taken when using ascorbic acid because if it oxidises it develops into hydrogen peroxide - a powerful oxidising agent – which is why it needs to be used with SO_2. Since it can be unstable a lot of winemakers avoid using it. Others find it very effective when used properly as a means of maintaining white wine freshness with less SO_2 additions. Recent research by Denis Dubourdieu and Valerie Lavigne at Bordeaux University suggests that sotolon, an aroma compound responsible for the character of wines suffering from premature oxidation (premox), is formed by the oxidative degradation of ascorbic acid, which could link ascorbic acid use to premature oxidation.

ASSEMBLAGE In wine-speak, assemblage is the French winemaking term for the blending. For more information, see "blending".

ASTRINGENCY / ASTRINGENT Astringency is a feeling of dryness in the mouth, particularly on the sides of the mouth where it often creates a puckering sensation with greatest prominence in the finish. The term is unusually used to describe the impact of tannins but some tasters also use it in reference to acidity or a combination of tannins and acidity. Because tannins play a lesser or non-existent role in white wines, the term is generally (but not always) reserved for red wines. An overly astringent tannic profile often indicates under-ripe and/or over-extracted tannins in the wine and is usually accompanied by tell-tale bitterness in the flavour profile. Riper, polymerised tannins tend to feel suppler and less astringent than smaller, under-ripe subunit types such as catechins for a given level of tannin extraction in the wine. Achieving balance in wine is the key to maintaining enough astringency to contribute structure, texture and ageability (if sought) without an overly unpleasant or dominating drying / puckering mouth-feel.

AUTOLYSIS Autolysis is a biological process that is encouraged to occur in the production of some

styles of sparkling wine, most famously Champagne, whereby lengthy ageing (i.e 1.5 years+) on the wine's lees results in the enzymatic breakdown of dormant yeast cells. The successful use of this process imparts what may be described as toasty, yeasty or bready flavour elements in the wine and contributes "creaminess" to the mouth-feel / texture. For more information see "lees ageing".

AWRI AWRI is an acronym for the Australian Wine Research Institute based in Adelaide, Australia. This institution is well-known in the wine industry for its ground-breaking research and studies into wine chemistry and technology as well as for the conducting of laboratory testing for the aid of Australian wine producers and further afield.

B

BALANCE Balance in wine specifically refers to a wine's components all existing in harmonious proportions that complement one another so that no single aspect negatively dominates on the nose or palate. (For more information see "Chapter 4 – Balance")

BÂTONNAGE See "lees ageing".

BERRY SHRIVEL This is the sudden shrivelling or "raisining" of the grape berries on vines often caused by sunburn and/or dehydration. Particularly detrimental for red grapes / wines, it can result in wines with a paler colour and a baked berry or raisin-like character. Worth noting are other causes of apparent berry shrivelling on vines that have not been proven to be caused by excessive heat, sun exposure or dry conditions, known as "bunchstem necrosis" and "sugar accumulation disorder", each with different effects than straightforward sun exposure and dry heat related berry shrivel.

BIODYNAMIC First established by Rudolf Steiner in 1924, biodynamics is a set of farming practices that follow what remain to date more philosophically based (and some would claim spiritual) guidelines than those of conventional farming, which are based mainly on traditional and scientific principles. Biodynamic wine production essentially uses a foundation of organic farming methods such as the exclusion of the use of artificial chemicals and builds upon these taking into account for example the movements and phases of celestial bodies for determining the timing of key winemaking practices. Specially crafted composts and herbal infusions (called preparations) are also applied with rigour yet little if any scientific rhymes or reasons. Proponents swear by the methods not only as a means of producing superior wine from a given vineyard, a moot point, but for sustainable farming - a far more provable rationale. A small but important movement in modern wine production, biodynamic grape growing methods have been established in at least 47 countries to date. Internationally recognized biodynamic certifying organisations exist with Demeter International being the largest and best known. Certified biodynamic wine producers usually display the name and logo of the certifying organisation on their wine labels.

BLENDING / BLENDED / TO BLEND (V.)
(AKA ASSEMBLAGE IN FRENCH) Practiced by winemakers for centuries, blending – the process of mixing two or more grape varieties, fruit sources or wines - can be carried out in many ways, on many levels to achieve many different results. In truth virtually all wines produced around the world are now blended in some way, at some point prior to bottling. This is often but not always done to achieve a better balanced wine; it is also widely used to achieve a certain style of wine (e.g. a NV Champagne, Port or Sherry) and/or to standardise a product (e.g. a wine where the brand expression is deemed more important than that of the grape and/or terroir). Most often it is used or also used to improve the overall quality of the various individual wines by creating a sum that is better balanced and in some cases more complex than the individual parts. In modern winemaking, the production of wine and especially a branded wine often involves incredibly complex blending operations, incorporating components that can come from many different sources (e.g. various clones, parcels, blocks, vineyards and/or regions) and from a wide variety of other variables, such as: different grape varieties, juice from different pressings, juice possessing higher/lower acid/sugar/tannins, wines fermented at different temperatures, fermented with different yeasts, fermented in different vessels,

various percentages of MLF, different oak and other maturation treatments, wines from different vintages, etc. Apart from winemaker vision, the only limitations on the extent of blending lots are local labelling laws that restrict for examples the use of different vintages within a vintage labelled wine, non-permitted grape varieties within a wine that declares a variety restrictive region or mentions the grape on the label and the percentage of regionally sourced fruit within a wine that mentions a legally recognized, delimited region. For more information on blending and examples, see Chapter 2 – Balance.

BLIND TASTING A wine-speak term referring to the ubiquitous practice of tasting wines without seeing the label or otherwise knowing what the what the wine is, blind tasting is a popular sport amongst wine geeks, a means of testing the abilities of wine students and occasionally a manner of assessing wines by wine professionals. The object is to ascertain such features as the grape variety(s), origin, producer, vintage and/or quality purely through the acts of seeing, smelling and tasting the wine in the glass. Variations include a single-blind tasting, whereby one aspect such as region or grape variety is known or a double-blind tasting, in which case nothing is known about the wine. Apart from the opportunity to show-off, why might some wine drinkers and professionals want to taste blind? Of course there is the challenge of this exercise, which is entertaining for some and can serve as a rigorous means of testing tasting skills, experience and wine knowledge, as demonstrated by institutions that perform annual blind tasting exams for their students such as the Institute of Masters of Wine or the Court of Master Sommeliers. Beyond this, blind tasting can help to dispel any preconceptions the taster may have about a particular grape, label, region or vintage, for examples, though presumably such preconceptions shouldn't exist amongst professionals. Another reason can stem from latent insecurity when it comes to tasting "expertise" along with that dastardly duo of wine tasting deadly sins – pride & ego – that often lead even experienced tasters into supporting a revered label or vintage that isn't always all it's cracked up to be. Also a major and perhaps the most valid justification for blind tasting amongst professionals is to preclude the possibility of being swayed by the financial agendas of the taster's employing publication or company or any other personal bias considerations that may exist (disclosed or not).

BODY Body is the sensation of the wine's weight on the palate. In common wine-speak wines that seem lighter in the mouth are referred to as light-bodied while ones that feel heaviest are full-bodied whereas those somewhere in between are perceived as medium-bodied. For more details of what constitutes wine body and how to detect it, see Chapter 4 in the section, "What exactly do you mean when you talk about a wine's 'body'?"

BOTRYTIS CINEREA (AKA BOTRYTIS, GREY MOULD, NOBLE ROT, AND POURRITURE NOBLE IN FRENCH) Botrytis is a ubiquitous fungal disease that infects grape bunches. It is particularly detrimental to red wine quality, directly impacting the colour of wines. However, "good" botrytis, sometimes known as "noble rot", produces some of the greatest sweet white wines in the world by concentrating sugars and acids in the berries while lending a distinctive "botrytised" character. For more information, see "botrytised".

BOTRYTISED This is a wine description used in reference to a wine that has been positively affected by botrytis cinerea, presumably lending recognizable botrytis related characters. These characters usually include sweetness, increased acidity, decreased/degraded grape derived aromas ("fruity esters") and/or increased levels of glycerol, depending on the level of botrytis infection and the style of wine produced. Botrytis also generates higher than normal levels of acetic acid and some new aroma compounds, the best known / most widely studied being sotolon, an aromatic lactone that lends a distinctive honeyed character to many botrytised wines. For more information, see "glycerol" and "sotolon".

BOUQUET This is a common wine-speak term for a collection of winemaking, mature or evolved (bottle aged) aromas. A moot example of outdated jargon, there is admittedly a certain logic to the metaphorical blossoming of primary fruit aromas into a complex "bouquet" of mature / aged wine notes. But this somewhat imprecise, sentimental term is tritely trotted-out by wine snobs and too often misused by the very nature of the image it conjures, so I prefer more specific references that say what they mean such as: "evolved fruit characters", "mature notes", "winemaking derived", "bottle aged" or "secondary" and "tertiary" aromas.

BRANDED WINE / BRAND While the term "brand" has many definitions and applications beyond wine, the expression of "brand" can be viewed as a purpose within the context of wine quality. Therefore while just about all if not all wines can be viewed as "brands" to some extent, a "branded wine" is a wine where the brand expression, standardisation of style and the consistency of perceived quality are deemed more important than the individual expression of the grape variety and/or terroir (i.e. regionality, vintage, etc.), even in cases where the grape and/or regional style, for examples, are an integral part of the brand (i.e. Champagne or Fino Sherry).

BRETTANOMYCES (AKA BRETT) Brett is a yeast that exists in wineries and vineyards throughout the world. Some consider brettanomyces "spoilage yeast" that, if present, can instil by-products in wine that constitute a wine fault. Others are more tolerant of these naturally existing fungi and contest that a little brett (or rather its by-products) can be seen as seasoning and contribute to complexity. The two by-products of major concern to winemakers are: 4-ethylphenol (4EP), giving rise to sweaty saddles, barnyard, earthy and sometimes medicinal, Band-Aid or iodine notes, and 4-ethylguaiacol (4EG), producing smoky, charred, menthol or somewhat spicy aromas of cinnamon stick and cloves. Contesting views over its effect on wine (bad or harmless / a benefit in small does) render "brett" a grey-area fault.

C

CARBON DIOXIDE (CO$_2$) CO$_2$ is an inert (non-reactive) gas common to winemaking. Naturally produced as a by-product of fermentation, for use in the winery it is generally purchased in canisters and used to help protect juice and wine from exposure to oxygen (opportunities for oxidation to occur) as a "reductive" handling technique. It can for example be used to push juice or wine through hoses or "blanket" / cover a tank since CO_2 is heavier than air and will remain within a contained space. CO_2 is also sometimes used on the bottling line to fill the head-space between the wine and closure. The one drawback of this fairly cheap, accessible gas is that is soluble in liquids, meaning that over a period of days it can be incorporated into the juice / wine forming small bubbles in the liquid with a slight spritz effect, which may or may not be desirable. After it has fully dissolved into the juice or wine and is no longer blanketing the liquid, CO_2 will need to be added to the surface again if protection from oxidation is still sought.

CATECHINS A type of phenol, catechins are small tannin subunits that can lend bitter flavour, a harsh affect and some astringency to wines. They are mainly found in the seeds and stems and to a far lesser extent in the skins of ripe grapes. During grape berry ripening the catechins present in the skins throughout the early stages of berry formation polymerise into larger tannin compounds as the skins ripen, equating to a less bitter taste and more astringent mouth-feel. So in wines produced from fully ripe red grapes catechins almost exclusively come from the seeds of the grapes rather than the skins. Furthermore, as grape seeds ripen catechins become less extractable from them and therefore ripe seeds as well as skins are desirable for the production of red wines especially where tannins will make an important contribution to the wine's texture and ageability.

CHAPTALIZATION This is the practice of adding sugar (usually sucrose in the form of beet or cane sugar) to grape juice before fermentation to increase the alcohol level that can be achieved after fermentation. It is usually only practiced and permitted within limits in cooler climates and vintages where the growing season may not naturally produce enough sugar in the berries to yield a balanced wine with the sufficient levels of alcohol, weight (body) and texture that the sugar will eventually yield after it has been converted to alcohol.

CLOSED (AKA DUMB OR MUTE) This is a common wine-speak term for a wine that is in a state of revealing very little smell, occasionally this state being contrary to the taster's expectations or more usually it is as is to be expected as a consequence of the wine's youth. Otherwise in some cases the taster may judge that the nose has shut-down or entered a relatively non-volatile stage of its evolution and therefore is currently giving very little on the nose. The terms closed, dumb or mute suggest that the taster believes that the wine will one day "open" and more smells will be forthcoming at a later stage in its evolution, or else terms such as weak, subtle or delicate should more accurately have been applied.

COLD STABILISATION Cold stabilisation is winemaking process often performed on white wines prior to bottling in order to prevent tartrate crystals from forming in the bottle, which may be viewed as a harmless superficial fault or a quality detraction depending on the eye of the beholder. As the name suggests, the wine is essentially chilled to such a degree and over a period of time that encourages any potassium and sometimes calcium naturally present in the wine to combine with tartaric acid, forming insoluble tartrate crystals that precipitate out of the wine. These crystals can then be removed prior to bottling to stabilise the wine, preventing wholly or to a degree the precipitation of tartrate crystals after the wine has been bottled. The process therefore strips the wine of some of its acid and mineral salts, which in effect subtly alters the wine. This forced altering of the wine's natural profile is deemed by some fine white wine makers as unacceptable, though it should be noted that many finer white wines are stored under cool conditions for such a period of time in barrel and/or tank as to precipitate the tartrates out without an artificially instigated cold stabilisation procedure. Other winemakers see cold stabilisation as a necessary quality assurance step in commercial wine production particularly for early bottled wines.

COMPLEXITY / COMPLEX (WINE) A somewhat subjective concept though pretty much universally deemed as an element in all great quality wines and many very good ones, complexity implies an abundance of pleasant aromas and flavours that can come in layers, particularly on the palate where different flavours may manifest themselves in the first impressions, on the "middle palate" (flavours that develop while the wine is in the mouth) and in the finish. Lesser quality wines will often have simple flavours which are easily described, succinctly listed and always fall short of satisfying one's emotional and intellectual expectations of a wine (if any). Another important yet less oft sited element of complexity is mouth-feel – a wine term for the textural sensation that a wine creates in the mouth. Intrinsic levels and grades of viscosity and tannic textures often offer vital contributions to the interest and therefore complexity of a palate profile. Complexity in wine should be manifested first and foremost as grape derived aromas / flavours and textures – those characters reflecting the grapes and perhaps the terroir from which it's made. Supporting complexity contributions can further come from the winemaking and ageing derived characters. For more information see "Chapter 5 – Complexity", "grape derived aromas / flavours" and "terroir".

CONCENTRATION / CONCENTRATED (AKA INTENSE / INTENSITY) Concentration refers to the relative density of a wine component or collection of components, with particular importance placed on how dilute vs concentrated it is relative to the grape's major component: water. Concentration is a wine term largely interchangeable with the concept of intensity, which more often specifically refers to the colour, aromas and flavours rather than other wine components. For more information see "Chapter 3 – Concentration".

COOPERAGE Cooperage (a noun) can refer to the work of a "cooper" (barrel maker) or the place where wooden vessels, usually in the form of barrels for storage or tanks for fermentation, are crafted and constructed. Almost always these vessels are composed of oak, predominately of a French or American oak species, though occasionally other woods and species of oak are used. For more information see "American oak", "French oak" and "oak".

CORK Naturally produced from the renewable bark of oak trees (Quercus suber), corks have for hundreds of years existed as an excellent closure

for wine bottles. However they are far from perfect, giving rise to what many in the wine industry believe to be unacceptably high incidences of cork taint / TCA. Perhaps the even greater though less measurable risk is "random oxidation" caused by nature of tiny imperfections on the surfaces (different for each cork) of the cork and / additionally whereby over the course of 15-40 years+ the cork will gradually lose its elasticity and therefore its airtight seal allowing oxygen into the bottle, which oxidises bottles at varying rates. This means that every single bottle of wine "aged" under cork will be slightly different in its state of oxidation / maturity. For more information see "2, 4, 6, Trichoroanisole" and "oxidation".

CORKED / CORK TAINT A corked bottle of wine is one that possesses cork taint caused by 2, 4, 6, Trichoroanisole (or TCA for short) contamination arising usually from contact with a TCA instilled cork closure. See "2, 4, 6, Trichoroanisole" for more information.

CROSS-FLOW FILTERATION (AKA TANGENTIAL FILTRATION) Such filtration involves a cross-flow filter, which works differently from basic filtration principals that pass liquids perpendicularly through a filter medium to stop particles of a certain size from going through to the "filtered" side. A cross-flow filter works by passing the liquid tangentially over the filter medium (a perforated membrane). This is a very efficient means of quickly clarifying liquid to a high degree as it can quickly strip out very small particles without clogging-up the filter medium by virtue of its sweeping action. Cross-flow filtration is the principal behind reverse osmosis filters, though is not used exclusively for reverse osmosis purposes and is common nowadays as a standard final filtration step prior to bottling wine. The downside of using the cross-flow filters developed for the wine industry is that they can be a little too good at doing what they do. Almost all cross-flow filters are set at a pore size of 0.2 microns, which is small enough to strip out yeast and most bacteria. Here lies the major issue with using these - there is a big difference between a "light" final filtration with particle catchers that are only widely spaced enough to take out large particles such as those visible with the naked eye and "sterile" filters such as cross-flow filters that routinely strip such microscopic microbials from the wine plus inevitably a certain amount of wine flavour and textural nuances that can lend complexity to wines, though to what degree this alteration is detectable is a moot point. On the up side, cross-flow filters can usually clarify wine with one step meaning less handling and opportunity for oxidation to occur.

CULTURED YEAST Cultured yeast are commercially produced, artificially instilled yeast used in winemaking to conduct fermentation. Their origins are however natural since they are isolated from strains of yeast that exist in vineyards and wineries around the world. Normally of the Saccharomyces cerevisiae species and occasionally of Saccharomyces bayannus, cultured yeast strains are selected and propagated in laboratories from thousands of yeast strains that exist around the world, chosen primarily for their efficiency to convert grape derived sugars into alcohol under various fermentation conditions. They may also be selected for their unique ability to produce specific aromatic fermentation by-products in wine such as aromatic volatile thiols from previously odourless aroma precursors in grapes. Because of their ability to reliably and consistently produce results and therefore their predictability, cultured yeast today perform the majority of fermentations in modern winemaking. However it is their very predictability and uniformity of results for which cultured yeast are chiefly criticised by those that shun their use such as natural wine proponents and many fine wine producers. The alternative is to use wild or natural yeast, sometimes termed as "natural fermentation" (see "wild yeast" for more information).

D

DEACIDIFICATION Deacidification, the lowering of acidity with correlating increase in pH in grape must or wine, is performed occasionally where permitted in some of the cooler areas of Europe such as Germany and in cooler vintages in New Zealand. It is a chemical process that involves adding a harmless compound, normally calcium carbonate, potassium carbonate or potassium bicarbonate, which will encourage some of the tartaric acid in wine to crystallize as tartrates and come out of solution, after which it can be removed. Another

far more common, ubiquitously legal and arguably 'natural' means of lowering the appearance of acid in wines is malolactic conversation more commonly known as malolactic fermentation or MLF, performed on almost all red wines around the world and occasionally on whites. See "malolactic fermentation" for more information.

DÉBOURBAGE See "settling".

DESCRIPTORS On a basic level, the descriptors used in wine-speak are an attempt to verbalise specific smells, flavours and textures that are experienced during tasting and/or drinking. Nowadays there are a number of ready-made lists available to students of wine to help guide them towards generally accepted terminology. Common descriptors include a lot of fragrant / stinky food, spice, flora and fauna items (ubiquitous and regionally obscure) and earth/turf related smells that share aromas and flavours with wine. One of the drawbacks to the descriptors commonly used, recommended and taught by wine professionals is that they are mainly Western in origin / nature and are to some extent meaningless in Eastern cultures and elsewhere.

DETECTION THRESHOLD A detection threshold is the level at which an aroma / flavour compound is able to be organoleptically sensed by an individual or humans in general. References to detection thresholds usually give the lowest concentration at which the human nose can perceive that odour. Individuals can vary slightly-to-enormously in their detection levels of various aroma compounds from possessing a heightened sensitivity compared to the norm to having a specific anosmia for a particular compound. For more information see "anosmia' and "organoleptic".

DIACETYL Diacetyl is a by-product of yeast created during fermentation but usually only in very small, undetectable concentrations. Detectable to pronounced levels are however also created as a by-product by lactic bacteria (mainly Oenococcus oeni), which are either added or naturally instilled and encouraged in nascent wines during winemaking primarily in order to convert the very tart malic acid present into softer, less sour lactic acid through the process widely known as "malolactic fermentation"

(MLF). The compound diacetyl is a volatile aroma with a distinctly buttery smell / flavour that can either compliment a wine's grape derived flavours (e.g. many Chardonnays, whereby MLF is often encouraged) or detract (e.g. most Rieslings, whereby MLF is often discouraged). Its distinctive aroma is more prominent on white wines than reds wines, where the aroma is largely undetectable unless significant quantities are present in a very delicate red wine such as some Pinot Noirs. When lending a complimentary contribution to the complexity of a wine's nose, it is usually considered important that the diacetyl / buttery character is in balance with the other aromas and plays a supporting role to the grape derived aromas / flavours rather than dominating and overshadowing these. Other descriptors for the smell of diacetyl include nutty, caramel, butterscotch and cream. Occasionally an uncomplimentary rancid butter character can emerge, depending on the strain of bacteria used.

DIAM Diam is a brand of agglomerated cork that is made of tiny cork pieces, treated to get rid of TCA and glued back together into a cork shape.

DIMETHYL SULPHIDE (DMS) Mostly known as a foul odour generating sulphide found occasionally in wines as a consequence of reduction, dimethyl sulphide mainly manifests itself with smells of asparagus, canned corn, tinned peas or cooked tomatoes. Because of its somewhat unappealing nature it is usually considered a fault when present in wine at levels much above the detection threshold. However in some cases at lower levels it may lend appealing aromas to the wines of certain grape varieties. For example, the influence of dimethyl sulphide on Syrah's glycosidic aroma precursor has been shown to instil a lifted raspberry or blackcurrant aroma in some wines made from this grape. See "reduction" for more information.

DRINKING WINDOW Drinking window is a common wine-speak term for a period of time when a bottled wine is drinking at its best. More often than not this period begins soon after the wine is bottled. Many fine wines are however designed to develop and improve with bottle age, becoming better balanced and more complex. Note however that every wine has its day when it is at the peak of

its drinking window (although this "peak" is largely subjective) after which it faces a period of plateau and eventually decline, whereby the grape derived aromas are all but unrecognizable and all that is left are oxidised and aldehydic notes. In the declining stages of maturity the nose may progressively be referred to as "tired", "drying / dried out" and finally "past-it". Drinking windows for wines are sometimes offered by wine critics as part of a wine review, accompanying the tasting note. To be clear though, any drinking window proffered is at best a guesstimate relying heavily on two major factors: 1) the experience level of the critic and 2) the personal preferences of the consumer (e.g. at which stage of evolution the drinker prefers to enjoy his or her wine).

DRY A common wine-speak word, a dry wine is one that has very little or no detectable sweetness. This does not usually mean that the wine contains absolutely no residual sugar – nearly all wines contain trace amounts of residual sugar that was not able to be fully fermented by yeast. Other reasons for allowing up to a few grams per litre of residual sugar to remain in a dry wine include for the purposes of balancing higher levels of acidity and to contribute to the texture or mouth-feel of the wine. (Sugar in the wine will make it appear more viscous.) A little sweetness can also modify the taste of bitter / under-ripe tannins. By EU definition a wine can contain up to 9 grams per litre of residual sugar, depending on the acidity level, and still be labelled dry but this mainly applies to white wines, which will naturally have higher acidity than reds. In practical terms a dry red wine will have less than 2 grams per litre of residual sugar and normally just trace amounts. It is worth also noting that the terms "drying", "dry finish" or "drying on the finish" are sometimes used in wine-speak not in reference to sweetness but to an overly astringent or tannic sensation caused by a high level of tannins in the wine and/or harsh / under-ripe tannins that overwhelm the finish. Alternatively the term "dried-out" is commonly used to describe a wine that has become completely oxidised and/or has passed the peak of its drinking window.

DRY EXTRACT See "extract".

E

ÉLEVAGE See "maturation".

ELLAGITANNINS Oak derived tannins tend to consist of hydrolysable (soluble) ellagitannins with tannin levels imparted in wine depending on the species of oak (e.g. American or French), where it is grown, how it is seasoned and toasted, the amount of wine surface area in contact with the oak (e.g. size of the barrel) and the period of time that wine spends in contact with the oak. For the most part only new / first use oak gives any significant level of tannins. Ellagitannins can be broken down into 2 major groups: 1) monomers, which are relatively astringent and 2) dimers, which are relatively bitter. This bitterness and astringency imparted by oak tannins while generally approachable compared to unripe grape skin, seed or stem tannins, can be a marker for oak tannins and can therefore render them organoleptically distinctive from ripe grape skin tannins.

ESTERIFICATION Esterification in wine terms is a chemical reaction that can occur in wine during maturation and bottle ageing involving the combining of an alcohol (usually ethanol) with an acid resulting in the formation of an aromatic ester. Esterification can make a wine taste less apparently acidic with age because the acids that become combined take on more complex flavours drawing the drinker's attention away from simple acidity. The rate at which esterification occurs is influenced by a host of factors such as the wine's pH and level of antioxidants, both natural (such as polyphenols) and added (such as SO_2 and ascorbic acid). For more information see "Chapter 5 – Complexity" in the section, "How do some wines become more complex after ageing?"

ESTERS Esters are volatile aromatic compounds found in wine usually formed by the combining of the various alcohols with the various acids during winemaking and bottle ageing, a process known as esterification. Depending on their nature and concentration, esters can contribute to the complexity of a wine's nose or constitute a wine fault. For example the combination of ethanol with acetic acid can yield the ester "ethyl acetate", which in small concentrations can contribute a complex lift to wine but in higher concentrations lends an unpleasant nail varnish/polish remover character (being an actual component of some such solvents). The "fruity" esters in wine are said to give it its distinctly vinous character. More than 160 different esters have thus far been identified in wines.

ETHANOL (AKA ETHYL ALCOHOL) Ethanol is the technical term for "drinking" alcohol and is the major alcohol found in wine. Wines can contain as little alcohol (ethanol) by volume as 5% (or less), as is common in a very sweet Tokaji Essencia, or without fortification they can contain as much as 18%, as is the case in some dry, red table wines from hotter climates / vintages. In its pure form it is colourless and possesses very little odour. As a major wine component it does however contribute to the body and mouth-feel / texture of wine, being more viscous than water. At higher levels it can also affect the flavour profile imparting what many tasters refer to as warmth at the back of the palate otherwise known as a "hot finish" or "alcohol burn". At the highest end of the alcohol spectrum and certainly in the case of fortified wines (ranging from 15-20% alcohol by volume), the high level of alcohol offers protection against microbial spoilage and therefore increased stability.

ETHYL ACETATE Ethyl acetate is an ester commonly found in wine formed by the combination of ethanol with acetic acid, which in small concentrations can contribute a complex lift to wine but in higher concentrations lends an unpleasant nail varnish/polish remover character (being an actual component of some such solvents).

ETHYL MERCAPTAN (AKA ETHANETHIOL) A foul odour generating mercaptan found occasionally in wines, ethyl mercaptan generally smells of struck-match, cooked cabbage, onions and leeks. Because of its unappealing nature it is usually considered a fault when present in wine at levels much above the detection threshold. See "mercaptans" for more information.

4-ETHYLGUAIACOL (4EG) 4EG is a phenolic compound and the by-product of brettanomyces yeast. When present in high concentrations in wine it is generally considered a wine fault but at lower concentrations there is some debate as to whether or not it is a fault and therefore its presence in wine is something of a faultiness grey-area. It tends to instil smoky, charred, menthol or somewhat spicy aromas of cinnamon stick and cloves. Generally this compound is considered far more complimentary than its cousin 4-ethylphenol (4EP), which is usually produced at the same time. As yet it is impossible to control the proportions of the two compounds that the yeast will generate and therefore most winemakers play it safe and try to eliminate brettanomyces from wineries and wines.

4-ETHYLPHENOL (4EP) 4EP is a phenolic compound and the by-product of brettanomyces yeast. When present in high concentrations in wine it is generally considered a wine fault but at lower concentrations there is some debate as to whether or not it is a fault and therefore its presence in wine is something of a faultiness grey-area. It tends to instil sweaty saddles, barnyard, earthy and sometimes medicinal, Band-Aid or iodine notes. Generally this compound is considered far less complimentary than its cousin 4-ethylguaiacol (4EG), which is usually produced at the same time. As yet it is impossible to control the proportions of the two compounds that the yeast will generate and therefore most winemakers play it safe and try to eliminate brettanomyces from wineries and wines.

EUGENOL Eugenol is the main chemical compound responsible for the smell of cloves and is also found in lesser concentrations cinnamon, nutmeg, bay leaves, basil and wine. The eugenol content found in some wines comes from oak barrels during the maturation process.

EVOLVED See "mature".

EXTRACT (AKA DRY EXTRACT OR TOTAL EXTRACT) When used as a noun and in the context of wine, extract usually refers to the non-volatile compounds existing in solution in a wine, which includes sugars, tannins, anthocyanins, proteins, minerals, glycerol and non-volatile acids such as tartaric, malic and lactic acid (plus many, many more trace elements). Wine's extract contributes to the overall body of a

wine although it is worth noting that if a wine is very sweet it can have a high level of extract from sugars but still appear relatively light bodied, particularly if the alcohol level is low.

F

FAULT / FAULTY (WINE) A fault is the wine-speak term for a flaw in a wine. Generally this equates to an uncomplimentary character that is other than the desirable grape variety / vine and terroir (soil, climate, weather, grower, etc.) derived aroma and flavour compounds plus only the winemaking characters that a winemaker intentionally imparted (oak, desired fermentation derived flavours, malolactic by-products, etc.). Truth be told, the overwhelming majority of wines that we drink reside in a grey-area somewhere between faulty and faultless. Almost all wines possess a number of grey-area fault characters, which in small doses can contribute a bit of seasoning to wine, though in larger doses constitute a certain level of quality compromise. (See Chapter 1 – Wine Faults.)

FERMENTATION In winemaking fermentation is the metabolic process of converting the sugars (carbohydrates) in grape juice into alcohol (predominately ethanol) and carbon dioxide by the action of yeast. Fermentation requires certain conditions, most notably the absence of oxygen (anaerobic conditions) and other factors that are yeast species or strain dependent such as temperature range, level of acidity / pH, level of sugar and level of alcohol. Alcoholic fermentation can be conducted by "cultured yeast", mainly of the Saccharomyces cerevisiae species, and/or some species of "wild yeast". See "yeast" for more information and the dedicated entries for both of these yeast categories.

FILTRATION / FILTER (VERB) / FILTERING Something of a contentious topic in fine wine production and scorned by some wine critics, filtration is nonetheless a very common winemaking process. The issue with regards to wine quality is not so much whether or not to filter ever but how much to filter and when since nearly all wines produced for commercial sale will receive some degree of filtration at some point during winemaking, if simply to perform a light filtration to rid juice or wine of residual harvesting debris (leaves, stems, bugs, etc.) and/or lees for examples. The bone of contention largely has to do with the common and somewhat habitual practice of a final filtration prior to bottling. Here there is a big difference between a "light" filtration with particle catchers that are only wide enough to take out large particles such as those visible with the naked eye and "sterile" filters such as cross-flow filters that routinely strip out microscopic microbials like yeasts and bacteria plus inevitably a certain amount of wine flavour and textural nuances that can lend complexity to wines, though to what degree this alteration is detectable is a moot point. Nowadays many fine wine and natural winemakers opt for very little (light) or no final filtration prior to bottling, necessitating that hygiene conditions in the winery and especially on the bottling line be impeccable to allow any degree of assurance that that wine will not be bottled with any ambient microbials (e.g. yeast or bacteria), which could spoil the wine. Otherwise precautionary winemakers will sterile filter (with a cross-flow filter or several other means) prior to bottling, stripping any possible residual microbials from the wine but also, arguably, some of the delicate quality-enhancing nuances that contribute to complexity. The alternative to filtering is careful "settling" followed by "racking" and for more information see the separate entries dedicated to these practices.

FINE WINE Fine wine is an imprecise but nonetheless very handy wine-speak term that refers to an elite group of wines that sit at the pinnacle of wine quality purposes and therefore presumably within the upper echelons of intrinsic and often extrinsic wine quality greatness.

FINING Fining is a set of clarification and/or fine-tuning winemaking processes. Fining is performed for a range of very different purposes and therefore there are a variety of methods and means of achieving these purposes. The common aspect of all fining techniques is that they involve adding a substance or "fining agent" to wine which will bond with the target component in the wine that the winemaker wishes to remove and precipitates both as solid sediment, which can then easily be removed by racking and/or filtration. Fining is different from filtration because

it has the ability to isolate and take-out specific soluble components in the wine according to their chemical make-up, whereas filtration strips out components by nature of their size and is therefore much less specific in what is removed. The two major components that are commonly fined from wines are proteins (see "protein haze") and tannins. Tannin fining is in fact a very old and common technique for "fine-tuning" red wines, practiced traditionally on the red wines of Bordeaux and Burgundy and now throughout the world. And even today the old-school, traditional fining agent regularly employed to "soften" the astringency / tannic impact of red wines is egg whites. When mixed in red wines the egg whites combine with tannins via an electrostatic interaction to form large protein-tannin complexes that settle to the bottom of the barrel, off which the wine can be racked. Egg white fining is usually done towards the end of barrel ageing. Anywhere between 1-6 egg whites per 225 litre barrique is used, depending how much tannin the winemaker wishes to remove. Sometimes the egg whites are whisked with a little salt prior to use to increase their solubility. Generally employed with the best intensions to help forge a better balanced wine, fining is however not practiced by all winemakers. Like filtration fining is considered by some winemakers as an unnecessary stripping of natural wine components and is therefore avoided.

FINISH (AKA AFTERTASTE) Finish is a common wine-speak term used in reference to the measure of the amount of time that the tastes, flavours and textures (e.g. tannins) last in the mouth after the wine has been spat or swallowed as well as the discernable nature (e.g. relative complexity) of these elements. The evaluation of a wine's finish or aftertaste is one of the fundamental factors to assessing a wine's quality. The greatest quality wines have long-lasting, pleasant and often complex finishes. For more information see "Chapter 6 – Length and Nature of Finish".

FLAVOUR Flavour is the combined effect of taste and smell in the mouth. Smelling strongly influences flavour largely through the function of retronasal olfaction. In the context of wine, the terms aroma and flavour are often used interchangeably since the flavours of wines predominately consist of aroma compounds.

There is also evidence to suggest that mouth-feel / texture largely impacts the perception of flavour, although it does not affect flavour itself. The brain combines the effects of the two or three senses into one, resulting what wine tasters have come to recognize as flavour. For more information see "aroma", "mouth-feel" and "retronasal olfaction".

FORTIFIED (WINE) This is a wine that has had its alcohol level boosted by the addition of a distilled spirit, commonly a neutral flavoured grape based spirit such as a specially produced brandy usually made locally within the country or region of fortified wine production. Such wines are generally fortified up to 15-20% alcohol by volume. The most famous examples of fortified wines are Port, Sherry and Madeira. At the highest end of the alcohol spectrum for wines, fortified wines can rely on their yeast and bacteria prohibitive level of alcohol to protect them from microbial spoilage and therefore possess increased stability compared to non-fortified wines.

FORWARD A common wine-speak word, a forward wine is one that is showing more expression of aromas and/or evolution on the nose and palate than the taster expected for its state of maturity.

FRENCH OAK   French oak is a wine-speak term generally referring to European indigenous / reared oak trees used to make oak barrels and tanks for wine maturation and fermentation. There are in fact many species of oak used in wine production but in terms of "French oak" there are two of major importance: Quercus robur and Quercus sessilus (A.K.A. Quercus petraea and Quercus sessiliflora). In France, oak from the Limousin forest is mostly of the species Quercus robur - a "robust" flavoured, tannic oak best suited to nearby Cognac production. Other French forests are wooded with several species most notably Quercus sessilus / petraea, which is more commonly used to make wine barrels as it tends to be less tannic than robur and offer more desirable aromatic compounds such as eugenol and various lactones. The most significant forests for the production of oak suitable for wine production are in the Vosges, Sarthe, Nevers and Alliers departments or communes of France. Other localised forests in Burgundy, the Loire, Alsace,

parts of Eastern Europe and Champagne sometimes produce wood for the use of neighbouring regions. Of significance is the origin and climate in which the tree has grown as these will influence the quality of the grain, texture and suitability (as well as price) of the wood. European or French oak tends to have more tannins and astringency than American oak and the flavours are much more subtle, usually imparting suggestions of coconut and baking spices. The increased tannins available from European / French oaks can be useful in aiding colour formation, structure and aging potential of many wines destined for long cellaring. For more information see "American oak" and "oak".

FUNDAMENTAL (WINE) quality factors
"Fundamental Quality Factors" is my term for the tangible components of wine that are collectively assessed by most professionals (critics, wine buyers, winemakers, etc.) when making a wine quality assessment.

These Fundamental Quality Factors include:
• The relative absence of Faults
• Fruit Health & Ripeness
• Concentration
• Balance
• Complexity
• The wine's Length & Nature of Finish

While all are these factors are vital to a wine's implicit functionality, some may play more of a critical part than others when we look beyond the role of basic wine soundness and extend to the pinnacle of the "fine wine" experience as achieved through wine excellence (see the Wine Purposes Pyramid for more information on wine roles). For more information on each of these fundamental quality factors, see the individual chapters of this book devoted to them.

G

GC-MS (GAS CHROMATOGRAPHY-MASS SPECTROMETRY, SOMETIMES INVERTED AND ABBREVIATED AS MS-GC) GC-MS is a method of analysing samples of juice or wine for specific chemical substances. This is useful for studying the presence and concentrations of certain aroma compounds such as terpenes or possible faults such as 4-ethylphenol (4EP) and 2, 4, 6, trichoroanisole (TCA).

GEOSMIN Geosmin is a metabolite / organic compound produced by various moulds (fungi) and bacteria. Detectable in wine at very low concentrations, it can contaminate just a few bunches of grapes and still have a significant impact. It imparts an earthy (i.e. like wet dirt or petrichor), beets, turnips and/or sometimes musty/mouldy smell in wine. It used to be (and often still is) attributed as a "terroir" character. Sometimes it is considered to contribute to complexity and therefore could be included as a grey-area fault. This compound is thought to degrade over time and be barely detectable in wines after a few years of bottle ageing.

GLYCEROL Glycerol occasionally makes a minor contribution to wine body. This is a relatively thick, colourless, odourless, sweet liquid and a minor by-product of alcohol fermentation. It is normally present in most wines in un- or barely detectable concentrations, although botrytised wines sometimes have concentrations that can exceed the detection level. Only when it rarely exceeds levels above the textural detection threshold (i.e. 28 g/L) is it really of any significance when considering the major components of body.

GRAPE COMPONENTS Grapes can be broken down into component parts, collectively contributing in varying degrees to the overall experience and therefore quality that a wine offers. The grape components of major wine contribution significance include:

- Sugars (mainly glucose and fructose)
- Organic Acids (tartaric and malic account for around 90% of these acids)
- Phenolic compounds, inc.:
  - Colour pigments (anthocyanins)
  - Tannins (ranging from small sub-units that are more bitter to large or polymerised compounds, which are more astringent)
- Aroma and aroma precursor compounds
- Nitrogenous compounds (important for yeast nutrition and can be a nuisance if too much

protein renders the wine cloudy, these include: amino acids, ammonia, nitrates, proteins, etc.)
- Minerals / Cations (mainly potassium, which can affect pH and tartrate stability, but grapes also contain trace amounts of sodium, iron, calcium, etc.)
- Water (a whopping 70-80% of the grape's volume)

GRAPE DERIVED AROMAS / FLAVOURS / CHARACTERS / COMPONENTS This is my term for the aromas and other characteristics or components (e.g. tannins and sugars) that come initially and predominately from grapes as opposed to those that are winemaking derived. In their early stages (i.e. soon after bottling) such aromas are also known in common wine-speak as primary aromas, giving rise to distinctively fruity, vegetal, floral and/or herbal aromas and including some spice characters such as pepper (e.g. rotundone, a compound common to Syrah). Grape derived aromas / flavours and components should have the ability to be notably linked back to the vine variety / clone and may additionally link back to certain distinguishable terroir elements such as climate, weather, vineyard, etc. With barrel and/or bottle ageing grape derived aromas and other components may evolve due to slow oxidative and reductive reactions and possibly combine with other components in the wine and/or "marry-in" with the winemaking derived aromas and components, contributing to a mature wine nose and palate, what is known in wine-speak as tertiary aromas or characters. For more information see "Chapter 5 – Complexity", "grape derived aromas / flavours", "terroir" and "winemaking derived aromas / flavours".

GREY-AREA FAULT A grey-area fault is my term for a compound or character in wines that can sometimes be considered a fault and other times be considered to contribute to the style and/or complexity of the wine. The difference between its positive and negative contribution is largely dependent on key factors such as, 1) whether or not it complements the style and/or grape, 2) the concentration level of the grey-area fault, 3) if it is balance with the other components in the wines and 4) the subjective view of the individual tasting the wine (i.e. whether they consider it a fault or not). Truth be told, the overwhelming majority of wines that we drink reside in a grey-area somewhere between faulty and faultless. Almost all wines possess a number of grey-area fault characters, which in small doses can contribute a bit of seasoning to wine, though in larger doses constitute a certain level of quality compromise. Some of the most common grey-area faults include oxidation, reduction, volatile acidity and brettanomyces. For more information, see "Chapter 1 – Wine Faults".

H

HANG TIME This term refers quite literally to the amount of time the grape bunches are left hanging on the vine. In other words, it is the period of time between the flowering episode in early spring until harvest, which can occur from late summer until late autumn. In viticulture "hang time" is an important concept as it relates to the overall ripeness of the grapes including not just sugars and acids but "physiological" aspects such as tannin polymerisation and flavour compound formation. "Limited hang time" usually implies that there was a rush to harvest (usually forced by excessive heat or rains) equating to less than ripe tannins and flavours, which unlike sugars and acids are difficult if not impossible to correct in the winery.

HOLLOW Hollow is a common wine-speak word describing flavours that are lacking in the mouth, particularly in reference to the relative absence of grape derived flavours in the mid-palate impressions.

HYDROGEN SULPHIDE (H$_2$S) This is a wine fault that is very common (albeit temporarily) during fermentation. Particularly if there is a low level of yeast nutrients (namely nitrogen) available in the juice, some of the sulphur present in the wine is prone to be converted into the simple but very stinky reduced sulphur compound known as Hydrogen Sulphide or H$_2$S. A foul, 'rotten egg' or pronounced sulphurous smelling molecule, H$_2$S is thankfully a highly unstable / volatile fault and can usually be dispersed simply with aeration (e.g. racking the wine, decanting the bottle or swirling the glass), though this method does of course carry with it the risk of oxidation. It's formation can also be controlled by winemakers by adding nitrogen to the fermenting

wine, usually in the form of diammonium phosphate or DAP. However, if H$_2$S is allowed to form and left untreated in a reductive environment (in the absence of air such as in a closed tank or sealed bottle), it may combine with other elements in the wine to form more stable odorous "reduction" compounds such as other sulphide compounds (inc. dimethyl sulphide (DMS) and dimethydisulphide), mercaptans / thiols, methyl mercaptan or ethyl mercaptan. These compounds are incredibly varied, commonly manifesting themselves in a struck-match, rubber or burnt tire character but also sometimes giving notes of garlic, canned corn, olives, onions, truffles, dirty drains and sewage. Once these are formed in the wine they can be much more difficult to get rid of than simple H$_2$S and, depending on how they manifest themselves (pleasant or unpleasant) and the subjective views of the taster (adds complexity or represents a detraction), can be considered a fault.

HYPEROSMIA This is a physical condition referring to an increase in olfactory sensitivity. In other words, it's a hypersensitivity or increase in an individual's ability to smell. This can be genetic or it has been theorised that the condition can be brought about by the use of certain drugs.

HYPOSMIA This is a physical condition that involves a decrease in an individual's sense of smell. Like anosmia (the complete loss of the ability to smell) hyposmia has been known to occur with brain damage (e.g after accidents to the head), the onset of Alzheimer's disease or even certain viral infections can cause temporary or permanent loss of the sensitivity to odours / smells.

I

INDIGENOUS YEAST See "wild yeast".

IPMP (2-ISOPROPYL-3-METHOXYPYRAZINE)
2-isopropyl-3-methoxypyrazine (better known by the acronym IPMP) is a specific type of methoxypyrazine found in some grape varieties and that is excreted by the Asian ladybird / lady beetle, which is the cause of "ladybird taint" (LBT). Methoxypyrazines or pyrazines for short are volatile aroma molecules that can start forming in the berry at an early stage before veraison and

which degrade as the berry ripens. Known for the green / leafy / herbal character they lend to wines, methoxypyrazines are more common in some grapes than others, especially prevalent in Sauvignon Blanc, where it is often valued, and its close relatives Cabernet Sauvignon and Cabernet Franc, where it is best avoided. Research indicates that the easiest way to avoid the formation of this herbaceous methoxypyrazine character in grape skins and therefore minimise its presence in wines is to ripen the compounds out with plenty of sunshine on grapes (which can be aided by early shoot and leaf removal) and hang-time…but this is not always possible in all climates and/or vintages. Both under-cropping and over-cropping in the vineyard have been shown to exacerbate the methoxypyrazine problem.

L

LACTIC ACID Lactic acid is a major acid found in many wines. It is not present in wine grapes but is imparted in wines by the transformation of the naturally occurring grape acid malic acid into lactic acid via the action of lactic bacteria, predominately of the species Oenococcus oeni, during the malolactic fermentation (MLF). The major reason winemakers allow / perform malolactic fermentation is to convert what may be considered a very sour malic acid profile in the wine into the less tart, apparently softer lactic acid, ultimately to achieve better balance.

LACTIC BACTERIA Lactic bacteria are used in winemaking to perform malolactic fermentation (MLF). Naturally present in many wineries around the world, they may independently instil themselves in wine and, if left uninhibited and the conditions are right, perform MLF of their own accord. Otherwise winemakers may prohibit their activity through various means or encourage it by rendering the wine more conducive to MLF and/ or inoculating the wine with a commercial strain. The species of major importance for oenology is Oenococcus oeni, as the name suggests (Oeno being the Greek goddess of wine). Although MLF is mainly performed to soften the impression of acidity and increase the pH in wines, it also generates new flavour compounds and alters the aromatic and

flavour profiles of wines. Different strains of bacteria produce different results but generally speaking the major by-product produced by Oenococcus oeni is diacetyl, lending a distinctive buttery character especially to more delicate white wines.

LADYBIRD / LADYBUG / LADY BEETLE TAINT (LBT)
The Asian ladybird (Harmonia axyridis) is a type of ladybird / ladybug indigenous to eastern Asia and now present in Europe and North America. It feeds on damaged grapes in the run-up to harvest time and, if present, can be harvested and processed with the grapes. During crushing and pressing the bug releases hemolymph – a circulatory fluid containing foul-smelling defensive compounds, most notably a methoxypyrazine (IPMP). "Ladybird Taint" (LBT) is caused by the release of 2-isopropyl-3-methoxypyrazine (IPMP) into must (juice) imparting a distinctive green, leafy, herbal or bell pepper character reminiscent of under-ripe fruit. It is now believed the European ladybird species (coccinellidae) can also be responsible for the taint. Fruit sorting, lighter pressing and must heating can minimise the impact but once a significant amount is in the wine (above detection threshold) it is difficult if not impossible to remove and does not appear to degrade with time. Some believe many 2004 Red Burgundies are afflicted with LBT.

LEES In common wine-speak "lees" is a general catch-all term for sediment – any sediment - in a wine vat, barrel, bottle, glass, etc. Depending on the situation, lees may be comprised of anything from seeds and bits of grape skin in the bottom of a fermentation vessel to tartrate crystals and large, insoluble tannin complexes in the bottom of an old bottle of wine. More specifically to winemaking and their use as a character enhancing tool, lees are the dormant yeast cells that remain in wine post-fermentation, settling to the bottom of the fermentation vessel after the yeast have converted all the sugar they can or are permitted to convert in the wine. A good many wines across all colours and most styles can and often do involve at least some time spent on these lees. Which lees are employed (gross or fine lees), how long they left in contact with the wine and how they are used (e.g. simply left at the bottom of the tank / barrel or regularly "stirred" up with the wine, known as bâtonnage, etc.) can dramatically change the effect lees ageing has on wines.

LEES AGEING / CONTACT Lees ageing is the winemaking practice of allowing nascent wine to spend a period of time on its lees, in this case dormant yeast cells. Bâtonnage is a French winemaking term now used in common wine-speak in reference to the practice of ageing a wine for a period on its sedimentary lees in tank or barrel while routinely stirring / mixing the lees up with the wine. Otherwise some wines are simply left for a space of time on the lees without stirring, simply known as lees ageing, ageing on lees or sur lies (French). One of the most often touted benefits of lees contact for both still and sparkling wines is the building of texture or "mouth-feel" in wines. This can be detected as a boost to the wine's perceived "creaminess" with the effect of an apparent slight increase to wine viscosity and body. Apart from this, contact with lees can degrade grape aromatics and the impact of MLF generated diacetyl. So wines that have had significant lees contact can appear less overtly fruity and, if MLF has occurred, less buttery. Extended contact with lees, as is the case with many sparkling wines such as Champagne undergoing second fermentation in the bottle, lends a distinctly toasty or bread-like character to wines, most apparent after 18 months+ on lees, resulting from a lees degradation process known as autolysis. For more information see "autolysis".

M

MACERATION Maceration in winemaking is essentially the process whereby crushed grape skins and juice are left in contact with one another for a period of time, often involving a periodic mixing or stirring technique, in order to extract an increased amount of components from the skins such as colour, tannins and flavour compounds. Maceration therefore helps to build concentration in a wine (see "concentration" and Chapter 3 for more information). It can be practiced before fermentation (using cooling and/or SO₂ additions to delay fermentation – known as "cold soaking"), after fermentation (whereby the alcohol will act as a solvent) or both. Common maceration techniques include: cold soaking, pigeage (punching down),

pumping over and submerged cap, each yielding slightly different results.

MADERIZED Maderized is a wine-speak term used as a positive or negative descriptor depending on whether the wine being described is stylistically intended to reveal a maderized character or if the wine is faulty as a result of overexposure to oxygen (oxidation) and/or heat during shipping and/or storage. As a positive descriptor it is used in reference to a style of winemaking that involves the purposeful, considerable oxygenation and heating of sweet, fortified wine during maturation (barrel ageing). The word stems from Madeira wine, a style that famously evolved over prolonged periods in barrel during lengthy sea journeys. As either a positive or negative descriptor its connotations and smells are somewhat vaguely defined, generally referring to a cooked or dried fruit character and/or caramel, butterscotch, nutty or honeyed notes.

MALIC ACID A major organic acid and component in grapes, malic acid is naturally produced as part of the berry's formation and remains in the berry throughout ripening. The two major acids in wine grapes are tartaric, an acid unique to grapes, and malic, an acid common to other fruits such as apples. Although tartaric acid continues to be manufactured in the berry throughout ripening, the overall concentration of acid decreases relative to that of other components such as sugar and water. And in fact the more sour malic acid is respired or consumed by the berry during ripening, generally resulting in grapes that are higher in the less tart tartaric acid at the time of harvest. With its more tart profile, malic acid can and often does contribute necessary freshness to many white wine styles. However it is generally deemed too tart to exist in a balanced red wine and some white grapes such as Chardonnay benefit from a softer acid profile. In such incidences malolactic fermentation is performed to convert the malic acid in the softer, less apparently acidic lactic acid.

MALOLACTIC FERMENTATION / CONVERSION (MLF) Not actually a fermentation (no alcohol is created), MLF is the common wine-speak term for the transformation of the naturally occurring grape acid malic acid into lactic acid via the action of lactic bacteria, predominately of the species Oenococcus oeni. It is often allowed or performed on red wines and sometimes on whites. Under the right conditions MLF may occur naturally in nascent wines, or it may be encouraged by winemakers or otherwise performed by inoculating the wine with a lactic bacteria strain. The major reason winemakers allow / perform malolactic fermentation is to convert what may be considered a very sour malic acid profile in the wine into the less tart, apparently softer lactic acid. This will also result in an increase in the pH of the wine, the amount depending on how much malic acid was converted. MLF causes a slight loss of fruitiness to wines, which some winemakers embrace while others shun. Since higher or sharper apparent acidity is generally valued in white wines rather than reds, MLF is generally a routine step in red winemaking. Less commonly performed in white winemaking, the notable exceptions are cooler climate Chardonnay wines such as those from Burgundy and Chablis and certain sparkling wine styles such as Champagne. Also worth noting is that wines that have gone through malolactic fermentation are generally more stable since there is little or no opportunity for MLF to occur in the bottled wine if by chance the wine is bottled with some lactic bacteria.

MASTER SOMMELIER (AKA MS) An "MS" is someone who has passed the rigorous Master Sommelier exams and has been accredited by its governing institution, the Court of Master Sommeliers. Established in the United States in 1977, the Court of Master Sommeliers seeks "to promote excellence in hotel and beverage restaurant service". The MS differs from the Master of Wine qualification primarily with its focus on the service of wine within on-premise businesses (e.g. restaurants and bars). The Court of Master Sommeliers currently offers four levels of sommelier certification with the MS qualification sitting at the pinnacle. The MS exam consists of three parts: "a theory examination (an oral examination and not written), a blind tasting of six wines, and a practical wine service examination. The minimum passing score for each of the three sections is 75%". Furthermore, "The candidate is required to wear professional working attire and to also provide all tools of the sommelier trade for the examination.

The candidate should exhibit a high standard of both technical and social skills throughout the examination, and demonstrate the courtesy and charm of a Master Sommelier. It is also essential that the candidate demonstrate excellent salesmanship." All three exam sections must be passed to become an MS. More information is available on the Court of Master Sommeliers website: www. mastersommeliers.org

MASTER OF WINE (AKA MW) More commonly known simply by the two letters "MW", a Master of Wine is an individual who has passed the rigorous Master of Wine exams to qualify as a Master of Wine and has joined the overseeing institution as a member. The Institute of Masters of Wine (IMoW) is the facilitator and accrediting body of the Master of Wine educational programme and annual exams. The first exam was held in 1953 in London and today there are just over 300 MWs in the world. The origins and head office for the IMoW are in London, UK, although today there are also branches in the USA and Australia. Originally intended as a qualification for the UK wine trade, over the last 25 years the IMoW has expanded its scope to include wine experts of many nationalities and those employed in other professional fields. It is widely considered the most challenging endeavour in wine education in the world with very high standards and a notoriously low exam pass rate. To qualify as a Master of Wine, students need to pass three exam components: 1) a three part written Practical exam that involves a series of three blind tastings (12 wines each, 36 wines in total), 2) a written Theory exam conducted in four parts over four consecutive days testing students' knowledge of viticulture, vinification, the business of wine and contemporary issues involving the wine industry and 3) a Dissertation which has recently morphed into the Research Paper. After passing all three parts of the exam, students must then sign the institute's "Code of Conduct" before becoming a recognized MW, thereafter being allowed to use the two signifying and legally protected letters after their names. More information is available on the IMoW website: www. mastersofwine.org

MATURE (AKA EVOLVED OR DEVELOPED) In wine-speak the word "mature" or term "grape maturity" can be used interchangeably with the words "ripe" or "ripeness" in reference to the last stages of grape evolution or ripening when the grapes are deemed suitable for harvest, which is somewhat subjective. (See the entry for "ripeness" and "Chapter 2 – Fruit Health & Ripeness" for more information.) As a verb it is frequently used in reference to the performance of the stage of winemaking that occurs after fermentation and prior to bottling – known as the "maturation", "rearing", "raising" or "élevage" (French) – usually to develop desired "mature" characters described as follows. Otherwise when used as a wine descriptor, a "mature" wine nose (in reference to aromas / flavours) is one in which the grape derived and winemaking derived aromas have transformed through wine ageing from their initial expressions, sometimes referred to as primary and secondary aromas respectively, into distinctively different characters. With barrel and/or bottle ageing grape and winemaking derived aromas may evolve due to slow oxidative and reductive reactions and possibly combine with other components in the wine and/or "marry-in" together, contributing to a mature wine nose; what is known in wine-speak as tertiary aromas. In such incidences the youthful grape derived fruity, floral and/or herbal aromas will open out and evolve into less overtly "fresh" characters resulting in dried fruit / dried herb notes and often spicy, savoury and/or nutty characters. Esters and aldehydes are also likely to contribute to the nose of an evolving wine and, when complimentary and in balance with the other components in the wine, add to the complexity of a mature nose. Note however that every wine has its day when it is at the peak of its drinking window (although this "peak" is largely subjective) after which it faces a period of plateau and eventually decline, whereby the grape derived aromas are all but unrecognizable and all that is left are oxidised and aldehydic notes. In the declining stages of maturity the nose may progressively be referred to as "tired", "drying / dried out" and finally "past-it". For more information see "maturation".

MATURATION (AKA REARING, RAISING OR ÉLEVAGE IN FRENCH)

Maturation is the stage of winemaking that occurs after fermentation and prior to bottling. This "maturing" of wines can be performed in barrels (oak or other material, new or old, large or small, etc.) or tanks made of other materials (i.e. concrete or stainless steel) for a period of time and can include processes such as lees ageing, racking, micro-oxygenation, fining, filtration, etc. The term implies that the winemaker is seeking to further develop the wine by promoting desired "mature" characters and changes such as softening of tannins and setting of colour usually with the goals of producing a better balanced and more complex wine. The alternative to maturation is "storage", which generally seeks to minimise any changes happening to the wine between fermentation and bottling through the use of inert, temperature controlled storage tanks and protective / inert gases such as CO_2. For more information see "mature", "oak", "lees ageing", "racking", "fining" and "filtration".

MENTAL WINE LIBRARY

Admittedly "mental wine library" is my own term coined for want of a better one that doesn't exist in conventional wine-speak. The concept here is nonetheless a very important one that separates novice tasters from experienced ones. The novice taster and the experienced taster may in fact have the same "natural abilities" to smell and taste. A novice can indeed have more natural talent; perhaps they have a more sensitive nose or more taste buds per square centimetre than the experienced taster. Be that as it may, natural talent will only get a taster so far towards being an experienced taster because that requires, well, experience. Tasters must go through the process of tasting a lot of different wines in order to gain experience. Throughout this process an experienced taster's mental wine library - his/her stored memories of many wines and the ability to recall the memories of relevant wines when tasting - develops into a skill that is equally as important as her/his natural abilities to smell and taste in order to produce a wine evaluation that takes on a whole new level, which is based upon contextual relevance. To be able to assess the fundamental wine quality factors with contextual relevance, wine professionals will need a considerable mental wine library, particularly when evaluating such factors as concentration, balance, complexity and nature of finish and especially when giving a wine rating.

MERCAPTANS (AKA THIOLS) Mercaptans include a wide range of odorous compounds resulting from the reduction of sulphur compounds during winemaking and/or ageing. Otherwise known as thiols, these grey-area fault compounds are incredibly varied, commonly manifesting themselves with notes of garlic, leeks, rotten vegetables, onions, dirty drains and sewage. Once these are formed in the wine they can be much more difficult to get rid of than simple hydrogen sulphide – a common by-product of fermentation. Some common mercaptan / thiol examples found in wine include methyl mercaptan (methanethiol, generally smelling of burnt rubber, garlic or rotten vegetables) and ethyl mercaptan (ethanethiol, generally smelling of cooked cabbage, onions and leeks). While most mercaptans / thiols are foul-smelling and to be avoided some can contribute appealing aromas and complexity to wines. Aromatic volatile thiols are a set of reduction compounds that are sometimes actively sought-after by winemakers who may even choose specialised cultured yeast that are targeted specifically to generate aromatic thiols from previously odourless aroma precursors in grapes. For example, 3-mercaptohexanol is the reduction thiol of a grape-derived aroma precursor in Sauvignon Blanc that lends an appealing grapefruit or passion fruit like smell to the finished wine. 2-Furanmethanethiol is another aromatic volatile thiol thought to be generated from aroma precursors found in Petit Manseng, Cabernet Sauvignon, Cabernet Franc and Merlot lending the aroma of roast coffee to some wines produced from these grapes. Also see "reduction" and "Chapter 1 – Wine Faults".

METHOXYPYRAZINES (AKA PYRAZINES)
Methoxypyrazines or pyrazines for short are volatile aroma molecules that can start forming in the berry at an early stage before veraison and which degrade as the berry ripens. Known for the green / leafy / herbal character they lend to wines, methoxypyrazines are more common in some grapes than others, especially prevalent in Sauvignon Blanc, where it is often valued, and its close relatives Cabernet Sauvignon and Cabernet Franc, where it is best avoided. Research indicates that the easiest way to avoid the formation of this

herbaceous methoxypyrazine character in grape skins and therefore minimise its presence in wines is to ripen the compounds out with plenty of sunshine on grapes (which can be aided by early shoot and leaf removal) and hang-time…but this is not always possible in all climates and/or vintages. Both under-cropping and over-cropping in the vineyard have been shown to exacerbate the methoxypyrazine problem. Note that 2-isopropyl-3-methoxypyrazine (better known by the acronym IPMP) is a specific type of methoxypyrazine found in some grape varieties and that is excreted by the Asian ladybird / lady beetle, which is the cause of "ladybird taint" (LBT).

METHYL MERCAPTAN (AKA METHANETHIOL) A reduction induced compound and form of foul odour generating mercaptan found occasionally in wines, methyl mercaptan generally smells of burnt rubber, garlic or rotten vegetables. Because of its unappealing nature it is usually considered a fault when present in wine at levels much above the detection threshold. See "mercaptans" for more information.

MID-PALATE (AKA MIDDLE PALATE) A common wine-speak term for the flavours that manifest themselves between the first impressions (when the wine enters the mouth) and the finish (after the wine has been swallowed or spat).

MINERAL / MINERALLY / MINERALITY The terms mineral, minerally and minerality are contentious wine-speak descriptors commonly applied to a range of characters in wine with little or no unanimous agreement as to the precise nature of those characters. That said, these are handy terms for conjuring smell / taste images of general rock, chalk, slate, stone, dirt, earthy or flinty smells and flavours that do in fact appear to exist in the wines produced from particular grape varieties and terroirs. But that some of the vine's surrounding dirt or components thereof might actually make it into the grapes and therefore wines, imparting what many critics refer to as minerality, is highly doubtful and has not been scientifically proven. What's more, some common "mineral" descriptors have actually been identified as winemaking generated. For example, it has been suggested that the "gun flint" character in some wines comes from the production of benezenemethanethiol from the breakdown of an amino acid during fermentation. Those chalky or crushed stone aromas in certain wines have been suggested to be due to low pH / high acidity. Earthiness could be due to microbial activity from geosmin or Brettanomyces. But (and with wine there's always at least one 'but') there are some soil borne elements such as potassium and sodium ions which have been found to transmigrate to the grapes and profoundly affect the wine style / character. They don't quite give wines that complex "minerally" character everyone loves, in fact the former lowers the acid of wine while that latter can make it detectably salty, but at least we can't say nothing at all comes from soils.

MOUTH-FEEL (AKA TEXTURE) A somewhat imprecise wine-speak term for the textural sensation that a wine creates in the mouth, mouth-feel is essentially a consideration of major tactile components such as tannins and viscosity. There is also evidence to suggest that mouth-feel / texture largely impacts the perception of flavour can render flavours seemingly more or less intense, although it does not change the flavour per se. Mouth-feel contributes to both the balance and complexity of a wine and is therefore an important wine quality consideration.

MUST In wine-speak must is a winemaking term for grape juice that has not yet undergone fermentation.

MS See "Master Sommelier".

MW See "Master of Wine".

N

NATURAL FERMENTATION See "wild yeast".

NATURAL WINE To date, there is no legal definition of the wine-speak term "natural wine", though the implication is that it is a catch-all for wine that is made naturally. Technically of course this isn't possible; grapes don't ever actually ferment on the vine and drop effortlessly as wine into receiving vessels like truer natural products such as honey

that can be consumed straight from a honeycomb. Some human intervention is necessary to make even basic "natural wines" and so it has become understood that natural winemaking involves at best minimal human intervention, the degree to which is completely subjective. Usually natural wine proponents embrace organic or biodynamic grape growing methods and go so far as to shun the use of artificially instilled chemicals in winemaking and/or gratuitous use of technology to enhance the character (smell, taste, texture and quality). Contentious issues amongst less dogmatic critical factions include the prohibition of common antioxidant and antimicrobial additions and ameliorations including added SO_2, cultured yeast, acidification and chaptalisation, arguably to the detriment of wine stability, minimum standards of quality assurance and the pursuit of fundamental wine quality factors.

NATURAL YEAST See "wild yeast".

NOBLE ROT See "botrytis cinerea".

O

OAK Oak barrels and vats are used in both the fermentation and ageing or maturation of wine. Oak vat or barrel fermentation and especially maturation allows for slow oxygenation of wines and new(er) oak imparts tannins (see "Chapter 2" on "Tasting Tannins"), and flavours (see "Chapter 5 – Complexity") that are leached from the contact between the wine and the surface of the wood. Around 600 different species of oak tree with the genus "Quercus" exist in the world. Dozens are thought to be used in winemaking, although there are three species that are mainly used and therefore of major importance: Quercus robur, Quercus sessilus (A.K.A. Quercus petraea and Quercus sessiliflora) and Quercus alba. More commonly wine professionals refer simply French oak, which includes the first two species just mentioned, and American oak, mainly consisting of Quercus alba. Each of these oak species possesses different characters and attributes directly related to variations in the wood, all of which play a part in the interaction between the wood and the wine. Specifically, it is the differences between the varying textures and the grains that the species offer that determine their suitability to winemakers seeking a specific contribution from oak ageing. The type of oak used, the cooperage techniques employed to produce the barrel and how the barrel is used (e.g. racking and topping-up regimes) all play a role in the flavours, texture and style of a barrel matured wine. Furthermore the toasting level of the barrels as well as the age and size of barrels and the period of time wine spends in contact with the oak have a significant impact on the amount of flavours and tannins the wine will pick-up. Much more information about the use of oak barrels and their contribution to wine complexity during maturation is available in the dedicated oak textbox in "Chapter 5 – Complexity". Alternatives to oak barrel aging include the use of oak staves, chips / cubes and essence. Generally speaking staves – simply planks of oak wood placed within wine tanks for a period of time - when of a high quality and incorporated with various means of slow oxygenation to mimic barrel fermentation and/or aging can produce very good quality results in terms of tannin and flavour integration at a fraction of the cost of oak barrels. Oak chips / cubes (literally chips or cubes of oak that are usually encased in a "tea bag" and dunked for a period in burgeoning wine) are an even cheaper and easier alternative but the results can be variable and usually stand-out because the flavour pick-up is easily overdone, sometimes imparting a tell-tale "sawdust" character to wines, therefore chips are rarely if ever used in the production of fine wines. Oak essence can provide oak flavour but none of the other oak benefits such as slow oxygenation or tannic contribution, often yielding clumsy results of disappointing quality. Normally only the cheapest, mass-production wines are treated with oak essence.

OENOCOCCUS OENI This is a genus and species of bacteria of major importance in winemaking, as the name suggests (Oeno being the Greek goddess of wine), since it is mainly responsible for conducting malolactic fermentation. This bacterium is primarily used because of its efficiency to convert malic acid into lactic acid and its ability to produce the desirable by-product diacetyl.

OLD VINES (AKA VIEILLES VIGNES IN FRENCH)
"Old vines" is a common wine marketing term of nebulous meaning. There is no universally agreed definition of how old "old" is. It is usually used to insinuate that wines produced of old vines are of higher quality than those of younger vines, though beyond a basic need for a certain amount of vine age to stabilise vine productivity (yields) there is little if any scientific evidence that older vines make better wine. In the EU and other wine producing countries of world, vines usually need be at least 3 years of age to produce wine labelled with a delimited region's name. After around 20-25 years of age vine productivity begins to be significantly reduced at which stage the grower may grub-up and replant the vineyard, if certain minimum yields are sought. Yet although the 25 year+ vine may become less productive, it is said to produce smaller quantities of more concentrated grapes, which can (but not necessarily) be linked to quality. Older vines also have larger and often deeper reaching root systems that are more efficient at regulating the supply of water and, along with their larger cordons (permanent wood), have greater stores of carbohydrates to help stabilise the vines during difficult vintages (e.g. drought and periods of excessive heat), which could offer a ripening and therefore quality advantage. Vines can and do survive to produce wines for 150 years or more. For example, in phylloxera free areas of Australia such as the Barossa and Eden Valleys there are vineyards containing vines of such age.

ORGANIC In the context of wine production, the term "organic" usually refers to organic grape growing and often (but not always) does not apply to winemaking techniques. Organic viticulture involves a somewhat strict, legally regulated set of farming principals. However throughout the world where the use of the word "organic" is legally protected regulations vary. In order to certify a vineyard and/or wine label as organic, the producer will need to seek certification by recognized institutions within the country of production. Generally speaking, organic grape growing and winemaking (if applicable) preclude the use of artificial chemicals such as chemical fertilizers and synthetic pesticides in the vineyard and chemical additives in the winery. There are exceptions in cases where naturally occurring chemicals may be applied, such as the limited use of sulphur and copper spraying in vineyards for the production of wines from "organically grown grapes". Usually a vineyard will need to go through a 3 year conversion period of documented and randomly tested adherence to the national legal guidelines before certification can be granted. "Organic wine" (includes winemaking) in most countries bans the use of chemical additives in wine throughout winemaking, including the most ubiquitously used antioxidant / antimicrobial: sulphites (sulphur dioxide). Because it can be very difficult to produce a stable wine of quality without sulphites, "organic wines" are not very common.

ORGANOLEPTIC Organoleptic analysis of grapes, must or wine involves sensory perception to determine ripeness, style, stability and/or quality. Therefore a taster will sample the grapes, must or wine using the senses of sight, smell, taste and touch to draw conclusions. This is in contrast to laboratory analysis, which will involve scientific techniques such as assays and GC / MS to determine the chemical make-up of wine.

OUTDATED WINE JARGON This is my phrase for wine terms that are past their sell-by date. These largely include old-school words, comparisons or phrases that were spawned in more conservative and chauvinistic times and when we knew a lot less about wine and especially wine chemistry than we do now. Throw-back terms that I hate because they are meaningless, misleading, euphemistic or just plain pretentious include: old world, new world, masculine, feminine, bouquet, charming, manly, foursquare, mawkish, mellow, stringy, suave, supple, gout de terroir, honest, needs food and corky (as opposed to corked).

OVER-EXTRACTED A nebulous wine-speak term that generally refers to overzealous use of extraction techniques (e.g. cold soak, pigeage, pumping over, etc.) in the winery resulting in a poorly balanced wine that suffers from excessive components, most notably tannins and anthocyanins or fruit concentration that isn't matched by structure. It may also refer to the quality of tannins as being harsh and bitter usually as a consequence of prolonged skin contact, which can draw out the overly astringent compounds, and/or extract bitter catechins from prolonged contact with the seeds or over-use of stems. Occasionally over-extraction proclamations may simply refer to under-ripe (overly astringent and bitter) tannins in the wine especially when the wine has been artificially concentrated using techniques such as reverse osmosis.

OXIDATION A grey-area fault, oxidation - as opposed to an "oxidative" character forged from the deliberate "oxygenation" of wine during maturation - generally refers to a fault resulting from oxygen exposure / dosing gone too far and /or happening at the wrong time. One of the initial and most obvious signs of oxidation is the premature deepening and browning in colour of a white wine (i.e. the wine goes from a pale lemon yellow to an increasingly deeper straw, golden and then brown colour) or a red wine that begins to go orange or brown in the rim at an unusually early stage. However be aware that these occurrences can be natural consequences of the grape variety or winemaking. For example, the red grape Nebbiolo is notorious for going orange / brown early-on in its bottle development and oak barrel ageing of a white wine often deepens the colour. The confirmation of the deleterious impact of oxidation is in the smelling and tasting. When primary fruit characters in wine are exposed to oxygen either during wine processing or storage (e.g. once the bottle is opened or when a bottle's closure is compromised and air is allowed inside) they become dulled and/ or faded. Examples of the aromatic profile of an oxidised wine may include the smells of old apple core, straw, leather, dried berries / fruits, raisins or nuts when clearly these are not part of the wine's intended style. Furthermore the palate will lack freshness and vibrancy. In more advanced stages of oxidation the wine is likely to develop volatile acidity (see below) and/or an aldehydic character from the formation acetaldehyde caused by the aforementioned oxidation of the alcohol. Apart from those wines that are deliberately made to an oxidised style, another grey-area with oxidation is that many of the characters just mentioned will naturally develop over time during bottle ageing and as part of the way a wine may mature into a more complex, evolved, or mature nose, commonly referred to in our somewhat outdated jargon as a "bouquet". But certainly when present on a young wine, particularly one destined for early drinking such as most Beaujolais wines, Pinot Grigios or Sauvignon Blancs, oxidation is likely to dull and flatten the character of the wine, detracting from the wine's quality and constituting a fault.

OXIDATIVE / OXIDATIVE HANDLING / OXIDATIVE WINEMAKING Oxidative is a term used in reference to the deliberate employment of oxygenation during winemaking (e.g. oxidative handling) in order achieve a desired so-named style. Wines said to possess an oxidative character are usually forged from deliberate "oxygenation", usually during maturation, to express that particular style. For more information see "oxygenation" and "rancio".

OXIDISED An oxidised wine is one that suffers from the wine fault "oxidation".

OXYGENATION There are a lot of positive quality benefits to controlled oxygenation - the dosing of wine with oxygen. A great many red wines and some whites such as Chardonnay are barrel aged, which is a process that allows slow, deliberate exposure to small amounts of oxygen. Racking (moving the wine from one container to another) and micro-oxygenation (pumping tiny amounts of oxygen into the wine) are means of exposing the wine to even more oxygen. Slow oxygenation can change the primary or fruity aromas in wine into less vibrant yet more complex aromas and flavours including esters, which are formed of acids and alcohols combined in the presence of oxygen. The tannin compounds in red wines are encouraged by oxygen to combine or "polymerise", becoming larger units that appear softer in the mouth and eventually fall out of solution as sediment, resulting in a suppler / less tannic wine. Prolonged exposure to oxygen can further result in oxidative or "rancio" characters arising from the evolution of fruit aromas and formation of aldehydes such acetaldehyde (the oxidation of the primary alcohol in wine, ethanol). Some of these desirable descriptors include: nutty, dried fruit / berry, bruised apple, caramelised and raisin, characters that define distinctive wine styles such as Tawny Port, Vin Santo, Tokaji, Oloroso Sherry, Vin Jaune, Rutherglen Muscat, Madeira and Banyuls.

P

PETRICHOR A somewhat newly discovered scent, petrichor has been described as the smell of dirt or more specifically rain on dry dirt / dusty earth. In wine it is thought to be derived from incidences of geosmin contamination of grapes / bunches, occurring in the vineyard.

pH Representing the proportion of H+ to OH- ions in a liquid, in a broad chemical context pH is essentially used to measure how acidic or alkaline a solution is. The pH of grape juice and wine - generally in the range of 3.0 to 3.8 - are important quality considerations for several reasons. Perhaps one of the most important aspects is that lower pH levels (i.e. more acidic) offer increased wine stability in terms of protection from microbial and oxidation spoilage. Plus the effectiveness of SO_2 increases at lower pH levels meaning less SO_2 additions are necessary. Because of its close (but not exact) correlation with the total acidity level in wines, pH also effects wine flavour and balance contributing pleasant crispness to white wines at the lower end of the scale (less than 3.4), although usually a mid-range pH level (3.4-3.6) is more desirable for reds so that they don't appear overly tart. For red wines pH further impacts the hue and stability of wine colour, manifesting more stable brighter red colours at the lower pH range and duller blue-purple colours at the higher pH end.

PHENOLIC RIPENESS (AKA PHENOLIC MATURITY) A term often used interchangeably with "physiological ripeness", phenolic ripeness somewhat more specifically relates to the ripeness levels of the phenolic components (e.g. tannins and anthocyanins / colour compounds) in grape skins, seeds and stems, and is monitored in the run-up to harvest. Phenolic ripeness is more commonly and easily gauged organoleptically, as physiological ripeness monitoring implies, or laboratory testing can be performed to measure for anthocyanin and tannin content in skins and catechin content in seeds.

PHENOLICS / POLYPHENOLIC COMPOUNDS
See "polyphenols".

PHYLLOXERA This is a tiny, pernicious insect that feeds on the sap of grapevine roots and leaves. Infestations are nearly impossible to combat with pesticides since the nymphs can live below the ground feeding on the roots. Once a vineyard has fallen victim to infestation there is usually no cure as the insects will eventually strangle the vines by cutting off nutrient and water supplies. Indigenous to North America, American vine species such as Vitis riparia and Vitis rupestris have developed natural defences to phylloxera. However these species do not generally make the most palatable wines whereas the European species Vitis vinifera, used throughout the world for quality wine production, has no defence against phylloxera. In the late 1800s phylloxera found its way to Europe, devastating nearly every great vineyard throughout the continent at that time. The only viable solution to the plague was to graft American phylloxera resistant rootstocks to the bottom of Vitis vinifera vines and to this day this is the only way of controlling the damage and spread of phylloxera. Thanks to more recent quarantine regulations imposed at borders around the world, there remain some (but not many) areas of the wine producing world that are still phylloxera free such as South Australia and Chile.

PHYSIOLOGICAL RIPENESS (AKA PHYSIOLOGICAL MATURITY) A trendy though somewhat vaguely defined concept, physiological ripeness is a fairly new wine-speak term that mostly considers the ripeness of components beyond the basic sugar and acid levels, sugar / acid ratio and pH. Nowadays with must ameliorations (adjustments) such as chaptalization, adding water, acidification and deacidification commonly and often legally practiced where and when grapes are lacking, the focus in the last 20 or so years has turned to components that are not so easy if impossible to manipulate in the winery. These include: anthocyanins / colour compounds, tannins (in the skins, stems and seeds) and aroma / flavour compounds. The word "physiological" presumably has relevance here since in the early days when it was first coined with "ripeness" it involved tossing out the refractometer (used to measure sugar content) and pH meter and physically sampling the berries organoleptically in the run-up to harvest to assess the ripeness. Growers might therefore test for physiological ripeness by going out into the vineyard and randomly tearing apart selected grapes to sample the texture of the pulp, the feel and relative bitterness of the skins, the crunchiness and taste of the seeds and the brittleness of the stems, etc. This term is not generally considered to be exactly the same "phenolic ripeness" but it is often used interchangeably.

PLASTIC CORK See "synthetic closure".

POLYMERISATION / POLYMERISE(D) /
Polymerisation involves a series of chemical reactions joining smaller, molecularly similar sub-units into larger compounds. In wine-speak this term is usually used in reference to the polymerisation of tannins, which naturally occurs over time and is aided by the presence of oxygen. As small tannin sub-units increase in size they appear texturally softer and rounder in the mouth. Eventually polymerised tannins can become so large that they precipitate out of solution contributing to sediment in a maturation vessel (e.g. barrel) or in the bottom / side of a bottle of wine.

POLYPHENOLS (AKA PHENOLICS, POLYPHENOLIC COMPOUNDS) The term polyphenols refers to a structural class of compounds that consist of a number of phenols (organic compounds). Tannins are types of polyphenols and in reference to wines the words tannins and polyphenols (or phenolics for short) are largely interchangeable. However there are other notable types of polyphenols in wine, including anthocyanins (colour compounds) and aromatic acids.

POWDERY MILDEW (AKA OIDIUM) Powdery mildew is a fungal disease that starts in the green tissues of the vine and therefore affects ripening and yields. In worst cases powdery mildew can spread to grape bunches. It mainly affects the vine's ability to ripen bunches possibly rendering under-ripe characters in wines although in severe cases it can cause bunch rot with similar effects as detrimental Botrytis cinerea infections.

PREMATURE OXIDATION (AKA PREMOX)
Premature oxidation does what its name suggests: oxidises a wine before its time or at least renders bottles dried-out and "dead" ahead of many critics' best-before estimates and that the track-records for a wine's aging potential would suggest. Recent research by Denis Dubourdieu and Valerie Lavigne at Bordeaux University suggests premox is the very real prodigal son spawned of wine's ever-present oxidation tendencies and, those paving stones to damnation, winemakers' good intentions. The trends to sew cover crops and avoid nutrient additions in the vineyard are partly at fault because it seems as these can starve vines and grapes of nitrogen, which is important for the grapes' production of the natural anti-ageing compound glutathione and for ensuring a smooth and complete fermentation and ultimately a more stable wine. Harvesting riper / higher-sugar grapes with lower acid levels and increased pHs combined with a tendency to add less SO_2 and mature more wines for longer in barrel may have played to recent consumer preference trends but in doing so have further upset the delicate ageing balance. The use of cork probably doesn't help either. Other research also performed by Dubourdieu and Lavigne identifies the lactone sotolon as one of the major offending premox aroma compounds, its precursor produced in significant quantities by the oxidative degradation of ascorbic acid as well as a by-product of certain yeast strains. Continued research also by Dubourdieu seems to suggest that this is not just a blight affecting whites and that many red wines, especially from warmer / riper years like 2009 Bordeaux, could also be affected.

PRIMARY AROMAS / CHARACTERS In common wine-speak primary aromas are grape derived aromas manifested in the early stages of a wine's life (i.e. soon after bottling), giving rise to distinctively fruity, vegetal, floral and/or herbal aromas and including some spice characters such as pepper (e.g. rotundone, a compound common to Syrah). They should have the ability to be notably linked back to the vine variety and/or clone as well as certain distinguishable terroir elements such as climate, weather, vineyard, etc. They are therefore distinctive from secondary or winemaking derived aromas. Furthermore as wines age in bottle the primary aromas will either fade altogether, after which the wine will have passed its drinking window and is "dead", or develop further due to slow oxidative and reductive reactions into mature or evolved grape derived characters (possibly combining with other components in the wine and/or "marrying-in" with the winemaking derived aromas), resulting in what is referred to as tertiary aromas or, as they say in somewhat outdated wine jargon, a "bouquet".

PROP PROP (short for the compound 6-n-propylthiouracil) is bitter substance used to lace a tab / small piece of paper for the testing of "supertasters". Once placed on a subject's tongue, supertasters will find the bitterness of PROP distasteful whereas average tasters may think it's not so bad and "non-tasters" won't taste it at all.

PROTECTIVE HANDLING See "reductive handling".

PROTEIN HAZE Protein haze is a superficial fault that doesn't affect the smell / taste of the wine but can render it with a distinctly cloudy appearance. This can happen when residual protein molecules that are so small they are not visible in wine polymerise (combine), particularly when exposed to warmer storage conditions, to form larger visible particles, which give wine a cloudy appearance that is usually not advisable to rectify through filtration once it occurs. Red grapes generally contain far less heat unstable proteins than white grapes. Also the polyphenols in red wines usually precipitate protein molecules out of red wines during fermentation as they combine with tannins to form part of the sediment (lees) that can be separated from the wine after fermentation and/or lees ageing have completed. Therefore protein haze is far less common in red wines. Most white wines are stabilised against protein haze by fining them with bentonite. Some grape varieties such as Sauvignon Blanc are particularly prone to high levels of unstable proteins and therefore bentonite fining is pretty much a requirement. However some fine wine white wine makers avoid or at least minimise such fining if at all possible as it is felt that that over-fining with bentonite can strip some of the nuances from the wine that give it complexity. Most quality conscious winemakers nowadays test wines for protein instability prior to bentonite additions to minimise over-fining…but that is not to say that routine use and occasional overuse does not exist. In drastic cases it is possible to filter out protein particles using ultrafiltration (an extreme form of cross-flow filtration) but this is mainly used as a cure rather than prevention as this level of filtration also strips out some phenolic and aroma compounds.

PYRAZINES See "methoxypyrazines".

Q

QUALITY / PRICE RATIO (QPR) Quality / price ratio (QPR) is a somewhat scientific way of calculating a wine's value for money. It specifically relates the quality of a wine to the price that's being charged for it and rates it according to value. Our modern practice of allocating wine quality scores (see "Wine Ratings" in Chapter 9 and the entry in this Glossary) has made this rating a little easier to calculate, though it's far from an exact science because ultimately something is only worth what you're willing to pay for it. For more information and a specific example of how a QPR calculation can work see "Chapter 7 – Supporting Quality Factors" in the sections "Value for Money" and "*What is wine quality / price ratio (QPR) and how can I work it out?*".

R

RACKING Racking is a winemaking operation that involves moving a wine from one vessel to another for the major purpose of separating the wine from any sediment that may have naturally settled in the bottom of the original vessel. Vessels may include tanks (stainless steel, concrete or wooden) or oak barrels, although the term is usually coined after fermentation, when the new wine is racked off its lees, and during barrel maturation when wine is racked from one barrel to another. The journey from the original vessel to the receiving vessel can be achieved in different ways to the effect of either of two additional aims: 1) protective handling (keeping wine from oxidising by careful pumping using inert gases such as CO_2, nitrogen and argon and maintaining cooler temperatures during the procedure) and 2) oxidative handling (allowing a somewhat controlled, to the extent that it is controllable, amount of oxygen to be instilled in the wine during the racking procedure. This is usually executed with a wine pump, without the use of inert gas, but rather allowing air to be incorporated with the wine as it gushes into the receiving vessel – sometimes referred to as "splash racking").

RANCIO From Spanish, rancio can be translated as "rancid" but this English meaning and certainly its negative connotations are far from accurate. It exists in both Spanish and French as a wine-speak term in reference to an oxidative or maderized and usually fortified style of winemaking and wines, and its meaning has been thus been adopted by the English speaking wine community. Rancio can be used to describe the aromatic profile of classic sweet wine styles such as Madeira, Tawny Port, Banyuls, Oloroso Sherry, Vin Santo, Vin de Paille and Tokaji and some dry wine styles such as Vin Jaune and dry Olorosos. Usually used as a descriptor of multiple smells, its character is generally considered complex including scents that can include raisins, dried fruits, nuts, caramel, honey, maple syrup, treacle / molasses, burnt sugar and butterscotch. Sotolon, a lactone marker for oxidised wines and premature oxidation, is usually present and revered in the aromatic profile of rancio wine styles.

RANDOM OXIDATION A topical and contentious issue relating to the continued used of corks as a wine bottle closure, "random oxidation" is caused by nature of tiny imperfections on the surfaces (different for each cork) of the cork and / additionally whereby over the course of 15-40 years+ the cork will gradually lose its elasticity and therefore its airtight seal allowing oxygen into the bottle, which oxidises bottles at varying rates. This means that every single bottle of wine "aged" under cork will be slightly different in its state of oxidation / maturity. For more information see and "oxidation".

RATINGS See "wine ratings".

REDUCED / REDUCED SULPHUR COMPOUND A broad wine-speak word used in reference to a wine suffering from reduction. It is mainly used in a negative context suggesting a faulty wine.

REDUCTION Generally considered a wine fault though firmly within the grey-area fault category, reduction in a wine usually first occurs during the winemaking and continues during bottle ageing. In a nutshell, reduction is the opposite of oxidation; it's a chemical reaction within the wine that happens in the absence of oxygen. The main concern is the reduction of sulphur, an element common in wine (both naturally present and added), and common sulphur containing, fermentation by-product compounds such as hydrogen sulphide (H_2S). Further reduction of H_2S can result in more complex reduction compounds such as mercaptans and sulphides. For more information, see "mercaptans", "sulphides", "dimethyl sulphide" and "Chapter 1 – Wine Faults".

REDUCTIVE / HANDLING / WINEMAKING (AKA PROTECTIVE HANDLING / WINEMAKING)
Reductive is an adjective describing an oxygen deprived situation or environment. The exclusion of oxygen as a stylistic tool is known as reductive handling. In "Chapter 1" reduction is discussed as a grey-area fault, but the meaning of "reductive handling" is different in that it does not refer specifically to the reduction of sulphur compounds in the absence of oxygen in wine but the preservation of primary or grape derived fruit characters by avoiding contact with oxygen. This can be achieved most commonly through the protective uses of inert gases (e.g. CO_2, Nitrogen and Argon), inert / stainless steel tanks and cooler handling and storage temperatures. Reductive handling is mostly practiced on aromatic white grape varieties such as Riesling or Muscat or those where intense fruitiness is desired, such as Sauvignon Blanc. And it is precisely this intensity of aromas / flavours that give reductive handling away on the nose and palate when you're tasting.

RESIDUAL SUGAR (AKA RS) Residual sugar is strictly speaking the amount of sugar remaining in wine after fermentation however the term may also refer to any sugar present in wine that has been added after fermentation using the winemaking practices of back-blending, süssreserve additions or dosage. The amount of residual sugar in a wine is usually reported as grams per litre. For more information see "sugars".

RETRONASAL OLFACTION / SMELL The detection of aromas while drinking or eating via the oral cavity located at the back of the throat is known as "retronasal olfaction". When sniffing odorous items (i.e. volatile compounds) through our noses we smell in the traditionally recognised sense of the term, technically known as "orthonasal olfaction". But if the act of smelling is combined with our sense of taste within the mouth the result is a very different effect from smelling or tasting alone, one which we have come to understand as flavour. Because we can only actually recognize five basic tastes with our tongues, in fact most of the flavours we "taste" in this manner result from retronasal smell. Our brains tend to combine the effects of our 2 senses into 1, which we have come to know and value as the flavours that we "taste" even though the real heroes here are our noses and our remarkable sense of smell!

REVERSE OSMOSIS (AKA RO) Reverse osmosis essentially functions as a filtration device though it works differently than a standard filter. It possesses the ability to separate out the smallest of microscopic compounds even down to molecular dimensions. Based on the cross-flow filtration principal, it works by passing the wine tangentially over a semipermeable membrane. Pressure is created on the "wine" side of the membrane to cause very small particles (determined by the pore size of the holes in the membrane) through to the side of less pressure, ultimately performing "osmotic" effect in reverse. In a greater context it is a method used to purify or desalinate water, though with regards to wine is mainly used for one of two purposes: 1) to concentrate must by removing water molecules or 2) to dealcoholize wine by removing ethanol and water molecules after which this small amount of the concentrated, dealcoholized wine can be reconstituted with pure water and blended back with a larger batch of wine to produce a wine of lower alcohol. Reverse osmosis is also occasionally used to remove volatile acidity or more recently smoke taint or the major by-products of brettanomyces (4-ethylphenol and 4-ethylguaiacol). While reverse osmosis is a very advanced not to mention expensive piece of equipment, it is not exact in what it removes from wine since the removal is based on particle size, so there is probably some loss of other desirable components besides the main targets such as water, ethanol, 4-EP, 4-EG or VA based on molecular dimensions. Although legal to use in most major wine regions for particular purposes and not uncommon in those at the pinnacle of wine quality production such as Bordeaux and Napa Valley, the major criticisms against reverse osmosis are the use of excessive manipulation, the possible stripping out of some aroma compounds that contribute to complexity and, in the case of must concentration, the concentration of any under-ripe and harsh components that may exist in the must such as pyrazines and unresolved tannins.

RIPENESS / GRAPE MATURITY The ripening of grape berries refers to the evolution of wine grapes from flowering / fruit set until they are harvested. "Ripeness" or simply "ripe" are terms used in reference to the last stages of grape evolution or ripening when the grapes are deemed suitable for harvest. A concern of major quality importance otherwise known as "grape / fruit maturity", the ripeness of the grapes at the time of harvest is to a certain extent subjective. What may be considered an ideal level of ripeness by one winemaker might be over-ripe to another and under-ripe to still another. Furthermore, optimal ripeness greatly depends upon the style of wine being produced. For example the ripeness of grapes used for high quality sparkling wines would in most cases be considered far too under-ripe to make a still wine. The best sweet wine grapes conversely are generally ripened to sugar levels that would equate to alcohol levels too high for balanced dry styles. To understand how ripeness can impact style, balance, complexity and ultimately quality, it's important to have a basic grasp of what chemical changes occur both within the berry's flesh and in its protective outer layer, the skin, as the berry approaches maturity. The fundamental changes relating to ripeness are followed by the grower and/or winemaker particularly after véraison and in the run-up to harvest by monitoring and often measuring the ripening progress of key maturity indicator grape components including: acids, sugars, tannins and aroma / flavour compounds. For more information see "Chapter 2: Fruit Health & Ripeness".

ROTUNDONE Rotundone is a naturally occurring aromatic compound present in some herbs, spices, flowers and fruits. Most notably it is the compound that gives black and white peppercorns their distinctively "peppery" scents. It is also found in Syrah / Shiraz grapes, naturally instilling a distinct peppercorn smell to some wines produced from these grapes. Research conducted by the AWRI implies that a significant proportion (20%) of individuals tested for the ability to smell rotundone cannot detect it at all, suggesting that it is common as a specific anosmia.

S

SACCHAROMYCES CEREVISIAE With a direct reference to "sugar" in the prefix of its genus (Sacchar), Saccharomyces cerevisiae is indeed a sugar hungry yeast species that includes many strains ideal for converting sugar into alcohol (ethanol). It is the major species used for winemaking although is used in beer brewing too and, because it also generates large amounts of carbon dioxide, certain strains are used as baker's yeast. Thus far hundreds of different strains of have been isolated and while not all are suitable for winemaking, many are with varying tolerances to yeast performance factors such as temperature, level of sugar, level of alcohol, level of SO_2 and pH. The differing strains also account for different aromatic characters generated in wines and some "off" aromas or faults such as H_2S and VA. Most cultured yeast are selected strains of Saccharomyces cerevisiae. See "cultured yeast" and "yeast" for more information.

SCORES See "wine ratings".

SCREW CAP In recent years screw caps have become _the_ alternative wine bottle closure to cork if not _the_ closure of choice in some areas of the world such as Australia and New Zealand. Continued research indicates that they not only eradicate some of the common problems associated with cork – chiefly cork taint and random oxidation – but offer an effective long-term seal to minimise and control rates of oxygen ingress during bottle ageing, if not prevent it altogether. What's more, screw caps are also reasonably inexpensive, easy to open and resealable. Usually formed from an aluminium alloy possessing an inner liner composed of a tin oxygen barrier, a compressible plastic or paper wad and with an inert film contacting the wine, the seal is created physically by compressing the liner firmly against the rim of the bottle top during bottling. Early complaints against screw caps included incidences of reduction largely due to winemakers not adjusting SO_2 levels at bottling to account for less oxygen ingress than cork and the seals of the screw caps failing when bottles were knocked during transport. Both problems seemed to have largely been solved now. One of the best known and most successful brands of screw caps for servicing the wine industry is Stelvin (Amcor). Stelvin has recently released a range of screw caps that allow controlled oxygen transfer between the atmosphere and wines, possessing variable liners with different, controlled breathability levels.

SECONDARY AROMAS / CHARACTERS In accepted wine-speak secondary aromas generally refer to winemaking derived aromas and flavours. In other words these are aromas and flavours that are created or mainly created through winemaking processes as opposed to grape derived characters (primary aromas) and maturation or bottle aged characters (tertiary aromas). Some professionals consider secondary aromas to include those characters derived from barrel ageing / maturation prior to bottling while others consider these processes contribute to tertiary aromas rather than secondary aromas. Regardless of where the secondary vs tertiary line is drawn, what is agreed is that secondary aromas are notably different than distinctly fruity, herbal, vegetal, spice or floral notes directly associated with certain grapes and their level of ripeness. Common winemaking characters include those derived specifically from the use of sulphur dioxide and other additives, oak ageing, malolactic fermentation and lees contact. These could also include grape derived characters / components that are transformed so dramatically through fermentation as to have lost their detectable association with the grapes such as ethanol, higher alcohols, fatty acids, volatile acids and esters. As part and parcel of the winemaking, these secondary characters can be considered to include those grey-area faults such as volatile

acidity, brettanomyces and reduction. With barrel and/or bottle ageing winemaking derived aromas may develop further due to slow oxidative and reductive reactions and evolve / combine with other components in the wine and/or marry-in with the grape derived aromas, contributing to what is known in wine-speak as tertiary aromas or, in somewhat outdated wine jargon, as a "bouquet".

SEEDS (GRAPE) Grapes used in winemaking (predominately Vitis vinifera) usually contain 1-4 seeds per berry. Because of the types of tannins they possess and bitter oil they release if crushed, the use of seeds during winemaking is not sought but their presence is hard to avoid particularly in red winemaking whereby crushed berries are left to macerate: skins, must, seeds and all. In this context seeds can be very difficult to remove from the macerating mass and therefore they are generally tolerated, their potential contribution taken into account and necessitating efforts to be made to avoid over-extraction of seed tannins. Seed tannins largely consist of catechins and epicatechins with relatively very low degrees of polymerisation compared to grape skin or even stem tannins. Their harsh, bitter nature is avoided during winemaking by minimising contact during maceration and level of pressing. Like grape stems, seeds ripen from a green colour / harsher tannin sensation (largely due to their more extractable nature) to a less extractable nature and brown colour / apparently softer feel with increased hang-time on the vine.

SETTLING (AKA DÉBOURBAGE IN FRENCH) Settling is a winemaking term mostly used to refer to the juice clarification practice of allowing freshly pressed grape juice (must) of white grapes to "settle" in a tank for a period of time, seeking to precipitate any solid matter that may be suspended in the juice to the bottom of the tank as sediment. This procedure pretty much necessitates that the tank be chilled during the settling period, not just to help protect the juice from oxidation and microbial activity but to facilitate the physical settling of solids. Once the solid matter has separated to the desired degree, the clarified juice can be drawn off from the solids in preparation for fermentation. Since red wines tend to ferment for a period on their skins, juice settling (débourbage in French) can really only be practiced on white wines. However sometimes the English word "settling" is used as a catch-all term for the practice of allowing juice or wine to sit for a period and allow the suspended solids to precipitate to the bottom of a vessel (tank or wine barrel). In which case, settling may be considered to occur after red wine fermentation and maceration, when lees and post-fermenting debris settle to the bottom of a tank and the wine is drawn off (racked). Other examples include after barrel maturation when wine is racked off the "settled" lees in the barrel and after fining operations. Settling is the alternative to much faster and more volume efficient but harsher methods of clarifying juice from suspended solids, such as centrifugation and/or filtering, although settling is generally considered to yield higher quality juice or wine than either centrifugation or filtering since these methods can cause oxidation and stripping of aromatic compounds, respectively.

SO₂ See "sulphur dioxide".

SOTOLON (AKA SOTOLONE) Sotolon is an aromatic lactone (a type of ester) most commonly linked to the spice fenugreek but it is also found in a wide range of food and beverage products including curry, caramel, rum, cigar tobacco and maple syrup. In the realm of wine it can be a lactone marker for oxidised wines and premature oxidation. Or it is usually present and revered in the aromatic profile of botrytised wines and rancio wine styles, especially vin jaune and wines produced with flor yeast such as flor sherries.

SPONTANEOUS FERMENTATION See "wild yeast".

STABILISATION / STABILISE / STABILITY
Stabilisation is a winemaking term referring to a collection of practices that help to produce a finished wine that has a degree of protection against certain faults and spoilage changes, which can occur during wine shipping and storage. Two major categories of stabilisation techniques are: 1) protection against physical changes (e.g. oxidation, tartrates and protein haze) and 2) protection against microbial spoilage (e.g. refermentation by yeast, brettanomyces and volatile acidity). Common means of stabilising wines include SO₂ additions,

fining, filtration and cold stabilisation. For more information see "cold stabilisation", "oxidation", "tartrates", "protein haze", "yeast", "brettanomyces", "volatile acidity", "SO₂", "fining" and "filtration".

STELVIN Stelvin is one of the best known and most successful brands of screw caps for servicing the wine industry is Stelvin (Amcor). Stelvin has recently released a range of screw caps that allow controlled oxygen transfer between the atmosphere and wines, possessing variable liners with different, controlled breathability levels. For more information, see "screw caps".

STEMS Stems are the "woody" parts of grape bunches that collectively maintain the bunch as a unit and in winemaking are considered to include the stalks or pedicels, which connect the berry to the stem. In most cases stems are removed as one of the first steps in winemaking, these days by employing the use of a "crusher / destemmer" machine that does precisely what the name describes, with modern devises allowing for varying degrees of crushing to the extent that some machines can yield berries that are more or less intact (if a whole berry character without the stems is sought). Berries can also be removed from the stems by hand in order to maintain their integrity but this is very labour and time intensive, and therefore in most cases prohibitively costly. Otherwise grapes can be whole bunch pressed – common with Chardonnay and for making styles where skin contact is avoided (e.g. white sparkling wines made from red grapes) – whereby stems play very little role apart from providing drainage channels within the press. Prolonged contact between grape juice or wine and stems is usually avoided because grape stems contain high levels of tannins consisting mainly of proanthocyanidins and catechins and these are generally of a much lesser degree of polymerization than ripe grape skin tannins. Stems and especially green or under-ripe stems also lend a distinctive green, herbal or leafy character to wines which, like pyrazines, can be unpleasant if overpowering and not in balance with the other aromatic components of the wine. Nowadays stems are occasionally and increasingly used in red winemaking (especially with Pinot Noir and Syrah wines) by performing "whole bunch fermentation", either wholly or partially (i.e.

only a percentage of the bunches are destemmed). This is normally performed in order to enhance the aromatic profile of the wine (lend what is deemed as a "freshness" through the "stemmy" or herbal contribution) and boost tannin levels and therefore ageability. Therefore stems should be used judiciously because overuse can obscure some of the complex grape derived aromas and their tannins are generally bitterer and can give a harsher effect than grape skin tannins. Note that like grape skins and seeds, stems ripen with hang-time. As they ripen stems become browner, less green and less bitter to a degree. Therefore as with grape skins, it is important to aim to use ripe stems if stems are to be utilized. Another consequence of fermenting on stems worth noting is that they have a tendency to leach colour from burgeoning wine. Therefore wines fermented on stems will usually appear paler although this effect itself does not affect wine quality.

STRUCTURE Structure is a vague but admittedly useful wine-speak term that helps to describe how the palate of a wine is constructed and ultimately how balanced the components are while giving clues about the wine's stability and potential to age. Generally it refers to textural, sensory and taste components in wine other than its flavour compounds, which are largely based on aromas. Thus if the flavours in wine are viewed as its "flesh" then components such as acidity / pH, tannins, sugars (sweetness) and alcohol (ethanol) provide the "structure" for that flesh, otherwise referred to as the wine's "backbone", "frame" or "foundation". Each of these structural components can individually or in combination help to preserve the fruit derived aroma / flavour compounds in wine, contributing to ageability. For more information see "acidity", "pH", "tannins". "sugars" and "ethanol".

STRUCTURED Structured refers to a wine possessing a high level of "structure".

STYLE(S) (WINE) In wine-speak, the term "styles" generally refers to the major categories of wine types that are made and consumed throughout the world and are defined largely by similar appearances and tastes. These include the most common colours of wines available: red, white, rosé, blush and, a minor but trendy moot contributor to this colour sector, orange wine. Wine style can also make reference to winemaking technique including: still (table), sparkling or fortified. Sometimes "body" is used to define or aid in the definition of style, including the major categories: light-bodied, medium-bodied and full-bodied. Or style descriptions can refer to the sweetness level, such as: dry, brut, off-dry, medium or sweet (with many shades and descriptions of sweetness levels in between). Historically regional names were also ubiquitously used to describe taste and/or production styles such as Port, Sherry, Burgundy or Champagne, however these regional names are now legally protected and can only be used on labels, in marketing or advertising in reference to wines that are produced within those regions and meet the local legal criteria for production. Likewise nowadays grape varieties can only be used to aid a style description if the wine legitimately contains a minimum proportion of the named grape(s) as stipulated by local production laws, although terms such as "Bordeaux Blend" and "Rhone Blend" are still frequently used in casual conversation and some marketing. Arguably another relatively modern sub-group of wine styles that reference their method of production include the categories: organic, biodynamic and "natural" wine, although these styles are far less if at all defined by the tangible look and taste of the wines but rather by their underlying principles of viticulture and winemaking. In the cases of organic and biodynamic wines these principles can be backed-up by legally recognized certification, which is not so with purported "natural" wines.

SUGARS Grapes mainly contain two sugar types: glucose and fructose. At veraison there is more glucose present in grapes but as the grapes ripen the ratio becomes 1:1. Berries containing more glucose at harvest time can indicate under-ripeness while those containing more fructose suggest over-ripeness, though the precise ratio of glucose to fructose at ripening is also variety dependent. The two sugars are in fact nearly identical sharing the same chemical formula, $C_6H_{12}O_6$, although fructose does taste significantly sweeter. In most quality wines that contain sweetness this comes from "residual sugar" consisting of any sugar that was not converted to alcohol during fermentation. It's worth noting that yeast prefer glucose and therefore when low amounts of residual sugar remain in wines, this is usually mainly or all fructose. Sugar can be added to grape juice and wine to one of two effects: 1) increase the alcohol and/or 2) increase the sweetness. To increase the alcohol, sugar (usually sucrose in the form of beet or cane sugar) will need to be added before or during fermentation. When sugar is administered to increase the alcohol in wine, the process is known as chaptalization. It takes around 17-18 grams per litre of sugar to create / increase the alcohol in wine by 1%. If sweetness is adjusted after fermentation often sweet juice, known as rectified concentrated grape must (RCGM), is used rather than sucrose to lend a more "natural" and harmonious effect. Common practice in Germany for producing sweet white wines, this sweetness addition is generally known as the adding of süssreserve and the process is sometimes referred to as back-blending. The best quality results can be obtained when the süssreserve consists of the same juice / must that was used to ferment that wine but was held back for this later purpose. The adding of sugar (sucrose) to finished wine is generally banned in most quality wine producing areas of the EU with the major exception of Champagne (and other sparkling wines produced elsewhere) whereby sucrose is almost always added at the final bottling with the "dosage" (sugar mixed with wine) to top up the bottles after the disgorging process. In this case the level of sugar in the dosage will define the style of the sparkling wine in terms of sweetness. Another minor contributor of sugars / sweetness naturally produced in wines is glycerol, a type of sugar-alcohol present in detectable levels in a few wines / wine styles. For more information see "chaptalization", "glycerol" and "sweetness".

SULPHIDES / SULPHIDE COMPOUNDS Closely related to mercaptans / thiols, sulphides likewise include a wide range of odorous compounds resulting from the reduction of sulphur compounds during winemaking and/or ageing. Sulphides common to wines include "hydrogen sulphide" and "dimethyl suphide" (see separate entries for more information). Sulphides or the term "sulphide character" are also often used as generic wine-speak terms to describe reduction compounds in wines

such as struck-match and earthy notes, usually in the context of Chardonnay or Syrah, which are mainly viewed positively and when in balance with the fruit components are considered to contribute complexity to the aromatic profile of these varieties.

SULPHITES Sulphites are widely used in the food and beverage industries as preservatives (antioxidant and anti-microbial agents). They are normally added during winemaking in the forms of sulphur dioxide or potassium metabisulphite. "Contains Sulphites" on wine labels or the "E" number E220 is a label requirement in some countries. For more information see "sulphur dioxide".

SULPHUR DIOXIDE (AKA SO$_2$) Sulphur dioxide is the most common of wine additives and is regularly used in modern winemaking. Its two most important properties are that it is an antioxidant and it is antimicrobial. In other words, when used at the right time and in the right proportions during winemaking it helps prevent oxidation and microbial spoilage from rogue bacteria and yeasts. Sulphur (sulphate) is naturally found in grapes albeit in very small amounts. During the process of fermentation this gets converted into SO$_2$; so even without any additions wines will naturally contain a little SO$_2$. The problem is that wines naturally have very little "free" SO$_2$ available to handle a potential oxidation situation and this free SO$_2$ can get "bound" to rogue oxygen molecules very quickly so that it is no longer effective in tackling any other oxygen present or introduced during winemaking. That's why winemakers commonly send in the supports: added SO$_2$. There are a few drawbacks to using SO$_2$. Like most chemicals it is toxic at very high concentrations and therefore legal limits on the total SO$_2$ content in wines, which are generally well below the safe guidelines, are imposed in most countries around the world. In rare cases SO$_2$ can cause asthmatic reactions and therefore affected individuals should avoid any intake, which includes that which is added to a wide range of food and beverage products around the world. And it does cause a temporary loss of "fruitiness" to newly bottled wines. For these reasons and perhaps to dogmatically avoid additives altogether, some winemakers including many "Natural Wine" proponents do not add any SO$_2$ to wines as a matter of principal. Certainly it is possible to make wine without any SO_2 additions but it is a risky business given wine's propensity to oxidise and the difficulties with maintaining a microbial-free status throughout winemaking. Therefore wines produced without SO_2 additions are far less "stable" than their sulphured counterparts and prone to becoming "tired" before their time if not oxidised and/or spoiled by microbes. Careful shipping and handling at lower temperatures (e.g. 15 degrees Celsius or below) can help protect non-sulphured wines from spoilage, though this can be hard to maintain and guarantee. Consumers may know if the wine they are drinking has had added SO_2 by noting the words, "Contains Sulphites" on wine labels or by the "E" number E220, a label requirement in some countries.

SUPERFICIAL FAULTS "Superficial faults" is a term I use for occurrences that can mar the look / appearance of wine but not the smell or taste. The major types include sediment (from bottle age), residual CO_2 from bottling, protein haze and tartrate crystals. For more information, see "Chapter 1 – Wine Faults" in the section on "Superficial Faults".

SUPERTASTER Tongues, one of our primary tools for wine evaluation, are also markedly different amongst tasters. The major, most easily recognised taste difference amongst individuals is mainly due to the number of taste buds people have – some people can have up to three times more than others! This means there can be a huge variation in the intensity of flavours that people taste and for "supertasters", those with densely budded palates, bitterness in foods can seem particularly prominent whereas those with fewer taste buds may hardly taste a bitter substance or not detect it at all. It's estimated that around 25% of the population are supertasters, with a notable tendency towards women. Studies have revealed such basic differences in the tongue can significantly impact our food (and, consequently, wine) preferences and shape our lives as impacted by our diets. It is easy to find out if you are a supertaster. Simply place a drop of blue food colouring on your tongue, spread it round with a swish of water, then place a pre-prepared ring-binder made hole over your taste buds and count the number of taste buds within

the hole. (A magnifying glass helps.) If you have more than 30 taste buds within the hole, you're likely to be a supertaster. A more precise test is by placing a bitter PROP (short for the compound 6-n-propylthiouracil) laced tab on your tongue to determine if this bitter substance can be tasted. Supertasters will hate the bitterness of PROP whereas average tasters may think it's not so bad and "non-tasters" won't taste it at all.

SUPPORTING QUALITY FACTORS "Supporting quality factors" is my term for less universally agreed quality factors than, for example, the "fundamental wine quality" factors but which sometimes play a role in the final tasting assessment of many wine experts. They include:

- The wine's ability / potential to Age
- Regional typicality
- Value for money
- Drinkability
- Compatibility with Food
- And Uniqueness of grape variety, style and/or region

For more information on supporting quality factors, see Chapter 7.

SUR LIES See "lees ageing".

SÜSSRESERVE When sweetness is adjusted after fermentation often sweet juice, known as rectified concentrated grape must (RCGM), is used rather than sucrose to lend a more "natural" taste and harmonious effect. Common practice in Germany for producing sweet white wines, this sweetness addition is generally known as the adding of süssreserve and the process is sometimes referred to as a back-blending. The best quality results can be obtained when the süssreserve consists of the same juice / must that was used to ferment that wine but was held back for this later purpose.

SWEETNESS Along with acidity, salty, bitterness and umami, sweetness is one of the five major tastes relating specifically to the perception of sugars on the tongue. Sugars can generally be detected on the palate at levels above 3-4 grams per litre of residual sugar. In reference to wine tasting there are several factors that can affect the perception of sweetness in the mouth, most notably acidity, which at higher levels can modify / mute the appearance of sweetness and at lower levels can make it stand out as "sickly" or "cloying". Tannic content also modifies sweetness and vice versa, whereby sweetness can make tannic wines appear less bitter. Apart from sugars, the presence of detectable levels of glycerol can contribute to the sweetness profile of wine. Ethanol (alcohol) can also lend to the appearance of sweetness. For more information see "ethanol", "glycerol" and "sugars".

SYNTHETIC CLOSURE / CORK (AKA PLASTIC CORK) A synthetic closure is a wine bottle closure alternative to using natural cork that looks and acts like a cork but is instead composed of a synthetic / plastic compound material. They are therefore not biodegradable but some are recyclable. Synthetic closures are removed from wine bottles much like normal corks using a corkscrew. As they are not made from cork, they offer no risk of transferring TCA (cork) taint to wine and they were primarily developed for this purpose. However studies performed at the AWRI and University of Bordeaux have revealed that amongst various wine closures including real cork and screw caps, certain types of common synthetic closures offer the highest rates of oxygen permeability. Accordingly, most synthetic closures are not deemed suitable for long-term wine bottle ageing although a few viable options have recently been developed to offer longer ageing potential. Other good TCA free wine bottle closure alternatives to cork include "Diam" and "screw caps". For more information on these, see their separate entries.

T

TA TA is an abbreviation for "total acidity" and, rather confusingly, "titratable acidity", although these values are not exactly the same thing. These are differing means of measuring the acidity in grape juice and wine. The total acidity value – the number of hydrogen ions that all the disassociated organic acids in wine would contain – will always be slightly higher than titratable acidity as this is a more limited in the sources of hydrogen ions it can measure. But the test for titratable acidity is generally easier and

therefore the norm. The TA (titratable acidity) of wines can be expressed in terms of any of the acids present in wine (curiously the French like to use sulphuric acid), most often expressed in terms of the most abundant acid in wines: tartaric acid. It is common for wines to have a TA (titratable acidity) range of 5 – 8 grams per litre expressed as tartaric acid. Otherwise TA (titratable acidity) is often expressed as a straightforward percentage (grams of tartaric acid per 100 millilitres) with a normal range of 0.5 to 0.8% expressed as tartaric acid.

TAINT A taint can be defined as an undesired character usually constituting a fault that is totally foreign to a beverage or food, normally coming from an exterior source. A taint of major importance to the wine industry is "cork taint". Other taints of growing importance are "ladybird taint" (LBT) and "smoke taint" from bush / forest fires that occur during the growing season near vineyards.

TANNIC Tannic is a wine descriptor used in reference to a wine's tannin profile, a wine that has pronounced tannins or sometimes implies overly high tannins in a wine to the point of being unbalanced.

TANNINS Tannins are types of polyphenolic compounds (polyphenols or phenolic groupings) produced in plants, characterized by their ability to interact with and precipitate proteins. (In fact their ability to "tan" leather was how they got their name.) Part of the sensual effect tannins produce on the palate is their interaction with the proteins on the tongue and sides of the mouth, producing a drying feeling or sensation of astringency that is commonly described by wine experts as anything from sandy / grainy (more astringent) in texture to silky / velvety (less astringent). Tannins play an important textural role, as well as contribute to the body and structure of mainly red wines. Their antioxidant properties are critical factors in the ability of red wines to age. But unresolved or "unripe" tannins can be deeply unpleasant. Not only can they make a red wine hard, seemingly "rough" or coarse in the mouth with an overly astringent texture and generally lacking finesse but they're bitter – the one taste that wine shouldn't have.

TARTARIC ACID A major organic acid and component in grapes, tartaric acid is naturally produced as part of the berry's formation and remains in the berry throughout ripening. The two major acids in wine grapes are tartaric, an acid unique to grapes, and malic, an acid common to other fruits such as apples. Although tartaric acid continues to be manufactured in the berry throughout ripening, the overall concentration of acid decreases relative to that of other components such as sugar and water. And in fact the more sour malic acid is respired or consumed by the berry during ripening, generally resulting in grapes that are higher in the less tart tartaric acid at the time of harvest. During winemaking the level of tartaric acid will drop in the wine compared to that of its freshly squeezed juice as some of the acid will combine mainly with naturally present potassium forming insoluble salts known as tartrate crystals.

TARTRATE CRYSTALS (AKA WINE DIAMONDS) Tartrate crystals or wine diamonds at the bottom of a wine bottle or glass of wine are harmless, superficial faults that may detract from the look of the wine but not the palate. They are naturally formed during winemaking when tartaric acid combines with elements in wine, mainly potassium, to form insoluble salts such as potassium bitartrate. They are more common in white wines than red wines for two principle reasons: 1) the high levels of polyphenols in red wines inhibit the formation of tartrate crystals and 2) the crystals are less soluble at cooler temperatures and white wines are generally kept at colder temperatures than reds. Because they can looking unappealing and sometimes alarming to unwary consumers, many wines are now "cold stabilised" prior to bottling in order to force any unstable tartrate crystals out of solution and avoid incidences of their occurrence during bottle storage / ageing. A few fine wine makers feel however that cold stabilisation is an overly harsh treatment that can strip wines of nuances and they therefore avoid the practice. Since such superficial faults as tartrate crystals don't affect the nose or palate of the wine, it's up to the taster to decide if they are quality detractions.

TERPENES Terpenes are aromatic compounds naturally found in some grape varieties, most prominent in "aromatic" grapes such as Riesling, Muscat and Gewürztraminer. Terpenes tend to lend distinctly floral and/or fruity aromas to wine.

TERROIR Terroir can literally be translated from French into "soil" or "dirt", but in the context of wine it encompasses much more than this. It can be defined as the interaction of the unique elements of the vineyard habitat - Climate, Topography, Weather and Soil plus in some cases the ways and means of Managing the Vineyard – and their influence on wine style, character and quality. All vineyards have a terroir but not all wines convey their terroir, nor are they necessarily made this way. For more information see "Chapter 5 – Complexity" in the text box, 'Terroir FAQs'".

TERTIARY AROMAS / CHARACTERS With barrel and/or bottle ageing grape and winemaking derived aromas may evolve due to slow oxidative and reductive reactions and possibly combine with other components in the wine and/or "marry-in" together, contributing to a mature wine nose; what is known in wine-speak as tertiary aromas or less precisely in somewhat outdated wine jargon as a "bouquet". In such incidences the youthful fruity, floral and/or herbal aromas will open out and evolve into less overtly "fresh" characters resulting in dried fruit / dried herb notes and often spicy, savoury and/or nutty characters. Esters and aldehydes are also likely to contribute to the nose of an evolving wine and, when complimentary and in balance with the other components in the wine, add to the complexity of a mature nose.

TEXTURE (AKA MOUTH-FEEL) A wine-speak synonym for the term "mouth-feel", texture is essentially a consideration of major tactile components such as tannins and viscosity. There is also evidence to suggest that texture / mouth-feel largely impacts the perception of flavour can render flavours seemingly more or less intense, although it does not change the flavour per se. Texture contributes to both the balance and complexity of a wine and is therefore an important wine quality consideration.

THIOLS See "mercaptans".

TIRED In common wine-speak a wine that is described as tired is usually past its prime and/ or exhibiting signs of oxidation. The aromas and flavours of a "tired" wine will be starting to fade from their flush of primary and secondary aromatic youth without successfully evolving onto complex tertiary or mature characters. Otherwise a "tired" wine may be a mature wine that has had its day and is on the decline. For more information see "oxidation" and "mature".

TITRATABLE ACIDITY See "TA".

TOAST / TOASTED / TOASTING (OAK) To "toast" an oak barrel is to literally cook the inner walls of the barrel with a special burner that is usually lowered into the barrel and left for a period of time depending on the desired toasting level. Toasting happens during the construction of the barrel and has two purposes: 1) to stress-relieve the wood after it has been bent into the barrel shape and 2) to affect the type and amount of tannins and flavours that will be imparted into the wine once newly filled. The heating causes many changes in the wood's internal structure, creating different compounds and texture / flavour expressions at different toasting levels. Toast levels are usually classified as light, medium or heavy and the heads – top and bottom of the barrel – may or may not be toasted exclusively or included. Generally speaking, the green, woody flavours of untoasted oak develop into characters of vanilla, bread, nut, clove, cinnamon and/or coconut with light to medium toasting. Heavy toasting can instil a distinct "smoky" and often espresso / roasted coffee character. Furthermore increased toasting level softens the texture of oak tannins and tends to yield less tannic influence on the wine. For more information, see "oak".

TOTAL ACIDITY See "TA".

TOTAL EXTRACT See "extract".

TRADE-OFF A winemaker trade-off is my term for an important decision made throughout the winemaking process that will be a compromise between that which is practical/possible/affordable and that which is qualitatively desired.

2, 4, 6, TRICHLOROANISOLE (TCA) 2, 4, 6, Trichloroanisole (or TCA for short) is a chemical compound derived largely from the cork stopper in a wine bottle and to a lesser extent from other sources such as wood (oak barrels, roofs, floorboards, etc.) in a winery. There are a few other compounds responsible for "cork" taint, but this is the major one. TCA is generated by naturally-occurring fungi that often exist in the crevices of wood or cork (which is the bark of wood) coming in contact with chlorine compounds, which are ubiquitously present in pesticides, cleaning / sterilising / bleaching agents and wood treatments, etc. Chlorine is highly volatile; it disperses easily far from its original source and it's often difficult to keep offending fungi from coming in contact with chlorine. When the fungi meet the chlorine there's an ungodly engendering that occurs, TCA is formed and it ain't pleasant - pernicious in its ability to instantly spoil a wide range of food and beverage items including mineral water, coffee and apple juice.

U

UC DAVIS (AKA UCD) UC Davis is short for "The University of California, Davis", which is a branch of the University of California located in Davis, California (just west of Sacramento). Its "Department of Viticulture and Enology" is world renowned for its high level of educational instruction and research facilities. More information is available on the university's website: www. ucdavis.edu

UMAMI Widely recognized nowadays as the "fifth taste", this is a savoury flavour found in meats, cheeses, mushrooms, seaweed and oyster sauce (or other monosodium glutamate / MSG containing products, ignoring any added flavours such as salt and sugar), for examples. The taste is widely considered to exist in some wines. Because its presence in wines is difficult to isolate and measure, it is hard to say which wines tend to contain umami taste. Personal experience however suggests that savoury, meaty and/or mushroom / truffle-like flavours similar to the MSG taste can be found in some bottle aged red wines such as Rioja, Barolo and Chateauneuf du Pape.

L'UNIVERSITÉ DE BORDEAUX (AKA UNIVERSITY OF BORDEAUX) Known in English as the University of Bordeaux, this is one of the world's leading providers of higher education in oenology at its Bordeaux Segalen University and of scientific research relating to wine via its partner: l'Institut des Sciences de la Vigne et du Vin de l'Université de Bordeaux (the English translation is the Institute of Vine and Wine Sciences of the University of Bordeaux). More information is available on the Bordeaux Segalen University website: http://www.univ-bordeauxsegalen.fr/en/university/faculties-and-institutes/oenology.html and the l'Institut des Sciences de la Vigne et du Vin de l'Université de Bordeaux website: http://www.isvv.univ-bordeauxsegalen.fr/en/

V

VÉRAISON Véraison is a French viticulture term now used universally in wine-speak referring to the stage of grape ripening when the berries begin to change colour. The beginning of the stage is visually characterised when red / black berries will start to synthesise anthocyanins (colour compounds), although even white grapes will soften and change from a pale vibrant green colour to more of a deep green, yellow or gold colour. But colour is not the only change occurring in the berry - significantly malic acid degrades, sugar starts accumulating, herbal flavours degrade and fruity flavours synthesise while tannins polymerise and become less bitter. All of this of course happens in order to make the "ripe" grapes more attractive to animals, which by nature's design are intended to eat the berries once the seeds are ready and deposit these seeds far and wide. For grape growers this colour change at veraison is a visual marker that ripening is about to begin and for those that are more technically inclined anthocyanin accumulation in skins can be used as an indication of tannin and to a certain extent flavour ripeness. The period between veraison and harvest is of vital importance to grape growers as it is make or break time for quality.

VISCOSITY The body or weight of wine in the mouth is mainly due to its viscosity, which is detected by a textural thickening of the wine in correlation to increased levels of sugar, extract and/ or alcoholic strength. Viscosity is sensed on the palate in the form of resistance as the wine coats the mouth and passes over the tongue. Think of the difference between sipping tomato soup and water – the tomato soup is way more viscous. In wine terms a sweet, sugar-rich wine will be more viscous than a dry one, even if they have the same alcoholic strength. Alcohol (ethanol – the alcohol in "alcoholic" beverages) is more viscous than water, so it is closely related to body. And the dissolved solids in wine - its "extract" – also make wine more viscous and therefore fuller-bodied. In wine it is tannins, sugars, proteins, non-volatile acids (such as tartaric), colour compounds (anthocyanins) and trace minerals (e.g. calcium and potassium) that usually make up the dry extract in wine. The tannin and anthocyanin extract in red wine therefore render reds slightly fuller-bodied than dry whites for the same alcoholic strength. Glycerol occasionally makes a minor contribution to viscosity and therefore body. For more information see "body" and "glycerol".

VOLATILE Volatile refers to a liquid that quickly evaporates. In wine-speak if it precedes the word "aroma" then it generally refers to an aroma that vaporises easily at room temperature and is therefore detectable through the sense of smell. Used on its own, the word can mean a wine that has a notable level of acetic acid otherwise known as volatile acidity.

VOLATILE ACIDITY (VA) Volatile acidity is a grey-area wine fault. Volatile acids are naturally occurring components that are present in all wines. The most abundant in wine is acetic acid. When generated in high concentrations above the detection level, acetic acid can impart a distinct vinegar smell in wine. When the vinegar smell of acetic acid notably and negatively impacts the smell of the wine, it becomes a fault and is referred to as volatile acidity, VA, volatile or acetic. But at the more acceptable end of this grey-area fault, some wines and indeed styles possessing relatively high and detectable levels of VA may not call-for a negative tick against quality and there are occasional incidences when it can even make a positive contribution towards balance and complexity. Such is the case with Amarone or some older / mature red wines and styles like a mature Bordeaux or Bordeaux blend reds. Another style exception worth considering is botrytised sweet wine (where the grapes are infected with botrytis cinerea or noble rot in the vineyard) within which it is natural for a much higher level of acetic acid to be present than in a table wine and in this incidence a very slight whiff on the nose and tang on the palate can contribute balancing lift to the richness of the wine and enhance complexity.

W

WHOLE BUNCH FERMENTATION See "stems".

WILD YEAST (AKA NATURAL YEAST, INDIGENOUS YEAST, NATURAL FERMENTATION OR SPONTANEOUS FERMENTATION) Wild yeast is a winemaking wine-speak term for the yeast capable of fermenting wine (to a degree if not wholly), and which are indigenous to a place, specifically a vineyard and/or winery. Therefore these are the naturally present yeast that are able to start and carry out the alcoholic fermentation of grape juice (must) into wine. Of course before the advent of cultured yeast, this is how all fermentations were performed. But because there is an element of unpredictability with the use of wild yeast(s) (e.g. speed, efficiency and aromatic by-products), cultured yeast additions became more practical in modern winemaking. Although the use of wild yeast still viewed as "traditional", with the trend towards natural winemaking and/or the view that wild yeast(s) can contribute to complexity, nowadays wild yeast fermentations have gone from conjuring old-school preconceptions to garnering new-school ideologies. One thing is for sure with wild yeast – they are wild cards, meaning you never know exactly what you're getting. There are many yeasts that exist in nature but few are of the Saccharomyces species and most are not. Common thought is that yeast brought in from the vineyard, mainly consisting of the Kloeckera and Hansieniaspora species, begin the "natural fermentation" but are by nature only capable of taking it so far...to about 3-4% alcohol by volume to be precise because they cannot tolerate higher concentrations. Then any Saccharomyces present – usually the winery's ambient Saccharomyces

yeast (presumably lingering dormant on winery equipment from previous fermentations) - will take over and complete the fermentation of the remaining sugar in the nascent wine. One major question in all this is exactly how wild are the wild yeast in any given "natural" or "spontaneous" fermentation. For example, if cultured yeast are being used in the same winery, then the yeast performing the fermentation may not be very wild at all since the cultured yeast have a tendency to find their way into vats of sugar-laden juice. There are even cases where bees have carried over cultured Saccharomyces yeast from neighbouring wineries into strictly "natural" fermentation wineries and this has become established in the winery as the dominating yeast. In a true natural fermentation there are some major risks especially because of the low level of SO_2 additions they require (to encourage the jump-start by non-Saccharomyces species), the amount of time it takes to start the fermentation and the danger of a stuck fermentation...all which can lead to microbial spoilage. Still, a growing number of fine winemakers feel the risks are worth the rewards, which are mainly in the form of another layer of complexity and a certain uniqueness to wines produced by wild yeast.

WINE COMPONENTS Wine can be broken down into component parts, collectively contributing in varying degrees to the overall experience and therefore quality that a wine offers. The wine components of major significance include:

- Sweetness
- Acidity
- Body
- Grape derived aromas / flavours
- Tannins, which can come from grape skins, stems, and oak barrel, stave or chips or can simply be added tannins
- Alcohol
- Winemaking derived aromas / flavours, e.g. characters formed or derived from Yeast(s), MLF, Lees, Oak, Sulphur Dioxide (SO_2)
- Winemaking Grey-Area faults: VA, Reduction, Brettanomyces, Oxidation, etc.

Wine components differ significantly from grape

components. When transformed from juice to wine, the resulting product is very different from the raw materials and this change in components goes far beyond the basic creation of alcohol by yeast. So for example were you to take a glass of ordinary grape juice that you buy from the supermarket and blend it with a neutral tasting spirit such as vodka, you would notice that the resulting cocktail doesn't taste at all like wine. Pre-fermentation, fermentation, post-fermentation, maturation and storage processes transform the grape components and instil new aromas and flavours, ultimately all of which make wine, well, *wine*.

WINEMAKING DERIVED AROMAS / FLAVOURS / CHARACTERS / COMPONENTS This is my term for the aromas that come initially and predominately from the winemaking – chiefly pre-fermentation, fermentation, post-fermentation, maturation and storage - processes as opposed to the grape derived aromas. In their initial stages these are also known in common wine-speak as secondary aromas, giving rise to notable characters that are other than distinctly fruity, herbal, vegetal, spice or floral notes directly associated with certain grapes and their level of ripeness. Common winemaking characters include those derived specifically from the use of sulphur dioxide and other additives, oak ageing, malolactic fermentation and lees contact. These could also include grape derived characters / components that are transformed so dramatically through fermentation as to have lost their detectable association with the grapes such as ethanol, higher alcohols, fatty acids, volatile acids and esters. As part and parcel of the winemaking, these secondary characters can be considered to include those grey-area faults such as volatile acidity, brettanomyces and reduction. With barrel and/or bottle ageing winemaking derived aromas may develop further due to slow oxidative and reductive reactions and evolve / combine with other components in the wine and/or marry-in with the grape derived aromas, contributing to what is known in wine-speak as tertiary aromas or, less precisely, as a "bouquet".

WINE PURPOSES PYRAMID Created to facilitate the discussion of wine quality as it exists across many purposes, to a certain extent the **Wine**

Purposes Pyramid I've constructed for this book is an approximate model demonstrating how individuals' levels of involvement with wine affect their awareness of wine quality factors and personal expectations of what a wine of perceived quality should offer. Based on my own extensive experience of working with consumers in the wine trade (20+ years) and research such as that on perceived wine quality performed by S. Charters, et. al in 2007 and W.V. Parr, et. al. in 2011, quality factors of increasing relevance have been approximately placed amongst the 3 major levels of wine drinker involvement: Low, Medium and High. Irrespective of the precise placement of factors on this hypothetical pyramid, one thing is clear to most wine industry experts – with increased involvement, awareness and indeed knowledge of wine, drinkers develop expectations for wine to extrinsically (grapes, winemaking, marketing, etc.) and intrinsically (taste, complexity, drinkability, emotional effect, etc.) do more. For more information, see "Chapter 1 – What we talk about when we talk about wine quality".

WINE RATINGS (AKA SCORES) A fairly recent phenomenon in the history of wine, nowadays most wine experts and critics around the world have embraced the usefulness of not just alluding nebulously to wine quality with the chosen descriptors in tasting notes or stating it plainly with terms like, "average quality" or "excellent quality", but in assigning a rating to it or a score. When ratings are consistently applied with consistency they can be very practical because standalone tasting notes are wide open to a broad range of quality conclusion interpretations and one often doesn't really know for certain where the critic stands. There are a number of wine critics and critical publications that use a 20 Point Scale for rating wines and there are a few other idiosyncratic methods of rating wines such as the dishing-out of 1-3 "bicchiere"(wine glasses) by the Italian *Gambero Rosso* publication. Some people simply choose to use ticks, stars or other symbols as ratings. It really depends on the level of rating precision sought by the taster. But today perhaps the most widely implemented and powerful amongst systems of wine ratings is the 100 Point Scale. This was created and introduced by Robert Parker in 1978 in what was to become

Robert Parker's Wine Advocate magazine. It was devised partly to challenge shortcomings of other rating systems such as the 20 Point scale since Parker believed that a 20 point rating system did not provide enough flexibility and often resulted in compressed and inflated wine ratings. The other major benefit of this 100 point system is that it offers a figure that is immediately recognized and understood as a grade since it was based on the American scholastic grading system. Technically it is not a 100 point scale though, as in practice employs 50-100 point ratings. So a wine gets 50 points just for being called a wine. Since its inception, Robert Parker's 100 Point Scale has become the wine industry's standard and is now used by other major wine publications such as the *Wine Spectator* and *Wine Enthusiast*. For more information see "**Chapter 9** – Wine-Speak, Tasting Notes and Ratings".

WINE-SPEAK Love it or loath it, the ever-growing community of winos appreciating and communicating about wine has evolved what could / would have been an onerously exhaustive list of wine related gobbly-goo down to a relatively manageable lexicon of descriptors, old-school carry-overs, technical and industry words and terms specific to our world. This includes a lot of fragrant to stinky food, spice, flora and fauna items (ubiquitous and regionally obscure) and earth / turf related smells that share aromas and flavours with wine along with everything from scientific naming to doggedly employed outdated wine jargon. Our language of wine borrows from no less than seven different wine producing and drinking nations' languages and colloquialisms (especially France, the UK, Spain, Italy, Germany, Australia and the USA) and employs plenty of nick-names and acronyms. To an outsider, wine-speak must surely appear like the cryptic lingo of an elitist club. But there is really nothing subversive about it. Developed largely over the last century throughout a hodgepodge of admittedly mainly Western wine drinking nations, wine-speak is really just a language treaty amongst this myriad of idiosyncratic cultures to weed out many of the more obscure descriptors and foreign names for things and describe wine using the same "tongue".

WSET (AKA WINE AND SPIRIT EDUCATION TRUST) These four letters are a common acronym amongst the wine industry for the "Wine and Spirit Education Trust", what has become the largest and most global of wine education institutions. With its foundations and headquarters in London, United Kingdom, the teachings can be a little Anglo-centric but the organisation has worked hard in recent years to adapt the curriculum for more far-reaching purposes. The courses were originally intended for members of the wine trade and it still does largely service this sector although the scope of interest in attending WSET courses has recently expanded to wine consumers. Exams for the five levels of qualification are regularly conducted with a solid degree of rigour and passes are awarded with certificates of achievement, the highest being the "Diploma" followed by the "Honours Diploma". More information is available on the WSET website: www.wsetglobal.com

Y

YEAST Existing as specialised types of microscopic fungi, winemaking yeasts are responsible for converting the sugar (carbohydrates) present in grape juice into alcohol (predominately ethanol) and carbon dioxide through the process of fermentation. So in essence wine cannot be made without yeast. In the very early days of winemaking and occasionally still today, the ambient or "wild yeast" - present in the atmosphere, brought in from the vineyard via grape skins and/or instilled from the surfaces of equipment in a winery - can under the right conditions (e.g. temperature, amount of sugar, level of acidity / pH, etc.) conduct the fermentation of grape must without any manipulation or yeast additions. This is sometimes known as "natural fermentation". Alternatively certain actions such as warming of must or deacidifying can help to induce a spontaneous fermentation. Otherwise the must can be inoculated with cultured yeast to achieve a smoother, more predictable fermentation, usually employing a strain of the Saccharomyces cerevisiae species, which is most efficient at converting sugar into alcohol. For more information see "cultured yeast", "fermentation", "Saccharomyces cerevisiae" and "wild yeast".

YIELD With regards to viticulture, yield is a wine-speak term that usually refers to the measured amount of grapes harvested or wine produced per area unit of land measurement. Yield figures are often used as an indicators of wine quality but, as with so many things when it comes to wine quality, the devil is in the details. The most common means of reporting yields in Europe is tonnes (of grapes harvested) per hectare (of vineyard land) or hectolitres (of wine produced) per hectare. Elsewhere tons per acre is the popular means of measurement. For more information on yield and its correlation with wine quality, see **Chapter 2** in the text box addressing: "Is it true that lower yields make better quality wines?"

ASIAN FOOD LEXICON FOR WINE

....

First published on eRobertParker.com in September 2008.

MANY OF THE formal descriptors traditionally attributed to wine aromas and flavours are based on Western foods that simply aren't easily / widely found in many Eastern nations. For example: cassis, gooseberry, oatmeal, brioche and butterscotch, just to name a few. Since a lot of these foods are not readily available in Asia, wine associations with such foods do not come naturally for many of the locals. But there are a number of Asian ingredients and foods that share aromas and flavours with various wines. Since I first arrived in Asia I've become interested in isolating them. Here are a few of my discoveries that I sometimes incorporate into my localised tasting notes or discussions to bring wine to life within Asia's wide variety of cultures.

AZUKI / RED BEAN PASTE: Used in a lot of Asian sweets, pastries and breads, this dark, sticky mixture has a rich, dried raisin / date / fig combined with dark honey sort of character. I find this smell in some Oloroso Sherries, Banyuls / Vin Doux Naturels, Tawny Ports, Rutherglen Muscat and particularly in sweet Pedro Ximenez wines. This descriptive can also be used with some Reciotos.

CARDAMOM: This fragrant seed-pod is often used as a spice in Indian and Asian cooking. It has an incredibly aromatic aroma of mint or eucalyptus with some citrus notes and a whiff of dried herbs. This distinctive aroma / flavour can sometimes be caught in ripe, rich, minty red wines such as classic Barossa Shiraz and Napa Valley Cabernet.

CASSIA: Frequently used in Chinese cuisine and a constituent of five spice, Cassia is sometimes referred to as Chinese cinnamon and like cinnamon it comes from the bark of a tree. Its aroma is similar to cinnamon but even more pungent and spicy. I find this aroma on many cool to moderate climate Grenache and Syrah based wines such as Chateauneuf du Pape from a good vintage.

CHINESE STEAMED BREAD: A very subtle fresh-cooked bread aroma and flavour that is often found in young / NV Champagnes and some sparkling wines.

CHOMPOO / ROSE APPLE (THAILAND AND MALAYSIA): The skin and flesh of Chompoo are crunchy with a flavour sort of like a cox or Macintosh apple mixed with watermelon and a dash of rose water. This fruit is quite astringent / tannic with a pleasant hint of bitterness in the finish that is balanced by the sweetness. Chompoo is a

good descriptive for more aromatic rose wines such as Tavel and rose Champagne.

CORIANDER SEEDS: Coriander seeds give off a fragrant aroma of warm, spicy orange rind, particularly noticeable when they're dry-fried. I find this appealing smell in the wines of aromatic varieties such as Muscat, Gewurztraminer, Riesling and sometimes Pinot Gris and Torrontes.

CUMIN SEEDS: Cumin seeds have a distinctively spicy, almost sweet aroma. I find this aroma on a lot of barrel aged red wines as they mature. For example, mature, top quality Bordeaux reds often convey a touch of cumin as do Northern Rhone Syrahs.

Cumin seeds (top), Cardamom (bottom right), Coriander seeds (bottom left)

CURRY LEAVES: These highly aromatic leaves have a very distinctive smell of green capsicums and fresh cut grass blended with citrusy fragrances such as tangerine and lemon. This scent is found on the noses of many ripe, pungent Sauvignon Blancs but it can also be detected in some warmer climate Rieslings and Austrian Gruner Veltliner.

DRIED TANGERINE / MANDARIN PEEL: A key aromatic ingredient in many great Chinese dishes. The smell is intense and akin to some noble rot wines especially botrytised Riesling.

DRIED PLUM (SOUR PLUM / BLACK PLUM): Not to be confused with ordinary prunes, the smell of this Chinese snack / cooking ingredient is very distinctive incorporating a subtle plum character with fragrant earthy, forest floor aromas. I also get a faint whiff of olive groves and dried herbs in these strongly flavoured dried fruits. Since they're salted I tend to use them just as an aroma descriptor. Sometimes the complex smell of dried plum can be caught on right bank Bordeaux clarets, some southern French reds and occasionally on red Italian and Spanish wines.

FIVE SPICE POWDER (CHINESE): A fantastically fragrant seasoning blend usually of cinnamon, cassia bud, star anise, ginger and cloves. Sometimes fennel seeds and Sichuan peppercorns are used. You can find this aroma on better quality wines made from Syrah and/or Grenache and occasionally on developing Right bank Bordeaux wines.

FUJI APPLE: A large Japanese apple, similar to a Red Delicious but with less acid and more aroma / sweetness. It shares aromas and flavours with some evolving Chardonnays and evolved or late-disgorged sparkling wines.

GALANGAL / LANGKWAS / KRACHAI: This is a Chinese / South East Asian rhizome that is similar to ginger and with a pungent, somewhat ginger-like scent but with nuances of black pepper, spearmint and pine nuts. I find this aroma sometimes on ripe, New World Pinot Noirs and on more concentrated examples of Loire Cabernet Francs (e.g. Bourgueil).

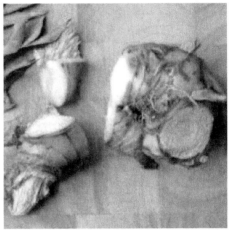

Curry Leaves (top) and Galangal (below)

GREEN OR UNRIPE MANGO: Used in many Thai dishes this ingredient has a fantastically tart, intense Granny Smith / green apple sort of smell and flavour with a slight tropical (pineapple) kick. The aroma and flavour can be found in New Zealand Sauvignon, late harvest Chenin Blanc and some warm climate Chardonnays, for example.

HOSHIGAKI (JAPAN), SHI-BING (CHINA), GOTGAM (KOREA) HONG KHO (VIETNAM): Dried persimmon. It smells and tastes kind of like a cross between dried figs and apricots. Similar aromas can be found in wines such as Vin Santo, Vin de Paille or Tokaji.

JASMINE: This is a perfumed almost honeysuckle aroma but with hints of exotic spice. It can be found in wines made from aromatic grapes such as Riesling, Muscat, Viognier, Gewurztraminer, Torrontes or Roussanne. Occasionally it can be found in Champagne or even young Nebbiolo and concentrated Pinot Noirs.

KAKI: Persimmons. These have a delicate aroma and flavour of ripe peach, cantaloupe and under-ripe guava. Its character can be found in examples such as Chardonnay, Viognier, Pinot Gris and Albarino.

KAYA JAM (MALAYSIA, SINGAPORE): This is a rich coconut and egg based jam commonly spread on toast in Malaysia and Singapore. The smell has a delicate scent of coconut with aromas of egg custard and caramel and can be found in mature or late disgorged Champagnes, mature Meursault or evolved Californian Chardonnay.

LEMON GRASS: As the name suggests, this unmistakable smell is both grassy and lemon-laced. I find it most in Australian Semillon but it is certainly present in many other exotically scented white wines.

LIME LEAVES (KAFFIR LIME LEAVES): An herbaceous, delicate lime scent that can be found in Semillon, especially young hunter Semillon and some youthful aromatic wines such as Riesling.

LONGAN / LAM YAI: A lychee-like fruit that is very popular in Asia. It is perhaps not quite as spicy as a lychee with a honeydew melon type of flavour with a touch of white pepper and fresh ginger. The aroma/flavours can be found in fine, cool climate Chardonnay, Pinot Gris and Albarino.

MIKAN / WENZHOU MIGAN: Japanese / Chinese tangerine with a ripe, fruity aroma that can be found in young Muscat and youthful sweet wines such as Saint-Croix-du-Mont or Canadian Ice Wine.

MANGOSTEEN: A South-East Asian fruit with a sweet flesh that is reminiscent of fresh peaches and honeydew melon with a citrusy tanginess. The aroma and flavour can be found in young, fruity Chardonnays, particularly those from the New World and warmer Old World climates.

MANGO PUDDING: This has wonderful creamy mango aromas and flavours. Can be found in very ripe Chardonnay or some NZ Sauvignons.

MOONCAKE (WITH LOTUS SEED PASTE FILLING): This is a traditional Chinese pastry commonly eaten in celebration of mid-Autumn festival. It has typical pastry aromas supplemented with a filling reminiscent of caramelised sugar or butterscotch. The smell can be found in a range of wines (and to varying degrees) from classic Marsala, Madeira and aged Sauternes to mature Champagne, aged Meursault and Tokaji.

Mooncakes

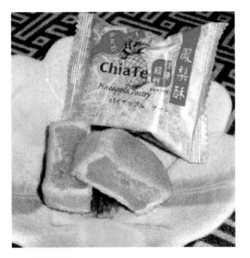

Pineapple Pastry

PINEAPPLE BUN: Doesn't actually contain pineapple, but rather looks like one. This is a sweet bun popular in Hong Kong and Macau. The aroma and flavour can be found in aged / late disgorged Champagne and mature Chardonnay.

PINEAPPLE PASTRY: A Chinese / Taiwanese sweet cake that consists of pastry casing containing a paste made of dried pineapple. The aroma can be found in ripe, oaked Chardonnay, some barrel fermented Sauvignons (e.g. from Bordeaux), Sauternes, and Beerenauslese.

POMELO (CHINESE GRAPEFRUIT): This is a very large green coloured grapefruit which is generally sweeter and less bitter than other grapefruits while maintaining tart acidity. Akin to ripe Sauvignon Blanc and warm climate Riesling.

MULBERRY (BLACK): The black mulberry is common to parts of Asia and possibly the closest native-grown approximation to a blackberry, which is not common in Asia. Black mulberries are sweet, strongly flavoured and seem lower in acidity than blackberries. They are commonly eaten fresh or dried. Similar smells / flavours can be found in Syrah / Shiraz, Malbec, Merlot and riper / warm climate Cabernet Sauvignons.

NASHI: A Japanese pear, though more like a cross between an apple and a pear. The aroma and flavour can be found in Chardonnay, Pinot Gris or Pinot Blanc.

NORI: Japanese dried seaweed, commonly used as a wrap for sushi or onigiri. Nori has a very distinctive savoury, sea/vegetal smell and delicate somewhat umami flavour. I find its aroma in better quality Koshus and occasionally in Gruner Veltliners and some evolved red wines.

OOLONG TEA: This is a Chinese tea widely consumed across Asia that is stylistically somewhere between black tea and green tea. It has a wonderfully earthy, savoury aroma with roasted nut nuances. I often find its distinctive smell in many mature old world reds, particularly on the nose of aged Nebbiolo and Sangiovese.

PRESERVED GINGER: Partially drying and preserving ginger (usually in a salt and sugar mixture) intensifies its aroma and reveals a sweet-spicy character found in many aromatic white wines such as Gewurtztraminer and Riesling.

SICHUAN (SZE CHUAN) PEPPER: To refer to this spice as "pepper" is actually a misnomer. Pepper comes from a species of climbing vine whereas this comes from a type of prickly ash tree. Sichuan peppercorns are more delicately scented than true peppercorns with a faintly citrus, orange peel smell. This aroma can be detected on the nose of some aromatic grape wines such as Muscat de Beaumes de Venise or Torrontes from Argentina.

SHISO: A Japanese mint, sort of like spearmint but more subtle. The smell can be found on warm climate / vintage Cabernet, Shiraz or Merlot.

SOURSOP JUICE: With a nose a bit like the cross between a strawberry and a pineapple this aroma / favour can be found in some of the more intense rose Champagnes. I've also found it in Gewuztraminers and New Zealand Pinot Gris.

STAR ANISE: This spice has an intense liquorice aroma and flavour that can be found in some wines made from red grapes such as Syrah or Grenache.

Shiso

TAU SAR PAU BUNS: I love these. They're basically Chinese steamed bread with a red bean paste filling. (See the separate descriptors for these foods.) I only mention them because these breakfast buns are quite accessible in Asia and a good way of familiarising yourself with the aromas and flavours of these ingredients if you've never had them.

THAI GUAVA (FARANG): This is a very common fruit in Thailand with a distinctive smell and taste that is a bit like a green apple laced with fresh thyme. The aroma and flavour can be found in Loire Chenin Blanc, Gruner Veltliner and more aromatic examples of Pinot Blanc.

TOFU: Fresh, silken tofu can have a rather distinctive earthy/nutty smell like Fino Sherry but I also find it has a delicate creamy/savoury character that is found in some young Cavas.

TURMERIC: This vibrant yellow coloured spice is a staple in many curries and broadly used in South East Asian dishes. It has a distinctive earthy smell with nuances of white pepper and sometimes mustard. The flavour is earthy / peppery. I often detect a touch of turmeric in some of the older vine wines of southern France and Spanish Garnachas.

STAR FRUIT / CARAMBOLA: The unusual star fruit gives subtle citrus and tropical fruit aromas like a cross between a lemon and a pineapple with a bit of grassiness. The most obvious grape with similar aromas and flavours is Sauvignon Blanc, particularly from the Loire, but the characteristics can also be found in Cortese or sometimes Pinot Grigio / Gris.

SUDACHI: This is a small, strongly scented Japanese lime that shares aromas with ripe Riesling, Semillon and some Sauvignons.

TATAMI MATS: Not a food per say, but this is a common, distinctively Asian smell. One step into a tatami room should immediately conjure aromas for wine drinkers of Loire Sauvignon Blanc or other cool climate examples of this grape. Tatami mats tend to smell predominately of straw with a slightly earthy / musky aroma.

UMAMI / XIANWEI: The "fifth taste", this is a savoury flavour found in meats, cheeses, mushrooms, seaweed and oyster sauce (or other monosodium glutamate containing products, ignoring any added flavours such as salt and sugar), for examples. I find nuances of this sometimes in aged Barolo or Southern French grapes such as Mourvedre or Carignan.

WINTER MELON: Consumed in Asia as a vegetable, the smell of raw winter melon is a cross between fresh mown grass and honeydew melon. Its aroma can be found in wines such as Sauvignon Blanc and Gruner Veltliner.

YUZU (JAPAN) / YUJA (KOREAN): This citrus fruit is like a hybrid of grapefruit and lemon. It is most commonly used for its aromatic rind which has a pronounced lemon-lime character. The smell in found in many white wines, notably those made from Koshu, young Chablis and some Sauvignons.

GENERAL REFERENCES

Coombe B. G., Dry P. R. *Viticulture: Volume 1 Resources*, Winetitles, 1988

Coombe B. G., Dry P. R. *Viticulture: Volume 2 Practices*, Winetitles, 1992

Jackson, R. S. *Wine Science: Principals and Applications*, 3rd Edn., Academic Press, 2008

Margalit Y. *Concepts in Wine Chemistry*, The Wine Appreciation Guild Ltd., 1997

Margalit Y. *Concepts in Wine Technology*, The Wine Appreciation Guild Ltd., 2004

Parker, R. M., Jr. *The Wine Advocate Rating System*, Available at: eRobertParker.com, 2014

Ribéreau-Gayon P., Dourbordieu, D., Doneche D. B., Lonvaud A. *Handbook of Enology Volume 1: The Microbiology of Wine and Vinifications*, 2nd Edn., Wiley, 2006

Ribéreau-Gayon P., Glories Y., Maujean A., Dourbordieu, D. *Handbook of Enology Volume 2: The Chemistry of Wine Stabilization and Treatments*, 2nd Edn., Wiley, 2006

Robinson J. (ed) *The Oxford Companion to Wine*, 3rd Edn., Oxford University Press, 2006

Zoeklein B. W., Fugelsang K. C., Gump B. H., Nury F. S. *Wine Analysis and Production*, The Chapman & Hall Enology Library, 1995

PROLOGUE, PART 1 – GO ON, I DARE YOU. SMELL IT.

Alberts B., Johnson A., Lewis J., Raff M., Roberts K., Walter P. *Molecular Biology of the Cell*, 5th Edn., Garland Science, 2007

Bushdid C., Magnasco M. O., Vosshall L. B., Keller A. "Humans Can Discriminate More than 1 Trillion Olfactory Stimuli", *Science* Vol. 343 No. 6177 pp. 1370-1372, 2014

Landis, B. N., Frasnelli, J., Reden, J., Lacroix, J. S., Hummel, T. "Differences Between Orthonasal and Retronasal Olfactory Functions in Patients With Loss of the Sense of Smell", *Archives of Otolaryngology - Head & Neck Surgery*, 131(11): 977-981, 2005

Shepherd G. M. *Neurogastronomy: How the Brain Creates Flavor and Why it Matters*, Columbia University Press, 2012

Turin L. *The Secret of Scent: The Adventures in Perfume and the Science of Smell*, HarperCollins Publishers, 2006

Villamor R. R., Ross C. F. "Wine Matrix Compounds Affect Perception of Wine Aromas", *Annual Review of Food Science and Technology* Vol. 4: 1-20, 2013

PROLOGUE, PART 2 - BUT BEFORE WE BEGIN...ARE WE ALL ON THE SAME SMELL PAGE?

Albers, S. "Are you a supertaster?" *Comfort Cravings in Psychology Today*, June 25, 2010

Moore, V. "The role of smell in appreciating wine" *The Telegraph*, 2014

Spence C. Harrar V. and Piqueras-Fiszman B. "Assessing the impact of the tableware and other contextual variables on multisensory flavour perception", http://www.flavourjournal.com/content/1/1/7, 2012

Spinney L. "The smelling test: The genetics of olfaction", *The Independent*, 2011

Wood C., Siebert T.E., Parker M., Capone D. L., Elsey G. M., Pollniz A. P., Eggers M., Meier M., Vössing T., Widder S., Krammer G., Sefton M. A., Herderich M. J. "From Wine to Pepper: Rotundone, an Obscure Sesquiterpene, Is a Potent Spicy Aroma Compound", *J. Agric. Food Chem.*, 56 (10): 3738–3744, 2008

INTRODUCTION – WHAT WE TALK ABOUT WHEN WE TALK ABOUT WINE QUALITY

Charters, S., Pettigrew, S. "The Dimensions of Wine Quality" *Food Quality & Preference*, 18: 997-1007, 2007

Parr W. V., Mouret M., Blackmore S., Pelquest-Hunt T., Urdapilleta I. "Representation of complexity in wine: Influence of expertise" *Food Quality and Preference*, 22: 647-660, 2011

CHAPTER 1 – WINE FAULTS

Adams, A. "New Thinking in the Brett Debate: UC Davis researchers create Brettanomyces aroma wheel" Wines & Vines, April 2013

Australian Food and Grocery Council "Organohalogen Taints in Foods", 2007

Botha J. J. "Sensory, chemical and consumer analysis of Brettanomyces spoilage in South African wines", *Stellenbosch University*, 2010

Bramley, B. R., Curtin, C., Cowey G., Holdstock M.A., Coulter A. D., Kennedy E., Travis B., Mueller S., Lockshin L., Godden P. W., Francis, I. L. "Wine style alters the sensory impact of 'Brett' flavour compounds in red wines" *Proceedings of the 13th Australian Wine Industry Technical Conference*, 2007

Lavigne V., Dubourdieu D. "The premature oxidative ageing of wine" *Bordeaux Institute of Vineyard and Wine Sciences* research available at http://www.newbordeaux.com/#!dubourdieu-premox-in-whites/c1lot, 2013

Pons, A., Lavigne V., Landais Y., Darriet P., Dubourdieu D. "Identification of a Sotolon Pathway in Dry White Wines" *J. Agric. Food Chem.*, 58 (12): 7273–7279, 2010

Segurel M. A., Razungles A. J., Riou C., Salles M., Baumes R. L. "Contribution of dimethyl sulfide to the aroma of Syrah and Grenache Noir wines and estimation of its potential in grapes of these varieties", *Journal of Agricultural and Food Chemistry* 52:23: 7084-93, 2004

Takeuchi H., Kato H., Kurahashi T. "2,4,6-Trichloroanisole is a potent suppressor of olfactory signal transduction" *Proceedings of the National Academy of Sciences of the United States of America (PNAS)*, August 2013

Tominaga T., Blanchard L., Darriet P., Dubourdieu D. "A Powerful Aromatic Volatile Thiol, 2-Furanmethanethiol, Exhibiting Roast Coffee Aroma in Wines Made from Several Vitis vinifera Grape Varieties", *Journal of Agricultural and Food Chemistry* 48 (5) pp 1799-1802, April 2000

CHAPTER 2 – FRUIT HEALTH & RIPENESS

Bogart K., Bisson L. "Persistence of vegetal characters in wine grapes and wine" *Practical Winery & Vineyard Journal*, March/April 2006

Bordeu, E., Troncoso, D. O., Zaviezo, T. "Influence of mealybug (Pseudococcus spp.)-infested bunches on wine quality in Carmenere and Chardonnay grapes" *International Journal of Food Science & Technology*, 47: 232–239, 2012

Kögel S., Gross J., Hoffmann C. "Sensory detection thresholds of 'ladybird taint' in 'Riesling' and 'Pinot Noir' under different fermentation and processing conditions" *Vitis* 51 (1), 27–32, 2012

Krasnow, M., Matthews, M. A., Smith, R. J., Benz, J., Weber, E., Shackel, K.A. "Distinctive symptoms differentiate four common types of berry shrivel disorder in grapes" *California Agriculture* 64(3):155-159, September 2010

McRae J. M., Kennedy J. A. "Wine and Grape Tannin Interactions with Salivary Proteins and Their Impact on Astringency: A Review of Current Research" *Molecules*, 16, 2348-2364, 11 March 2011

Michel J., Jourdes M., Giordanengo T., Mourey N., Lorrain B., Teissedre P. "Oak Wood Influence on the Organoleptic Perception of Red Wine" *Quad. Vitic. Enol. Univ. Torino*, 31, 2009-2010

Villamor R. R., Ross C. F. "Wine Matrix Compounds Affect Perception of Wine Aromas" *Annual Review of Food Science and Technology,* Vol. 4: 1-20, February 2013

CHAPTER 3 – CONCENTRATION

Blanchard, L., Darriet, P., Dubourdieu, D. "Reactivity of 3-Mecaptohexanol in Red Wine: Impact of Oxygen, Phenolic Fractions, and Sulfur Dioxide" *American Journal of Enology and Viticulture* 55:2, p. 115-119, 2004

Wood, C., Siebert, T. E., Parker, M., Capone, C. L., Elsey, G. M., Pollnitz, A. P., Eggers, M., Meier, M., Vossing, T., Widder, S., Krammer, G., Sefton, M. A., Herderich, M. J. "From Wine to Pepper: Rotundone, an Obscure Sesquiterpene, Is a Potent Spicy Aroma Compound" *Journal of Agricultural and Food Chemistry* 56 (10), p. 3738–3744, May 2008

CHAPTER 4 – BALANCE

Molina A. M., Swiegers J. H., Varela C., Pretorius I. S., Agosin E. "Influence of wine fermentation temperature on the synthesis of yeast-derived volatile aroma compounds" *Applied Microbiology and Biotechnology* 77:675-687, 2007

CHAPTER 5 – COMPLEXITY

Cook, D. J., Hollowood, T. A., Linford, R., Taylor, A. J. "Oral shear stress predicts flavour perception in viscous solutions" *Chemical Senses,* 28, 11-23, 2003

Ebeler S. E., Spaulding R. S. "Characterization and Measurement of Aldehydes in Wine" *Chemistry of Wine Flavor,* 13: 166-179, 1998

Mabberley D. J. *The Plant-Book,* 1st Edn., Cambridge University Press: UK., 1987

Nykanen L., Suomalainen H. *Aroma of Beer, Wine and Distilled Alcoholic Beverages (Handbook of Aroma Research),* Springer, 1983

Rodríguez-Rodríguez P. Gómez-Plaza E. "Effect of Volume and Toast Level of French Oak Barrels (*Quercus petraea L.*) on Cabernet Sauvignon Wine Characteristics" *Am. J. Enol. Vitic.,* 62:359-365, 2011

Ross, J. "Minerality, Rigorous or Romantic?" *Practical Winery & Vineyard Journal,* Winter 2012

Ugarte, P., Agosin, E., Bordeu, E., Villalobos, J. "Reduction of 4-Ethylphenol and 4-Ethylguaiacol Concentration in Red Wines Using Reverse Osmosis and Adsorption" *Am. J. Enol. Vitic.,* 56:1, 30-36

White R. E. *Soils for Fine Wines,* Oxford University Press, 2003

Wilson, W. *Terroir: The Role of Geology, Climate, and Culture in the Making of French Wines,* Mitchell Beazley, 1998

CHAPTER 9 – TASTING NOTES, QUALITY CONCLUSIONS & RATINGS

Cooke G. M., Lapsley J. T. "Evaluating Wine Quality" *Home Winemaking,* 7: 30-32, UC Davis, 1988

Noble A. C. *The Aroma Wheel,* UC Davis, 1995

Noble A. C. "Wine Tasting is a Science" *California Agriculture,* July 1980

Index

CPSIA information can be obtained at www.ICGtesting.com
Printed in the USA
LVOW02s0822250515

439758LV00042B/1570/P